Becoming an *Exceptional* Executive Coach

USE YOUR KNOWLEDGE, EXPERIENCE, AND INTUITION TO HELP LEADERS EXCEL

Michael H. Frisch, Robert J. Lee,
Karen L. Metzger, Jeremy Robinson,
and Judy Rosemarin

AMERICAN MANAGEMENT ASSOCIATION

New York • Atlanta • Brussels • Chicago • Mexico City • San Francisco
Shanghai • Tokyo • Toronto • Washington, D. C.

Bulk discounts available. For details visit:
www.amacombooks.org/go/specialsales
Or contact special sales:
Phone: 800-250-5308
Email: specialsls@amanet.org
View all the AMACOM titles at: www.amacombooks.org

Library of Congress Cataloging-in-Publication Data

Becoming an exceptional executive coach : use your knowledge, experience, and intuition to
help leaders excel / Michael H. Frisch ... [et al.].
    p. cm.
Includes bibliographical references and index.
ISBN-13: 978-0-8144-3758-2
ISBN-10: 0-8144-3758-3
1. Executive coaching. I. Frisch, Michael H.
HD30.4.B43 2011
658.4'07124—dc22
                    2011011577

About AMA
American Management Association (www.amanet.org) is a world leader in talent development, advancing the skills of individuals to drive business success. Our mission is to support
the goals of individuals and organizations through a complete range of products and services,
including classroom and virtual seminars, webcasts, webinars, podcasts, conferences, corporate and government solutions, business books and research. AMA's approach to improving
performance combines experiential learning—learning through doing—with opportunities
for ongoing professional growth at every step of one's career journey.

Printing number

10 9 8 7 6 5 4 3 2 1

Contents

CONTENTS

Acknowledgments

First, we would like to thank an early but pivotal contributor to the realization of this book. At the 2008 annual meeting of the American Psychological Association, Richard Hackman gave a presentation about the dos and don'ts of producing a book based on topically focused discussions of a long-standing group of colleagues. We don't know what other attendees at that session took away, but for us the messages were clear: Turning intentions and interesting points into tangible text requires the tyranny of a project manager, due dates, funds, and a professional editor. Just as in coaching, a solid process that puts ideas into action is a necessary condition for aspirations to become reality.

More immediately, we would like to thank our students, supervisees, and the organizational sponsors of coaching assignments connected with our courses. During our ten years of teaching executive coaching, their support and encouragement have provided us with the impetus to continually question, refine, and articulate our ideas about executive coaching. We would also like to thank our organizational clients, who have relied on us to support their internal coaching efforts, as well as our academic partners, Baruch College (CUNY) Zicklin Business School's Management Department and the graduate programs of the New School University. In addition, we would like to thank our editor, Claire Wyckoff, who participated in innumerable "book" meetings, showing enormous patience in providing guidance on both the product and the process. We would also like to thank Christina Parisi, our Executive Editor at AMACOM, who supported our proposal and was decisive in helping us resolve key questions even as she nurtured her other projects. Finally, we would like to thank our families, who unflinchingly supported this extracurricular effort with their encouragement and flexibility.

List of Figures

Introduction

Our Journeys

We five authors came to executive coaching in ways similar to those who participate in our coach training courses—from organizational psychology, consulting, organization development, career counseling, and the personal helping professions. At the time we began to coach there was no formal practice of executive coaching. The need for individualized, just-in-time executive development emerged in the 1980s, in the form of requests for help from our human resources contacts. Taking a cue from *A Chorus Line*, a musical of that era, we responded with, "We can do that!" With very little definition or guidance, we originally provided those individual development services under various headings, such as *developmental counseling, mental health consultation, occupational clinical psychology,* or *retention work.* By the early 1990s, however, executive coaching had become the preferred label, and somewhat consistent expectations had been defined.

Although there was no training for executive coaches back then, there were many streams of skill, knowledge, and practice that fueled and shaped coaching work, including individual psychotherapy, leadership development courses, organization development (OD), and human resources consulting. At the same time, there were new ideas about management and leadership that were synergistic with the increasing demand for executive coaching. Managerial competencies beyond technical skills were gaining prominence, including an emphasis on the manager as coach and developer of talent. Approaches to leadership began focusing on soft skill areas such as communication and interpersonal dynamics rather than formal authority or command and control. Human resources practices were moving beyond personnel administration to include sophisticated succession planning systems and 360-degree feedback tools for individual development. Consulting and training firms and executive education branches of business schools were responding to, and advancing, these new ideas about leadership and HR practices and incorporating them into management and executive training experiences for clients.

Our early opportunities for executive coaching work evolved out of those swirling applications. Under the prevailing *zeitgeist*, executive coaching coalesced with a surprising degree of consistency around a confidential one-on-one relationship, informed by 360-degree and other assessments, organizationally sponsored, and anchored in on-the-job action planning. Certainly there were branded labels for coaching, reflecting a particular theoretical model or the desire to be differentiated in the marketplace, but the rough outlines of accepted executive coaching practice became clear quickly. Supporting that clarity was the fact that *coaching* was not yet a term used for services outside of organizational contexts. In other words, the term *coaching* had not yet ballooned to apply to personal, life, and career interventions.

By the early 1990s in the United States, coaching had become an accepted option for executive development. Even those firms offering more traditional classroom courses saw coaching as a complement to their efforts and grafted it on. The Center for Creative Leadership was an early innovator in executive development courses and used coaching to facilitate interpretation of assessment feedback as a basis for individual development planning. In addition, coaching found its way into increasingly sophisticated human resources practices. Competency-driven human resource planning, performance management systems, and action learning teams all triggered identification of leaders who would benefit from individualized, accelerated development. As executives and managers were selected for development, demand for coaching grew. Coaches were screened, introduced to prospective clients, and offered coaching opportunities, typically for six-month engagements.

In these early years, coaching qualifications were undefined, but some were favored: affinity for the business enterprise; insight about organizational life, especially at the top; the ability to engage executives one-on-one in a self-discovery process; and organizational sponsor management. Industry-specific knowledge, assessment tool facility, professional/human resources networks, and consulting experience were also immediately useful. Experience as a professional counselor and advanced training in psychology or other human service fields added to credibility but were not required. Eventually, a parallel phenomenon emerged as HR professionals began offering forms of coaching to managers in their organizations, and the role of the internal coach was born.

The authors participated actively in the growth of executive coaching and also were called upon to help improve its practices. Starting in the mid-1990s, we supported the development and case supervision of less experienced executive coaches. For all of us, these cases became very gratifying aspects of our professional lives. We discovered we enjoyed, and were effective at, guiding others in their coaching work. We also found a synergy between *coaching the coach* and our own coaching practices: Our cases became opportunities to extract lessons and provide examples, while the cases our students provided drew us into broader coaching issues and considerations of how to train coaches, whether they would be based inside their home organization (internal coaches) or become independent coaches offering their services to a variety of organizations (external coaches).

Key Principles from Our Executive Coach Training Programs

These experiences led us to deliver courses on executive coaching starting in 2002. Since then, we have refined and clarified our ideas about coaching and how coaches learn. These insights are the basis for the design and content of this book. A core idea is that executive coaching is a whole-person activity. All coaches bring unique knowledge and experience to their practices, but in a more profound way we bring our personalities, values, implicit beliefs about adult growth, and our own individual styles of connecting with others. Thus, this book does not advocate any specific coaching methodology but rather helps you, the reader, define your own approach and model. We are confident that becoming overtly aware of what you bring to executive coaching will provide you with a richer foundation than training in a standardized technique.

In creating this book, we have been very aware of the importance of doing and applying, as well as learning and understanding. To the extent a book allows, we have tried to capture the essence of an apprenticeship experience rather than only providing guidelines. We have included numerous examples of coaching casework. Every coaching topic is accompanied by a detailed illustration from a case, and that case is further explored from the perspective of a case supervisor. As our students have discovered, learning is enhanced both by application and by reflecting on the experience. Case supervision is the best way we have found for new coaches to use actual experience as a springboard to understanding how executive coaching actually works and, by extrapolation, discovering their edge as a coach.

Anchored in our whole-person philosophy and *no-one-best-way* approach is a strong emphasis on helping coaches to individualize their approaches. Our preferred method is to ask every coach to reflect on, and actually define, his or her own model of executive coaching. The Personal Model, which you will find detailed in Chapter 1, is an organizing principle for our courses and for this book.

We believe that this learning approach prepares coaches to deliver executive coaching services better than any other method available. To the extent possible, we have included all essential input to help you build your executive coaching practice; however, most of the success is up to you. Coaching is a competitive field and growing more so every year. Our experience is that those coaches who are willing to carve out time from their noncoaching work to pursue the type of coaching that they want to do and promote their coaching using professional networks are the ones who get traction and engagements. This applies equally to internal and external coaches.

Goals of This Book

This book is intended to give all coaches at whatever level, internal as well as external, fresh ideas about how to improve their executive coaching skills, expand their personal ranges, and grow their coaching practices. You, as a reader, may have little, some, or substantial coaching experience. Our goal is to provide varied stimuli to engage you, whatever your level, in the search to define coaching in ways that feel right to you. We hope that even if you have no executive coaching experience, this book will help you determine your interest in tackling issues that are part of delivering coaching in organizational contexts. The book also speaks to challenges for internal coaches by recognizing both similarities and differences from their external coaching colleagues. Finally, the book would be useful to students in coach training programs or to those who lead and train internal coaches within organizations.

Recording your thoughts and reactions is always a good way to begin the process of mastering content, and we encourage you to keep a journal as you move through the book. In addition, think about what you are willing to do in addition to reading this book. Doing some actual coaching and receiving case supervision will significantly catalyze your learning as you read. Attending forums and professional meetings, as well as doing additional reading, will further facilitate your learning.

The goal of this book is to expand the choices and options for your exceptional approach to coaching. Part I consists of three chapters that build a foundation for all that follows. Chapter 1 outlines the process of defining your Personal Model of coaching; Chapter 2 describes what being an executive coach requires in terms of interests and competencies; and Chapter 3 defines key terms and provides perspectives about the field of executive coaching.

Your Personal Model of coaching is informed in part by insights you gain from the important content areas of coaching, which are presented in Part II.

Each chapter in Part II includes our latest thinking on topics within the practice of executive coaching, influenced by the questions, reactions, and suggestions of the students in our courses. These topical chapters also contain case examples illustrating the options and case supervisors' perspectives about more subtle elements of the cases. The last chapter in Part II, Chapter 20, is an exception because, instead of a topic, it outlines the increasingly important role of the internal coach.

In Part III, we prompt you to consider key questions that are essential to drafting the three outputs of your Personal Model of coaching. Chapter 21 presents how to describe your emerging approach to coaching; Chapter 22 covers building your executive coaching practice; and Chapter 23 outlines planning for your future development as a coach. Chapter 24, the final chapter in the book, brings all the pieces of the Personal Model together by telling the story of one rising executive coach.

We expect that you will find some surprises in this book and possibly even ideas you disagree with. From our teaching experience, however, we are confident that this approach to teaching executive coaching will engage you. Based on our experiences, we also know that your real learning will happen as you reflect on and apply these ideas to actual coaching engagements and, in so doing, shape your own approach to executive coaching.

FOUNDATIONS FOR

BECOMING AN EXCEPTIONAL

EXECUTIVE COACH

1

Your Personal Model
of Coaching

N O TWO COACHES WORK IN QUITE THE SAME WAY. NOR SHOULD THEY. WHETHER OFFERED FROM AN INTERNAL OR EXTERNAL PERSPECTIVE, EXECUTIVE COACHING ASSUMES A SPECIAL BOND BETWEEN COACH AND CLIENT that is genuine and well defined. It is a human partnership aimed at achieving results by exploring the individuality of you and your client. As a result, exceptional executive coaching goes well beyond just knowing about established coaching practices and techniques. Those coaches who are most successful bring insights about their own identities to the activity, including awareness of their goals, their feelings, and their interpersonal styles. They draw on a combination of professional experience, personal characteristics, and self-awareness, as well as formal training, to help shape their observations, questions, and hypotheses about their clients.

Ideally, your unique combination of knowledge, experience, and intuition can be woven together into a pattern that will be both similar to, and different from, other coaches. Having created that pattern, you will be better able to describe your services to others, deliver them consistently, and stretch toward handling more complex coaching challenges. This pattern making is the basis for articulating a Personal Model of coaching, and it has both immediate practical utility as well as a broader value as a foundation for your coaching.

Crafting your Personal Model does not happen in the first weeks of your career as a coach. It takes time, practice, feedback, and reflection to pull one together. On the other hand, it is never too early to begin considering elements of your Personal Model of coaching so that it will evolve as you gain experience and reflect on what you are learning.

Especially for anyone new to coaching, shaping a Personal Model of coaching asks a lot of you. Early in a coach's career, there is a tendency to rely on established protocols, techniques, and procedures that others recommend. While this is understandable, it fails to leverage the *whole person* that will show up when you meet with each client. Consciously or not, who you are has a significant impact on your relationships with clients. In effect, creating a Personal Model asks you to reach beyond impersonal descriptions of coaching into your actual coaching experience and catalog what you know and do not know about how you perform as a coach. The sooner you gain insights about what is unique in your application of coaching processes, the more you will be a thoughtful learner and practitioner.

A Personal Model can be compared to an iceberg: Some aspects of your approach are visible to clients, but a lot of it is under the surface and out of sight. The visible parts cannot exist without the underpinnings, and together they make up a unified whole. Carrying the metaphor further, the visible parts are likely to be more readily modified by external conditions, while the foundation also needs to be acknowledged so that all the contours can be redrawn.

Clients cannot be expected to know what coaching is or how to differentiate coaching from other helping and consulting experiences they may have had. They certainly cannot know what any particular coach will do during an engagement. It is your responsibility to explain what your approach includes and what it does not. Coaches can more effectively do that when they have invested the time and energy to articulate their own Personal Models.

The importance of creating a Personal Model rests on a core belief that *there is no one best way to coach*; coaches, clients, and contexts are all involved in designing the process. Learning to coach must be an active pursuit of internalizing, not just absorbing, wisdom about coaching. A Personal Model describes what you are trying to do with your clients, how you believe coaching works to create insight and change, and what *you* feel is relevant to bring to the coaching relationship, as a human being and as a professional. This foundation allows you maximum flexibility to tailor your approach to the challenges of any particular case.

In this book, the concept of a Personal Model of coaching is comprised of six key components, shown in Figure 1-1, that define who you are as a coach. Three of the components are *inputs* to your thinking that emerge in answer to the following broad questions:

1. What characteristics of who you are as a person may be relevant to executive coaching?

2. What sensibilities and skills do you bring to work in organizational contexts?

3. What concepts and practices in executive coaching have resonated with you and you would like to adopt?

Your responses to these three input questions are often under the surface and not apparent to clients, but they need to be explored by you in defining the underpinnings of your Personal Model.

Three other components of your Personal Model are called *outputs* because they can be described, discussed with others, and used to conduct your coaching activities. They are revealed in formulating ideas and answers to these questions:

1. What are the elements of your preferred approach to delivering coaching services?

2. How do you intend to promote your coaching practice and secure more experience as a coach?

3. What skills and abilities need to be further developed by you in order to continue growing as a coach?

Figure 1-1. Personal Model inputs and outputs

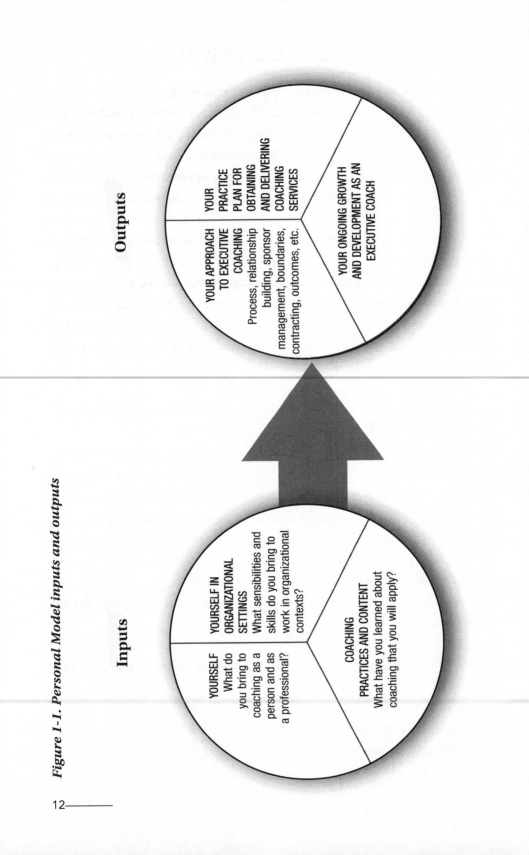

Inputs

YOURSELF
What do you bring to coaching as a person and as a professional?

YOURSELF IN ORGANIZATIONAL SETTINGS
What sensibilities and skills do you bring to work in organizational contexts?

COACHING PRACTICES AND CONTENT
What have you learned about coaching that you will apply?

Outputs

YOUR APPROACH TO EXECUTIVE COACHING
Process, relationship building, sponsor management, boundaries, contracting, outcomes, etc.

YOUR PRACTICE PLAN FOR OBTAINING AND DELIVERING COACHING SERVICES

YOUR ONGOING GROWTH AND DEVELOPMENT AS AN EXECUTIVE COACH

The inputs to a Personal Model may seem fixed, but in fact they do change, since reflection stimulates clearer self-observations so that new self-insights emerge. Even more dynamic are the outputs. They are works-in-progress that continue to benefit from adjustment and updating as your client experience, learning, reflection, and preferences build.

This book is intended to support that process by providing a structure for your model, illustrations of coaching content, and examples of coaching cases. You can use the questions outlined in this chapter to help you capture your reflections about the first two inputs in a learning journal. As you go through this book, you can also record impressions, ideas, questions, and other reactions to the coaching content chapters in Part II. Doing so will prepare you to assemble your coaching model, guided by Part III, Chapters 21 through 23, which explore the three output areas of creating a Personal Model of coaching.

Input 1—Yourself: What Do You Bring to Executive Coaching as a Person and as a Professional?

Coaching is a *whole-person* activity. You bring your various talents and life experiences to your assignments. Although not everything in your life story is relevant to coaching, it is important to identify and acknowledge those aspects of yourself that may have an impact on your coaching practice and on your client relationships. Your personality, formative life experiences, career history, interpersonal style, interests, notions of success, skills, and talents may all influence your approach to coaching.

Consider the following questions in reflecting on this input area to your coaching model:

1. How might your early history, family of origin, early formative events, role models, personality, and characteristics influence your approach to coaching? For example, you might have grown up in a household that shaped your helpfulness, self-reliance, or introversion, all of which would have implications for your coaching.

2.   How does your education relate to coaching? How might the contents of your undergraduate, graduate, continuing or professional education, and other coursework relate to your practice as a coach? What notions about personality, motivation, leadership, and business that you learned in school have application to coaching?

3.   In what ways has your career brought you to coaching? Internships, part-time jobs, full-time employment, or any work experiences may have a direct or indirect connection to coaching. For example, you may have worked as a leadership development consultant and been exposed to concepts and models relevant to coaching.

4.   What are your assumptions about adult health and growth? Consider courses, books, mentors, and theories about adult development that resonate for you and are likely to apply to your work with managers and executives in coaching relationships. For example, you may have found that emotional intelligence or cognitive-behavioral concepts appeal to you.

5.   How might your own personal priorities about what is important in life, the values that guide your interpersonal dealings, and the principles you aspire to in your interactions influence your approach to coaching? For example, if work/life balance and connection to family are priorities for you, they are likely to shape the topics that you emphasize with clients.

6.   What is your *growing edge* as a person? How are you leveraging strengths, targeting areas for learning, identifying biases and blind spots, and addressing personal skill gaps? Consider the connection between your own areas of personal growth—such as being more assertive or being better organized—and coaching. What are the ways that coaching as a practice may align with areas you have targeted for personal growth?

Input 2—Yourself in Organizational Settings: What Sensibilities and Skills Do You Bring to Work in Organizational Contexts?

Executive coaching almost always occurs in organizational settings. Each coach has had different experiences in organizations. Whether employee, manager, consultant, adviser, senior leader, board member, or coach, you have had experiences that are likely to influence how you interact with coaching sponsors and others in the organization. For those readers who have done some executive coaching, either internally or externally, your prior contact with the organizations in which you have coached is especially relevant to your Personal Model.

Related to how you function in organizational contexts, these questions are relevant to your coaching:

1. Since executive coaching benefits both individuals and organizations, what is your motivation to do such work? What experiences within organizations have you had that indicate the usefulness of coaching? How motivated are you by the organizational and individual outcomes of coaching?

2. What are your feelings about business and other types of organizations in which you may be coaching? What preferences do you have for the types of organizations you may coach in? What if those preferences cannot be fully followed in your coaching work?

3. What do you know about the ways in which individual coaching objectives tie into organizational expectations? How should the connection be managed between business or organizational goals and individual growth objectives that you help your clients articulate?

4. How do you respond to authority and organizational hierarchy? Your client's work world will probably have levels and structure—up, down, and across the organization. It will be regimented to some degree, with reporting lines, processes, and cycles. What has been your experience in dealing with structure, formal authority, power, organizational politics, teams, and leadership?

5. What has been your experience in dealing with human resource professionals and other staff groups in organizations? What prior experiences and assumptions about HR staff will you bring to those interactions?

How do you feel about their oversight as they screen clients and coaches and monitor coaching engagements?

6. What is your approach to dealing with those managers and leaders who sponsor coaching and make decisions about funding it? How comfortable are you in interacting with the sponsors of your coaching work at the same time that you maintain your closest tie to the person you are coaching?

Input 3—Coaching Practices and Content: What Have You Learned About Coaching That You Will Apply?

The third input to your Personal Model prompts you to consider your preferences about coaching practices, theoretical underpinnings, emerging coaching topics, research questions, and other coaching content areas. While there is a large amount of published material on executive coaching, each coach will find certain topics and ideas more compelling and relevant than others.

The content chapters in Part II of this book discuss a number of these topics. Here you will find concrete and practical descriptions of foundational concepts that tap into theories about behavior; contextual considerations in working within organizations; leadership challenges; and approaches to building productive relationships with clients.

If you are an experienced coach, you may want to select specific chapters of particular interest to you or relevance to your practice. Whether you jump to specific content chapters or read them in sequence, you will probably find that the relevance of certain chapters changes with your coaching practice and clients. Going back and forth in reflecting on the first two inputs to your model and becoming familiar with coaching practices may be a productive way to begin to describe the foundations of your Personal Model.

We encourage you to capture your responses to this material in a journal, both to activate your learning and to prepare yourself to pull relevant ideas and practices into your own Personal Model. Consider these questions as you delve into coaching topics:

1. What are your reactions to the practices described in each content

chapter in Part II? What is engaging and may be applicable to your work as a coach? What is appealing but would need to be tried before deciding on its value? Which practices do not seem to be useful, in your judgment?

2. What surprises did you have as you read about the practices described in each chapter? In what ways do these practices differ from the coaching that you might have already done? How might you explore those differences to determine if they should be part of your Personal Model?

3. What is your reaction to the coaching cases and supervisors' observations presented in Part II? What subtle practice points are highlighted in the cases? What does the supervisor bring out that may be especially relevant for your coaching?

4. What topics that are not covered in the content chapters but are allied to coaching—such as counseling, individual assessment, action learning, and organizational change—do you want to explore?

At some point we hope you will feel the need to pull your inputs together to provide a basis for your Personal Model outputs. Detailed descriptions of how to populate those outputs are discussed in the final chapters in Part III of this book. To provide a preview, however, they are described briefly here.

The first *output* to your Personal Model, explored in Chapter 21, is the broadest. It taps insights and inclinations from all three input categories, asking you to weave them into a description of your approach to coaching. Your ability to articulate an engaging definition of coaching enables you to answer the predictable question, "What's your approach to coaching?" More importantly, it requires that you be knowledgeable about your coaching process, practice boundaries, interpersonal presence, and other factors that are likely to define you in your coaching roles. These considerations and others provide an essential backdrop to productive conversations with clients and sponsors.

The second *output*, which is detailed in Chapter 22, explores the promotional and business aspects of coaching. It is your *practice plan*. Because executive coaching is usually done on the basis of contracts with organizations, it is valuable to know how to manage your coaching as a business partner. A successful coaching practice has a structure, marketing plan, materials, references, and professional affiliations. This second Personal Model output provides guidance about these matters so that you can successfully promote and deliver the coaching that you want to do.

Chapter 23 covers the third *output*, which is an active *development plan* for your role as coach. Just as your clients, you need to be an involved adult learner, committed to your professional growth and constantly curious about alternative approaches and new ideas. Coaching has many roots and branches for you to explore. Some of those will require further study, courses, and guidance from more experienced coaches, case supervision, and other learning interventions.

Your Personal Model of coaching is both a concept and a roadmap. This book and our teaching philosophy are based on the importance of connecting who you are as a person with how you conduct yourself as a coach. There are no universally useful techniques, so having the broadest possible foundation for your coaching work is the best preparation you can have. A Personal Model is a concrete plan for how to operationalize these points. Reflecting on the three inputs and then extrapolating them into the three outputs brings impressive depth and breadth to your role as a coach. As you read subsequent sections of this book, the Personal Model framework is used frequently to guide your learning and help you become an exceptional executive coach.

2

Executive Coach Competencies

THIS CHAPTER IS MEANT TO HELP YOU EXPLORE THE FIRST INPUT TO YOUR PERSONAL MODEL—THE PERSONALITY CHARACTERISTICS, INTERESTS, SKILLS, AND ABILITIES THAT YOU BRING TO EXECUTIVE COACHING. UNDERSTANDING this input requires a wide-ranging reflection on your education, professional accomplishments, career path, and other formative experiences, as well as an analysis of the qualities you have developed from those experiences.

As a framework to make your self-assessment more targeted and productive, this chapter identifies a number of key competencies that are relevant to executive coaching. While no coach will be equally strong in all these qualities, knowing which ones are strengths and which ones you struggle with can be immediately useful in anticipating the challenges of a coaching practice.

A Key Requirement

Sometimes a question arises as to whether there are make-or-break prerequisites for doing executive coaching. Although it is difficult to isolate any one factor, the competency that seems to be most pivotal is effective self-management. While it is appealing to be spontaneous and natural with clients, a professional posture that provides focus, intentionality, and discipline is very important. Those coaches with problematic self-management are emotionally reactive to clients in observable ways and may offer advice or solutions impulsively. By contrast, coaches who manage themselves well are able to identify an emerging theme and maintain a focus on it both within and across coaching sessions.

In your self-assessment, self-management may be a difficult dimension to appraise. However, in addition to being as honest as possible with yourself about this dimension, seek feedback from trusted colleagues. Ask them for their observations about your interpersonal style. If self-management appears to be a challenge for you, having an active development plan can help you improve your ability to contain reactions and maintain focus. As you improve your ability to follow themes and be reflective about your own feelings in response to clients, you can apply this important characteristic to all your professional roles, including coaching.

In addition to self-management, there are groups of competencies and characteristics, listed in Figure 2-1, that deserve your attention as you develop your coaching abilities. These competencies fall into three categories: building relationships, communicating, and fostering learning.

In addition to determining the extent to which you possess these competencies, three other qualities are especially important to your effectiveness as a coach. The first is the ability to foster hope and optimism. There are never guarantees of success in life or in coaching, but coaches who find ways to increase their clients' positive outlook and sense of ownership tend to empower clients to persevere. Clients face many challenges that they have little actual control over: career disappointments, poor organizational leadership, political maneuvers, business downturns, reorganization, acquisition by another firm, and other setbacks. Your compassion may be triggered by your clients' external challenges, and you may even empathize with their discouragement. However, when clients are overwhelmed and pessimistic, it is important for you to provide a counterbalance, encouraging useful action while avoiding empty cheerleading. When you convey optimism about your clients' strengths and assets, you foster hope and help them see new options and alternatives.

Figure 2-1. Coach competencies

Competencies Useful in Building Relationships
- Insight into interpersonal relationships and organizational dynamics
- Acceptance without judgment of the full range of feelings that may be experienced by others
- Sincere desire to help others
- Transparency and integrity in dealings with others
- Curiosity about clients and their career stories
- Respect for the uniqueness of clients
- Relating to a new client so that safety is experienced and trust builds quickly
- Being fully *present* while focusing on others

Competencies Useful in Communicating
- Ability to ask thought-provoking, probing questions
- Ability to foster client storytelling with curiosity, questions, and restatements
- Facility at summarizing and moving a conversation toward a conclusion and at reframing issues
- Ability to provide useful feedback based on observations and sensitive interpretations of data
- Ability to avoid judgment and willingness to continue trying to understand the client
- Ability to manage time within sessions
- Ability to ask for feedback and be open to what clients suggest

Competencies In Fostering Learning
- Flexibility in designing a coaching engagement to fit the client's needs
- Helping clients without needing much credit
- Restraint in regard to giving advice
- Ability to ask clients about their learning and noticing how they learn
- Knowledge about theories of adult development, motivation, and learning
- Ability to find an appropriate balance between support and challenge
- Ability to adapt to a variety of personalities and organizational cultures

Coaching Effectiveness Competencies
- Optimism about human development and behavior change
- Attuned to own reactions and choosing in what ways to channel the reactions
- Consciousness of and use of *self*
- Reaching out for guidance
- Openness to feedback

Second, those coaches who are able to be insightful about their own feelings, and then use those reactions to understand others, display a talent that serves them well in coaching. This ability comes from using your own insight, empathy, and intuition to tune into a client's mindset and then to find ways to use those perceptions in the service of your coaching. Sometimes referred to as *in the moment feedback* or *use of self*, this ability allows coaches to be genuine and bring immediacy to their work. For newer coaches, use of self can be challenging to apply, but it can be learned, and it does have a significant impact on strengthening the coaching relationship. This is covered in greater depth in Chapter 13.

Third, and connected to use of self, is the willingness to ask for help. There are many challenges and potential pitfalls in a coaching engagement. Yet its structure and confidentiality requirements are not conducive to getting help when it is needed. Effective coaches know how to seek help when they are struggling. They understand that these are important moments in their learning and that being isolated when faced with a challenge is counterproductive. However, only you can sense a need for collegial/supervisory dialogue, new perspectives, or direct help in dealing with a challenging client or situation.

To prepare for that eventuality, many coaches forge relationships with mentors or case supervisors. Typically, these are experienced coaching practitioners and instructors. In this book, supervisory perspectives based on descriptions of cases are included at the ends of Chapters 4 through 19 in Part II. These snapshots provide samples of the added insight and value that can come from discussing cases with a supervisor. This dialogue process is an essential tool in managing the challenges of the coaching role and the continuing development of your coaching skills. In addition, the willingness to ask for guidance models a characteristic you want to instill in your clients.

The Leadership Experience Myth

Newcomers to executive coaching may assume that a requirement for success is direct experience as an executive. This is not the case. While there is a legitimate need for executive coaches to be students of leadership and orga-nizational behavior, experience in an organizational leadership role is more of a "nice to have" than a requirement. While it is true that having been an executive can boost a coach's credibility in a prospective client's opinion, this value is short-lived.

Other factors, such as those characteristics described previously, have more positive relevance to coaching outcomes. Furthermore, a significant background in leadership can actually be counterproductive when it leads to dominating conversations, telling stories, and offering advice. In other words, having been an executive may help you win a coaching assignment, but using your executive experience directly will not make you a better coach. Draw on your leadership experiences to inform your questions, hypotheses, and contextual understanding of your client's world. However, remember that those experiences hold no more weight in your effectiveness as a coach than any other relevant experiences that contribute to the foun-dations of your Personal Model.

Judging your capacity for these various competencies and characteristics is challenging, but the effort has considerable value as inputs to your Personal Model and to guide your development as a coach. In particular, we recommend that you reflect on past feedback you have received—whether from a 360-degree survey or other assessment processes—and use those results as indicators of your capacity on these dimensions. Such self-knowl-edge will serve you well both in providing the best coaching you can for your clients and in learning from your coaching experiences.

3

Foundations and Definitions

THREE STREAMS OF PROFESSIONAL PRACTICE CONVERGE IN EXECUTIVE COACH-ING. THE FIRST STREAM IS REFLECTED IN THE ONE-TO-ONE STRUCTURE OF COACHING AND COMES FROM THE CONFIDENTIAL TALKING PROCESS THAT therapists and counselors employ. As therapy became more common and acceptable in the United States in the 1960s, some of those clinical practitioners were invited to apply their skills to the needs of corporate executives, even before executive coaching was labeled as a practice in its own right.

A second stream taps activities of consultants who were engaged to help with organizational and human resources challenges. They normalized the general use of external professionals when special expertise was needed by organizations. As coaching gained traction, the precedent of consulting made it easier to use outside experts to help individual managers and executives with their leadership challenges.

The third stream contributes content and processes that were designed for leadership development programs. Paralleling the growth of coaching, organizations were also experimenting with defining leadership competencies. They relied especially on assessment tools and individual development planning processes. Once competencies were identified, it was possible to design leadership courses that often combined content, individual feedback, and action learning elements for a complete development experience. Executive coaching draws directly from the concepts and content of the leadership development movement, which has continued to generate new ideas about what it means to be an effective leader.

Along with these streams of influence (illustrated in Figure 3-1), banks or boundaries were defined to differentiate executive coaching from other interventions. Specifically, executive coaching is unique because it embraces the following characteristics:

Transparency: The process is open and observable.

Shared Responsibility: The coach leads the process while the client leads change.

Facilitative Style: The coach helps identify client choices while minimizing being directive.

Client-Focused Narrative: The client's stories and perspectives dominate discussions.

Organizationally Sponsored: Engagements are supported by representatives of the organization, such as human resource professionals and client managers.

Work-Related Goals: Client development goals target important managerial and leadership areas, and implementation occurs in day-to-day performance changes.

Nonhierarchical Relationship: The coach has no formal authority over the client.

Limited Confidentiality: Coach-client conversations are private, although the process is transparent and plans are shared with the organization.

Staying within the banks of executive coaching requires the following coaching skills:

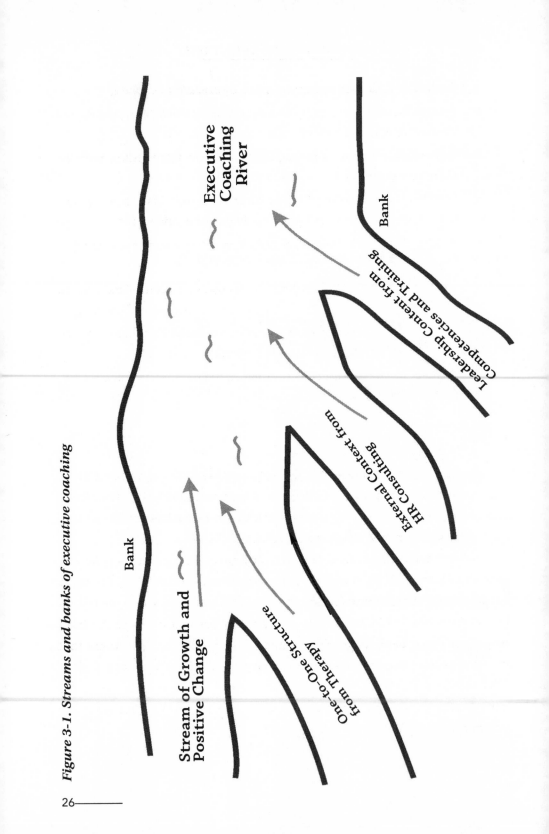

Figure 3-1. Streams and banks of executive coaching

Executive
Coaching
River

Bank

Leadership Content from
Competencies and Training

External Context from
HR Consulting

Stream of Growth and
Positive Change

Bank

One-to-One Structure
from Therapy

- Being able to describe what you mean by *executive coaching*
- Establishing your credibility as an expert on the coaching process, not the client's issues or field of work
- Remaining proactive in managing the evolving relationships with the client and sponsors
- Establishing appropriate goals as the coaching unfolds and being open to what emerges, while maintaining an outcome orientation
- Shifting the responsibility for process ownership toward the client during the course of the coaching
- Maintaining hope and optimism about positive outcomes and change, even as the client faces practical reality and organizational challenges
- Tying coaching to current challenges to increase the client's longer-range career potential and learning appetite
- Finding ways to be personally authentic, neither impersonal nor clinical, but always professional

Definitions of Coaching

The streams and banks metaphor provides coaches with ways of describing coaching and differentiating it from other interventions. This helps clients and coaches understand both what coaching is and what it is not. Doing so is part of the larger task of shaping a Personal Model.

In definitions of executive coaching, the term *client* is particularly important. For some coaches, the client is the organization; for others, the *client* designation is shared between the organization and the person in the coaching relationship. In this book, the word *client* refers exclusively to the individual seeking growth and development through coaching. It assumes that the coach-client relationship is the primary vehicle for change rather than the coach's relationship with the organization or its representatives (e.g., the client's manager or the Human Resources partner), who are referred to here as *sponsors*.

WHY WE DON'T USE THE TERM *COACHEE*

This book uses the term *client* for the person who is seeking growth through the relationship with a coach. The term *coachee* is not used since it implies something being done to the person, rather than a relationship of relative equals.

Some people might view this as merely a semantic distinction, but it is much more important than that. The position you take in defining the word *client* will show up in your coaching in important ways—in confidentiality, in goal setting, and in the involvement of others, especially if the coaching process comes under scrutiny or pressure. It is therefore important for you to consider and decide how the client designation will be used in your coaching model and practice.

Here is the definition of *executive coaching* that underlies this book:

Executive coaching is a one-to-one development process formally contracted between a professional coach, an organization, and an individual client who has people management and/or team responsibility, to increase the client's managerial and/or leadership performance, often using feedback processes and on-the-job action learning.

This definition implies several important distinctions between executive coaching and other activities. First, it recognizes that the activity of managers coaching their employees is different from executive coaching because of its authority structure and lack of confidentiality. Second, while the term *mentoring* is sometimes used synonymously with coaching, this book views it as a different activity. Mentoring is valuable in supporting career access and advancement but does not focus on performance improvement. Third, training and development programs can have similar content to coaching, but they are delivered in group settings rather than the one-to-one structure of coaching.

There are, of course, a variety of other definitions that have been given to *executive coaching*. Several alternative definitions by other practitioners are shown here. Each one reflects that practitioner's favored theories or approaches (indicated in parentheses) to fostering learning and change:

The essence of executive coaching is helping leaders get unstuck from their dilemmas and assisting them to transfer their learning into results for the organization.[1]

—MARY BETH O'NEILL
(organization development, or OD, values)

Action coaching is a process that fosters self-awareness and that results in the motivation to change, as well as the guidance needed if change is to take place in ways that meet organizational needs.[2]

—DAVID DOTLICH AND PETER CAIRO
(relationship focused on business results)

Coaching is not telling people what to do; it's giving them a chance to examine what they are doing in light of their intentions.

Our job as coaches will be to understand the client's structure of interpretation, then in partnership alter this structure so that the actions that follow bring about the intended outcome.[3]

—JAMES FLAHERTY
(phenomenology)

A masterful coach is a vision builder and value shaper ... who enters into the learning system of a person, business, or social institution with the intent of improving it so as to impact people's ability to perform.[4]

—ROBERT HARGROVE
(transformational change)

The aim of coaching is to improve the client's professionalism by discovering his or her relationship with certain experiences and issues ... to encourage reflection ... to release hidden strengths ... to overcome obstacles to further development ... to investigate the extent to which aspects of the client's behavior are causing or prolonging the issues.[5]

—ERIK de HAAN and YVONNE BURGER
(learning, human potential)

The Intersection of Executive Coaching and Consulting

The goals of executive coaching usually can be categorized under one or more of the following headings: strengthening a client's self-management; interpersonal effectiveness; and leadership impact. When useful, traditional managerial skills such as contracting for performance, delegating, and providing feedback can be included under the leadership heading.

Of course, case-specific coaching goals are always tailored to the client's needs and interests. Examples of a client's needs might include being a stronger team leader; influencing in complex systems; clarifying a vision and goals; taking on larger or global responsibilities; or managing multilayer execution. There may be other aspirations as well, tied to that leader's unique blend of skills, personality, career aspirations, and challenges.

Some executive coaches bridge their work into the content areas of executive roles—areas such as business strategy, integration of acquisitions, or talent management processes, for example. This practice is particularly true of consultants, human resource professionals, and organizational psychologists who have added coaching to their practices. However, this melding can often be confusing to clients. While coaching and consulting can be synergistic, the activities are quite different. Coaching leverages the client relationship within a process that fosters self-discovery, whereas consulting brings particular content expertise to the foreground. In overly general terms, coaches ask in order to explore, while consultants ask in order to tell. In this respect, coaching is more aligned with the values of organization development (OD), which seeks to draw out answers that reside in the collective consciousness of the client.

Experience indicates that coaches who also consult need to make a clear separation between these two activities in order to prevent client confusion. In building your Personal Model, it is important for you to make a conscious choice about your coaching/consulting balance. Without acknowledging that boundary, you are likely to slip into consulting mode because it is what clients are used to. Said differently, it is important for coaches who also consult to be clear with themselves and with clients about their roles in every engagement and use different processes within those roles. It is also important to reaffirm roles during the course of coaching engagements if boundaries are challenged or become blurred. For detailed distinctions among executive coaching, consulting, personal coaching, and therapy, see Exhibit 1, which appears among the supplementary materials at the end of this book.

Understanding Adult Change and Growth Through Theories that Apply to Coaching

Most people have strongly held beliefs about how people change and grow. Some may be rooted in philosophical tradition (e.g., *What doesn't destroy me makes me stronger*), while others may come from religious teaching (e.g., *Turn the other cheek*). Still others may reflect values imprinted from an individual's upbringing (e.g., *Education is the key to success*). These belief structures exist for coaches, clients, and sponsors, whether articulated or not, and they act as lenses through which behavior is interpreted. In order for you to articulate your Personal Model and apply consistent professional judgment, you need to identify your own philosophy of how people change and grow and make it overt and describable, at least to yourself. For example, you may believe that clients experiencing transitions (e.g., into leadership roles or entering midlife or a second career) are particularly open to growth, or you may know you would rather coach younger managers before they are set in their ways.

In reflecting on your own point of view, it is useful for you to become conversant with a repertoire of broader theories of adult change. These formalized theories of adult change and growth represent eddies in that first stream from therapy and counseling that flowed into coaching. They encapsulate many useful concepts and models about adult growth.

Six of these theories are highlighted here because they have been important influences on coaching practice; we encourage you to try on these lenses. The six theories are psychodynamic, life stage, behaviorist, emotional intelligence/positive psychology, existential/phenomenological, and cognitive.

None of them is inherently more accurate than any of the others; each provides a useful perspective, or lens, about how adults establish and change behavior, while at the same being applicable to coaching.

All of the approaches are likely to be familiar to executive coaches with graduate training, but you may not have realized that all have been applied to coaching. In addition, any of them could be part of shaping your Personal Model or definition of coaching. As you try on these different lenses, you may find one or more of the theories especially engaging and helpful in increasing the acuity of your observations. In this regard, studying them helps you articulate your own change philosophy and expand the range of your thinking.

Since the descriptions of each approach could take a book by itself, this chapter merely highlights how each could translate into a coaching approach:

- Coaches who apply *psychodynamic thinking* to their work are focused on revealing insights about the client's motivations, choices, and defenses, especially through exploring the client's formative emotional experiences. They may also leverage the relationship between coach and client and transference reactions, in which the client may experience thoughts and feelings in response to the coach that are reminiscent of other important relationships, such as with a parent.[6]

- Coaches who apply *life-stage conceptions* of change look for the accomplishment of life-stage challenges and successful transitions. They also encourage clients to view change as a natural part of growth and plan for transitions and challenges likely to be prominent in future stages.[7]

- Coaches who emphasize a *behaviorist approach* target specific, manageable, behavioral change goals and foster an environment that reinforces those desired changes. They focus on putting aside past ineffective behavior by changing the context and the feedback, rather than by increasing the client's self-insight.[8]

- Coaches who use *emotional intelligence* as a lens emphasize helping clients improve their emotional self-management, social awareness, empathy, and effectiveness in relationships. Related to emotional intelligence is the *positive psychology* movement. When used in coaching, positive psychology emphasizes strengths and uses insights about them to chart a path toward effective leadership. These ideas have been very appealing to coaches and clients who want to tap into the energy generated by building on success.[9]

◎   Coaches who leverage *existential/phenomenological thinking* explore the client's view of the world and empower the act of choosing, even though uncertainty can never be eliminated. Some coaches may view these ideas as bleak or fatalistic; others are truly energized by supporting choice in the face of real-world pressures.[10]

◎   The most widely used approaches in clinical and counseling psychology, *cognitive perspectives* about change (sometimes called cognitive behavioral or rational emotive) are favored by coaches as well. They combine behavioral outcomes with self-insight about negative or self-limiting thoughts and the behaviors they engender.[11]

While each of these six conceptual lenses has unique elements, they also naturally overlap. Examples include a cognitive approach that leverages emotional intelligence ideas, life-stage transitions that incorporate an existential stance, and, of course, behaviorist thinking overlaps with almost all of the other approaches in terms of tangible, behavioral outcomes to coaching.

In addition, there are other useful conceptions of adult development, which come from streams other than individual change but have been applied to coaching, such as learning models and systems approaches.[12] Increasing your awareness of the many ways that change can be understood is a valuable endeavor. It will help you articulate your own beliefs about adult growth and influence how you will apply those beliefs in your coaching model and practice.

Consider the following questions as prompts to your own conceptions of adult change:

1. What do you believe are the most important influences shaping personality and interpersonal style?

2. What are the most powerful leverage points in fostering changes in behavior?

3. In your own experiences, what influences have helped you change and grow?

4. How do you conceptualize the connections between feelings, thoughts, beliefs, and behavior?

The Range of Coaching Services

Even though descriptions of coaching usually focus on those services that are delivered in a typical three- to six-month engagement, there are related interventions that fulfill our definition of *executive coaching*. Coaching has been viewed along a continuum, from shorter and more targeted, to longer and more emergent interventions. This book envisions seven distinct types of coaching that range along this continuum (see Figure 3-2). Each one differs from the others in important respects. All have a focus on individual development in the work context, although breadth and other features vary. You may not be familiar with all of them, but becoming familiar with more of them could expand your practice, whether you are an internal or external coach.

Moving from left to right in Figure 3-2, the types of coaching are arranged by degree of coaching skill and experience required, as well as the likelihood that an internal coach would be delivering this type of coaching versus an external coach. Type I coaching is similar to a tutorial but focused on an important management or leadership skill tailored to the needs and abilities of the client. While this type of coaching may not arise frequently, internal coaches connected with leadership development functions readily deliver this type of coaching in a few sessions. Types II and III coaching are similar because they are tied to a developmental experience (e.g., leadership development program, assessment feedback, or 360-degree surveys) and because they are aimed at having the client draft a well-founded development plan.

Figure 3-2. Executive coaching continuum

Type I	Type II	Type III	Type IV	Type V	Type VI	Type VII
TARGETED SKILLS COACHING	FEEDBACK/ DEVELOPMENT PLAN COACHING	FEEDBACK COACHING WITH FOLLOW-UP	TRANSITION/ ASSIMILATION COACHING	LEADERSHIP EFFECTIVENESS COACHING	HIGH-POTENTIAL COACHING	LEADER'S AGENDA COACHING
One-on-one communication, interpersonal, people management, or leadership skills training (e.g., presentations, listening, giving feedback; could be several sessions)	Interpretation of 360-degree survey results and/or self-insight questionnaires, simulations, and other feedback from leadership training or other experience to help a client move toward action planning for on-the-job development plan	Same as Type II but with scheduled follow-up meetings/ calls focused on progress in drafting and implementing previously discussed development action plan; could be several sessions; may include facilitating a 3-way meeting with client's manager	Coaching program aimed at helping a newly hired (on-boarding) or promoted manager or executive make an efficient and productive transition to a new role; may draw upon client self-insight, early feedback from colleagues, and transition planning tools; knowledge of organizational culture and values helpful; usually 4-6 sessions	Full coaching engagement of 3-6 months focused on improving managerial and/or leadership performance in the context of the client's current job; often there is an issue or obstacle that needs to be addressed if the client is to be fully successful in that role	Full coaching engagement of 3-6 months focused on readiness for future opportunities, often linked with the organization's Talent Management Planning process	Open-ended engagement determined by the client's agenda; almost always a C-suite executive or member of the senior executive team; less emphasis on stakeholders, tools, and formalized development planning, more emphasis on discussion and insight, with the focus on the executive's unique leadership challenges. Note: This is NOT consulting on organizational or business challenges, except as a vehicle to help the executive grow

The difference is that Type III coaching includes follow-up meetings after the initial feedback discussion. These follow-up meetings require additional coaching skill in order to adjust and confirm the implementation of a productive development plan.

The specifics of Type IV coaching are unique for each organization. What is common is the goal of making a transition to a new job smoother and quicker. It may be applied to current employees or new hires (i.e., on-boarding) but the structure of these engagements can vary widely. Type IV coaching has become very widely used and gives internal coaches an opportunity to leverage their organizational knowledge, although external coaches deliver it as well.

Types V and VI coaching are most often thought of when the term *executive coaching* is used. They differ only in the need that triggers the engagement: Type V focuses on improving current performance, and Type VI supports a client's promotability to a likely future job or organizational level. What is profound about this distinction is its effect on how coaches will contract and conduct the engagement. Type V, in particular, can be challenging for all parties because job jeopardy may be implied, depending upon the severity of the need for behavior change. Type VI, on the other hand, challenges the coach and client to extrapolate to future job challenges and create a development plan with that vision as the focus. Typically, both types of coaching are six-month engagements.

Last, Type VII coaching is uniquely delivered to those senior, or C-suite, executives (e.g., chief executive officer, chief financial officer, and so forth) who control their own budgets and developmental agendas. Goals are quite variable—from leadership style concerns, to career quandaries, to just having a confidential *discussion partner* for leadership issues facing the executive. As long as the client remains the focus, this intervention stays within the boundaries of executive coaching. As indicated by the flow of the continuum, highly experienced external coaches almost always deliver this type of coaching.

All of these coaching interventions are in active use across the spectrum of the executive coaching field. You may choose to specialize in one or more of them while at the same time targeting your growth toward those you would like to add to your practice.

Part II of this book is aimed at the third input to your Personal Model: your awareness of and preferences for executive coaching practices. As such, Part II divides the challenges of an executive coaching engagement into sixteen major topics, from contracting to concluding the engagement and everything in-between. Some chapters are not aligned with the sequence of an engagement but are important to consider, such as dealing with differences and professionalism. Each of these content chapters includes a case study that illustrates aspects of that chapter's focal topic, followed by a case supervisor's commentary. The concluding chapter of Part II addresses the special challenges of being an internal coach, a role of increasing importance in management and executive development.

PART

II

TOPICS IN

EXECUTIVE COACHING

4

Managing the Coaching Engagement

E NGAGEMENT MANAGEMENT DESCRIBES THE ENTIRE ARC OF THE COACHING PROCESS. AS THE COACH, YOU ARE RESPONSIBLE FOR MANAGING THIS PROCESS IN ITS ENTIRETY, FROM INITIAL INTRODUCTIONS TO THE CLOSURE MEETING. This chapter provides an overview and introduces the many topics that are part of an executive coaching engagement. Figure 4-1 provides an overview of the typical phases of an executive coaching engagement. As you read this chapter, you can observe the flow of the elements and be confident that those that interest you are explored in greater depth in subsequent chapters within this section.

If coaching can be compared to building a house, your role is equivalent to that of the general contractor—working closely and respectfully with those who will live there as well as with the neighbors, being guided by plans that the owners have contributed to, conforming to various practices or codes, staying within a budget and time frame to complete the project, and supporting the transition to the new space. The following are some important considerations to keep in mind regarding that role:

⊙ You are the expert about the coaching process; your clients are the experts about themselves and their situations.

Figure 4-1. *Typical phases of executive coaching*

1. Someone feels a need or a problem
   - Client or manager calls Human Resources, who calls you, or …
   - Encouraged by the sponsor, the client calls you directly to arrange a meeting.

   Gather initial information from HR and/or manager.

2. Entry—first meeting with client
   - Engage in conversation to learn about each others' backgrounds and experience and to start building trust.
   - Check for suitability; arrive at a tentative agreement to have a working relationship.
   - Introduce contracting, the coaching process, confidentiality, sponsor involvement, possible data gathering, and such.

   Gather initial self-insights and developmental perspectives from client.

3. Next set of meetings
   - Draw together further information from client and sponsors.
   - Look for opportunities to reframe presenting issues ["Aha" experiences].
   - Offer your impressions; hypothesize about client and context.
   - Revise statement of the "problem" or "development need" in positive terms.
   - Identify strengths, gaps, fears, and blind spots.

   Use openness, empathy, and authenticity to foster insight, trust, and motivation.

4. Data collection and feedback session(s)
   - Contract about data to collect, whom to sample; involve sponsors in that decision.
   - Collect information, prepare summary, discuss with client.

   Help the client distill information into engaging headlines/themes; further refine and articulate development needs.

5. Draft of developmental action plan with the client
   - Shape developmental goals to meet both client and organization needs.
   - Brainstorm on-the-job action ideas, including timing, resources, outcomes.

   Orchestrate sharing the plan with sponsors; obtain consensus and support.

6. Monitoring development progress in subsequent appointments
   - Provide cognitive, tactical, and emotional support.
   - Acknowledge success; debrief and learn from setbacks.
   - Adjust development plan as needed; look toward closure.

   Help client obtain other support and ongoing feedback.

7. Evaluating progress and discussing next steps with client and sponsors

   Reflect on learning; hand off development plan to client and sponsors.

8. Bringing closure to the engagement.

   Arrange follow-up support as needed.

- As process expert, you are responsible for anticipating the flow and providing the client and sponsors with guidance about each step and expectations for it.

- Doing *process checks* with the client and sponsors will help you stay attuned to their reactions and needs, allowing you to address any concerns that arise.

- While there may be pressure to define coaching goals early in the process, it is more important that goals feel right to the client and motivate action, even though that may take longer.

- The essential challenge of engagement management is alignment: you and the client, the client and sponsors, and you and sponsors. This can be tricky but it is what makes executive coaching challenging and gratifying.

Pre-Engagement Events

Although you cannot begin the engagement until the organization contacts you, the events that led up to the decision to find a coach influence how you set up and manage the engagement. Whether triggered by a problem, an opportunity, or possibly both, the possibility of coaching for your client was likely to have been discussed by the client's manager, human resource professional, and others in leadership development or a related function.

They have agreed that coaching would be the intervention of choice for your client. You can therefore assume that they considered and rejected other alternatives. Their decision implies a consensus that both the client and the need are important enough to warrant the expense and effort of retaining an executive coach. You can also infer that they believe coaching has a higher probability of success than other possible interventions. However, the strength and consistency of their agreement may be more uneven than it appears. Exploring the events and decision process that preceded your arrival may provide valuable information about how your client is perceived, the goals that have been discussed, and the ways that sponsors work together and with the client.

Effective Communication Is Key

How well you are able to manage the engagement depends on how well you communicate with the sponsors and the client about their expectations and vision for the process. In particular, you need to know what factors caused them to call you in and what they hope will be different after coaching is finished. With this knowledge, you can propose a coaching process that is most likely to achieve what is envisioned.

Some sponsors may have clear opinions about process requirements and others will defer to your judgment and your recommended engagement steps. As you become a more experienced coach, you will be able both to explore options with sponsors and to offer variations based on the details of the case. It is through such give-and-take that you have the best chance of reaching agreement on the coaching process and milestones that everyone believes will support successful outcomes.

Initial Steps in the Process

Engagement management begins from the minute a sponsor calls you to discuss using your services. In addition to the issues described thus far, there are other important topics to cover even before you meet the client. Among these are the client's prior development efforts, assessment data about the client that may be available, and existing development plans. This history may provide you with indications about the potential challenges in the engagement. It is also important to explore the client's key relationships, such as those with sponsors and with others in the client's organization (such as dotted-line managers, mentors, talent management professionals, and coaching coordinators).

Building on information from the sponsors, you can then use your initial meeting with the client to get a sense of whether this is going to be a workable coaching assignment with a good likelihood of success. In particular, it is important to evaluate whether:

- The need, as described by the sponsors, is an acceptable starting point for the coaching even if it differs somewhat from the client's articulation.

- There are no major personal or professional impediments to the client making a commitment to coaching.

- The organization has the capability and willingness to support the client's development in terms of sponsor involvement and organizational values that encourage development.

- There is mutual interest in a coach-client developmental partnership, sometimes called *positive chemistry*. (Typically, coaching clients are interested or even excited to engage in coaching, even though feelings of uncertainty and nervousness may be present, too.)

- You are comfortable with the proposed terms of the contract—time frame, fees, deliverables, and general objectives.

When all these variables have been explored and found to be acceptable to you, to the client, and to the sponsors, the coaching process has an excellent foundation for more detailed contracting, which is discussed in the next chapter. However, even before those details are agreed to, you are beginning to build a working relationship with your client. Rapport may emerge easily out of this collaboration, or it may take longer. Either way, there is information to be noted about your client on variables such as communication style, interpersonal comfort, openness, and self-insight. These early impressions may prove useful later as you gather other perceptions about your client and provide feedback.

An especially pivotal discussion is about what you and the client should work on. In most cases, this is a substantive exchange that has several discernable stages. These stages fall under the heading called *goal evolution*, and they represent an important aspect of engagement management. They are summarized here and discussed in detail in Chapter 8.

Goal Evolution: Starting with Felt Needs

Identifying goals begins in the earliest stages of coaching as you and the client explore ideas about what to focus on together. We call these ideas the client's *felt needs*. The sponsors are likely to also articulate their own versions of felt needs for the client's development. In most cases, there is conceptual, if not literal, overlap between client and sponsor felt needs. Alignment between the client's and the sponsor's felt needs should occur at some point, but it does not have to be forced in the early stages of coaching.

With the client's felt needs as a starting point, you and the client will begin to discuss goals for the coaching assignment: "What should we focus on together? What goals are realistic to achieve?" Those discussions are likely to result in greater clarity and understanding of what you and the client will work on. When that happens, we say that *negotiated goals* have emerged. These goals are often felt needs reframed to be engaging and actionable for clients. They may contain client aspirations and ways to expand the client's repertoire of behaviors. For example, a client's felt need might be to *Become a stronger leader*, or *Step up to the challenges of my new role*. Your early coaching conversations might have helped these felt needs evolve into negotiated goals such as *Set and maintain higher performance standards for my team*, or *Build relationships with my new peers*.

Articulating negotiated goals often triggers interest in confirming that these goals are worth working on. You may already have the sponsor's felt needs to guide you, but gathering the perceptions of a wider group becomes relevant. Consider these two questions:

1. Who can provide a perspective about the client's strengths and development areas?

2. Who can confirm and clarify the negotiated goals?

You and the client can discuss these questions and reach agreement about a data-gathering process (often anticipated by the contract and with support from sponsors). This process may utilize coach informational interviewing, a multirater or 360-degree survey, client self-report questionnaires, and other assessment tools.

Providing feedback from data sources leads to the next stage of goal evolution, identifying *designed objectives*. These are clear statements of what the client would like to achieve. By their nature, they imply on-the-job actions that will support their implementation. The objectives and the linked action ideas are often shared with sponsors in a document called a *development action plan*. Its creation brings the goal evaluation process full circle and links original felt needs with an articulation that is compelling and contains detailed action plans.

Implementing the actions generated by development planning is a tangible way to foster the client's growth. Coaching supports that by providing the client with a confidential forum to debrief efforts and make adjustments. You, your client, and the sponsors then can use the development plan as a shared guide to keep your coaching on track and to evaluate progress as coaching reaches closure.

The Importance of Alignment

Alignment occurs when everyone in the process—coach, client, and sponsors—share the same or a similar vision for the engagement and, equally important, for the development objectives. Success in managing the engagement requires paying close attention to alignment and taking steps to reestablish it when gaps occur.

Giving clients positive feedback is an important aspect of sustaining their involvement and demonstrating that you and they are focused on the same objectives. Acknowledging support from sponsors helps to encourage their active participation in the process. Sponsor reward and acknowledgment of the client's progress brings greater alignment between the sponsors and the client. Your role is to orchestrate as much of these alignment-supporting activities as possible, although some will be outside your purview.

When misalignment occurs, it is usually because one or more of the participants fails to fulfill commitments to the process. Examples include a lack of involvement by the sponsors, scheduling problems, inadequate follow-through by the client, and shifts in the level of enthusiasm exhibited by the client or the sponsors. All of these factors signal the need to address expectations with the appropriate person so that issues can be discussed and alignment be reestablished.

Both gravitas and sensitivity are required in handling these situations. If the client, or sponsors, or both are not meeting their commitments to coaching, you need to call attention to that gap and invite dialogue about it. At the same time, it is important for you to remain flexible. Even with everyone's commitment to coaching, clients and sponsors have many other demanding obligations. Approaching misalignment diplomatically and with curiosity is always preferred. Most of the time, raising the question is enough to resolve it, although adjusting the contract based on emerging situational constraints or shifting roles is also an option.

Achieving Closure

Near the end of the engagement, both you and the client may reflect on it: What has the client learned? How has behavior changed? What requires further developmental attention? How can sponsors continue to support development? Updating the development plan to indicate progress and areas of opportunity is a useful step as the engagement ends. In addition to what happened for the client, you can consider your learning from the engagement: What worked well, what was difficult, and how did your Personal Model fit this assignment? Formal follow-up evaluation of the coaching is also recommended. This is often achieved by polling the sponsors about the effectiveness of the process, goals achieved, and follow-up that would be useful.

This chapter has illustrated that executive coaching is much more complex than just a series of conversations between coach and client. The process must engage sponsors, produce tangible results, and provide for the client's continued development, as well as trigger the client's self-insight and increased awareness. Coaches often place less importance on those macro aspects of their work, preferring to focus on the micro aspects of building productive relationships with clients. Our position is that for you to be an *exceptional* executive coach, you need to manage the overall engagement as well as apply excellent coaching skills within coaching sessions. Subsequent chapters present more detailed considerations about both the macro and micro challenges of executive coaching.

CASE ILLUSTRATION: ENGAGEMENT MANAGEMENT TOUCHES ALL PARTS OF COACHING

Engagement management requires attention to many aspects of the coaching process. There are the major steps of relationship building with your client and sponsors, contracting the process, shaping a development plan that aligns with both client and organizational needs, and conducting progress checks along the way. Some of these may be straightforward, but often there are unexpected challenges that call upon both your problem-solving skills and assertiveness. The following case illustrates both standard and unique engagement elements that the coach must manage to achieve success.

Mark, the coach, was called by Gail, the VP of HR, about a potential coaching case. He met with her and they discussed coaching for Cindy, the head of sales. Gail described Cindy as a very dynamic person who was somewhat eccentric, but generally competent and productive. At the same time, high turnover among the sales staff, along with a series of complaints about Cindy's behavior, highlighted the need for a coach.

When Mark met Cindy several days later, he found her to be energetic, socially skilled, and eager to discuss her situation. Disarmingly, she readily admitted that she could be a difficult boss. She reported being demanding and especially tough on low producers. She brushed aside Gail's reports of complaints about her and wrote them off as "collateral damage" when holding people to higher performance expectations. To Mark's surprise, however, she was happy to engage with him about a developmental challenge that was of her own choosing, but also reflected sponsor concerns: namely, broadening her range of people management skills. While this was a general goal, Mark agreed that they could begin their coaching engagement with that focus.

Gail requested that Mark get in touch with Margaret, the COO and Cindy's direct manager, and Althea, the HR generalist dedicated to Cindy's department. However, Mark found out that Margaret was about to go on maternity leave and couldn't be very involved in the coaching. Therefore, it looked like Althea might be the primary sponsor contact. Although she was willing to take on that responsibility, her time was limited because she had several other departments to cover. Mark was concerned about the lack of organizational involvement, and after checking with Cindy, he arranged an appointment with Margaret and Gail to clarify sponsorship of the engagement.

During the meeting, Mark reviewed Cindy's felt need of broadening her people management skills, and they agreed it was a useful start. Gail emphasized, however, that the bottom line was that the complaints should stop. They agreed on a coaching process that would include informational interviewing of Cindy's colleagues and direct reports, regular process check-ins, and a meeting to review a development action plan. Mark emphasized that he would require their active participation during the engagement. Change would take both time and their involvement.

Given Margaret's impending maternity leave, she was hesitant about her commitment and suggested closer involvement by Gail and Althea. Gail was willing to stand in for Margaret. However, Mark noted to himself that Margaret didn't sound like a very strong supporter of Cindy. Even with Margaret's impending leave, he felt certain he had to find ways of keeping Margaret involved, even if less frequent than usual for a manager. At the end of the meeting, Mark expressed thanks to the sponsors for their support and noted that he looked forward to subsequent conversations as the process unfolded. He also reminded them that he would review the engagement details with Cindy so that everyone was on the same page.

Surprisingly to Mark, both the data-gathering process and the developmental planning with Cindy went quite smoothly. Direct reports respected Cindy, but they said her demanding style was too "one size fits all" and often resulted in demotivation. Cindy's peers also found her to be too direct, so there were development issues with them as well. Mark was able to get Cindy to experiment with more facilitative ways of communicating and, for her part, Cindy was willing to take more time with people if it resulted in stronger engagement. These ideas and experiments resulted in a development action plan that expanded Cindy's repertoire of communication skills both downward and across the organization. She was actually quite open to learning and brought both successes and setbacks to her sessions with Mark.

As soon as possible after the development plan was drafted, Mark was able to arrange a four-way meeting, including Margaret by phone and Gail in person, to get everyone's reactions and suggestions. There was strong support for the plan and for Cindy's efforts.

After their commitment was on the table, Mark followed up with Gail and Margaret to encourage them to provide Cindy with continuing support and feedback. During one of their calls, Mark perceived a warming in Margaret toward Cindy, and he hoped this was a positive sign for their future relationship. He also checked in with Althea regularly to learn how Cindy was managing her staff and used that feedback to fine-tune Cindy's action plans.

At the end of six months, Mark moved the coaching toward closure with a final meeting that included just Gail and Althea, since Margaret was unavailable. The complaints about Cindy had largely stopped. It was acknowledged that turnover in Cindy's organization might have contributed to the improvement, as had the coaching. However, Cindy reported that she now believed it was possible to balance her high standards with the need for positive rapport with her team. Still, since she didn't find it easy, she expected some backsliding. She also talked about managing herself in stressful situations and seemed more attuned to her inner indicators.

Cindy and the sponsors considered the coaching to be a success for the reasons they reported, although everyone was realistic about the need for continued attention to the changes. With Gail's approval, Cindy and Mark agreed that they would check in by phone every month for the next six months to support Cindy's development, and Gail would meet with Cindy regularly, too, in preparation for Margaret's return.

Supervisor's Observations

Engagement management isn't one element of coaching—it's all of them! There isn't a complete checklist, although the coach has to think about all aspects of coaching and how they come together: How to do the contracting? Who should be involved? Who has a hidden agenda? Where are the pitfalls? What does the client really want from the coaching? What is the process for making it all happen within the allotted time frame?

Complicating matters, sometimes a coach has his own agenda to get the process going quickly in order to *close the sale*. The danger here is that moving too quickly can limit the coach's perspective to understand all the concerns from client to manager and Human Resources. One can easily see how rushing ahead and assuming standard contracting may actually lengthen the time it takes for the client to fully engage and for sponsors to be as supportive as needed. Coaches need to have the presence of mind to build the best foundation possible given the constraints of the participants and the situation. Of course, stepping away from an untenable process should always be an option as well.

Coaches become increasingly confident about managing engagements based on learning from experience, whether that experience is positive or frustrating. Still, even for coaches who have completed dozens of engagements, it takes a measure of courage to advocate engagement management choices that may contrast with what sponsors envisioned. In this case, Mark leaned on Margaret to stay involved to the extent that she could, even as he kept Gail involved as a senior sponsor and relied on Althea for close-in support. Mark accepted that the organization's felt need (stop the complaints) was different from Cindy's (broaden her style) and trusted that the process had a good chance of bringing the two goals together. Was that too big a risk? It might have been If Margaret had had a hidden agenda and/or became distant from the process or if other unknown obstacles had surfaced. Still, it is important for coaches to use their intuition in making decisions about engagement details. It is somewhat reassuring that most of these decisions are adjustable, if addressed on a timely basis.

There was much in this case that a supervisor could commend. Mark effectively connected with Cindy as a client, despite Cindy's tough demeanor and the difference between her own goal and management's. He took a leadership role in designing a process and getting others involved. He anticipated how the assignment would flow. He maintained good transparency and managed everyone's expectations. There was solid progress in terms of Cindy's learning; her leadership behavior also appeared to improve. The organization's felt need, the cessation of complaints, also appeared to have been met, although as with all outcomes, the causes were multidetermined.

The unexpected can happen and challenges sometimes emerge—in this case, the concerns were Margaret's potential distance from Cindy and whether those voicing complaints would be quickly responsive to Cindy's behavior change. To deal with these possibilities, coaches need to pay close attention and build in process checks along the way. When a coach makes all that happen and then makes adjustments as feedback is received, the ending is not a surprise to anyone. That's good engagement management!

Takeaways

- ⊙ Engagement management refers to the entire arc of the coaching experience. It is a process you lead from design through closure.

- ⊙ As the expert in the process, you suggest and monitor the structure of the engagement. You anticipate steps and obstacles and establish clear process expectations.

- ⊙ You encourage periodic reflection about the process and progress toward change to reveal questions or concerns as early as possible.

- ⊙ You facilitate the evolution of development goals—from felt needs to negotiated goals to the designed objectives in a development plan—as the client gains insight and commitment to change.

- ⊙ It's important to initiate coaching with as much clarity as possible; even so, adjustments and realignments may be necessary.

- ⊙ You are an advocate for greater alignment between your client and organizational stakeholders. If the client, sponsors, or others involved are not meeting their commitments, you can be a force to resolve gaps.

- ⊙ Each engagement is an opportunity to learn more about yourself as a coach.

CHAPTER

5

Contracting the Coaching Process with Clients and Sponsors

ONTRACTING CAN BE COMPARED TO PREPARING A ROOM FOR PAINTING: IT MAY SEEM TO DELAY THE START OF THE NEEDED WORK, BUT PREPARATION ALWAYS PAYS OFF LATER IN BOTH EFFICIENCY AND QUALITY OF RESULTS. That same principle applies to contracting the coaching process, even though you may be tempted to bypass this step out of urgency to get started. Nonetheless, this step, whether simple or complex, needs to be part of the start of every coaching engagement.

As mentioned in the previous chapter, various discussions and decisions may have preceded your initial meeting with the sponsors of the coaching engagement. In order to inform your contracting, you need to uncover what was previously discussed by asking several questions:

- ⊙ How is the development need described and by whom?

- ⊙ Why was coaching selected and why now?

- ⊙ What preferences, if any, do sponsors have about the coaching process?

- ⊙ What is the organization's experience with coaching?

Contracting provides an opportunity for you to discuss these questions with sponsors, and later with the client, so that the coaching process can be designed to fit both organizational and client needs.

Contracting: Definition and Challenges

Contracting is the step that enables the sponsoring organization, the client, and you, the coach, to reach agreement on the coaching engagement process—in other words, how coaching can best achieve the results that are envisioned. The contract may be written as a letter or as a more formal document, or it may even be left as an oral understanding if you and the organization have worked together before. As the first step you will take to manage the engagement, contracting is aimed at aligning expectations for all those involved in the process (see Figure 5-1).

In organizations where coaching is well established or where you have coached before, contracting may be a matter of confirming your usual process and highlighting any exceptions within a particular case. In organizations where you have never coached and/or where there is little experience with coaching in general, you may need to clarify your approach and discuss important details before you start. In fact, it is in those situations when a written contract or letter of agreement is particularly important.

The Contracting Process

There are three parties to contracting with overlapping interests: the client, the sponsoring organization, typically represented by a human resource professional and/or the client's manager, and you. All parties can, and should, play a role in shaping the contract. The contract reflects your mutual agreement about the implementation and the general outcomes of the coaching process that are critical to establishing a working relationship among all the parties.

The client's involvement in pre-coaching contracting may be minimal, but it is no less important. Client-coach contracting usually occurs during the initial meeting with the client. Progress on your Personal Model of coaching

Figure 5-1. Contracting: Setting process expectations

What is typically in a contract?

- Reason for initiating the coaching
- Probable duration of the engagement
- General flow of the coaching assignment: data gathering, feedback, revision of goals, action planning, implementation, review
- Frequency and length of meetings
- Privacy, confidentiality, and reporting issues
- Relationships with significant stakeholders
- Data-gathering methods: interviews, assessments, observation, and the like
- Fees and terms

What are possible formats of the contract?

- Letter of agreement or formal contract between coach and the organization
- An agreement letter to the client
- Outline shared by the coach
- Discussion and oral agreement

What other documents might be requested by sponsors?

- Nondisclosure agreement (NDA) provided by the sponsoring organization
- Progress reports (subject to confidentiality guidelines)
- Action/development plan shared with sponsors
- Closure review: coaching evaluation, wrap-up, and development ideas for the future

will prepare you to discuss the elements of your preferred process with the client and negotiate any modifications requested. If a written contract has already been drafted, it can be shared with the client, although fees usually are not included in that draft copy. Typically, clients have already been briefed about their organization's approach to coaching, but it is always useful for you to confirm process elements, especially about confidentiality. Clients can be encouraged to express reactions, ask questions, and suggest process adjustments that they prefer.

This early discussion before coaching has begun to reach mutual consent about the coaching process also serves a more profound purpose: It allows you to establish whether the right *chemistry* exists for you and the client to work well together. If this appears likely, even though coaching has not officially started, you may choose to move into a coaching interaction with the client. You might explore the client's felt needs for coaching, making observations about them or even reframing those needs to make them clearer and more actionable. In this way the client can immediately experience what working with you would be like. You might even label the interaction as a sample of your coaching and explore the client's reactions to it. Making this *chemistry meeting* substantive will also give you a sense of the client's openness, self-insight, and readiness for coaching. Agreeing on the coaching contract is important, but getting a coaching relationship started with the client may be an equally important aspect of your initial meeting.

The broad and specific topics that are usually addressed in a standard coaching contract include:

1. Scheduling—when you might be available to start the engagement and the frequency of meetings
2. Nondisclosure—your assurance that you will never disclose any organizational information you may be exposed to
3. Confidentiality—how you will handle information you obtain about the client, including interview and assessment results, feedback summaries, and development plans
4. Time frame for the engagement
5. Location for the coaching
6. Frequency of coaching sessions
7. Data-gathering processes or instruments that the organization typically uses
8. Deliverables expected from the coach
9. Evaluation of results
10. Definition of successful outcomes

11. Fee and payment options

12. Milestones in the coaching process

Although all the issues listed are potentially relevant to your agreement with the organization, it is especially important that the contract be explicit with respect to confidentiality and how client information used at any point in the coaching process will be handled. Most coaches prefer to keep the details of confidentiality agreements as simple as possible. When organizations require you to provide progress reports or other content information, it is also important to clearly agree on what topics those reports should contain and how they will be handled. Often you and the client will jointly produce them.

A typical way to contract about confidentiality is for you to be open about the coaching process but to hold all content confidential, except for the draft of the development plan. Such an approach encourages progress checks between coaches, clients, and sponsors but avoids pressure to reveal any client data or what has been covered in coaching sessions. Contracting for this level of privacy helps to establish and sustain the client's trust.

Organizations that are interested in hiring you as a coach tend to respect your experience in structuring engagements and therefore they are not likely to inject requirements that conflict with either usual coaching practices or your specific Personal Model. Occasionally, however, the organization has requirements that may not be part of your usual coaching process but that can be made acceptable. These might include the use of a particular assessment method or adhering to specific touch points during coaching.

More rarely, organizational preferences may diverge in important ways from your coaching model. For instance, the organization may specify a preference for telephone versus in-person sessions, or ask that an engagement be unrealistically brief given what is expected. Other examples of potential contracting conflicts: a manager who opts out of the coaching process, assessment results that are shared with the sponsors, expectations for you to also help the client's team, or a requirement that you teach organization-favored leadership models.

Contracting empowers you to bring your preferred coaching process to the foreground, even if to do so will highlight differences between your approach and the organization's preferences. In those situations, sponsors often relent when you explain your concerns. For example, an HR sponsor may have neglected to build in an opportunity for you and the client to share a development plan with the client's manager. The sponsors are likely to approve that step when you explain the importance of getting the manager's suggestions and support for implementation.

Hopefully, you can negotiate elements so that they are aligned with your preferred approach. If your requests are rejected or the process requirements are in stark contrast with your approach, you can consider declining the engagement. It is always better to reveal process expectations before coaching begins rather than stumble over them later and find yourself with process, or even ethical, quandaries.

Once engaged, you can begin monitoring the behaviors of the client and sponsors with regard to the standards expressed in the contract. When managers fail to honor their obligations to attend meetings or return phone calls, or clients consistently show up unprepared for sessions, alignment with the contracted process is potentially at risk. Often just a reminder about what was agreed to in the contract is enough to bring participants back into alignment. Having an active partnership with your HR sponsor can be very valuable both to communicate the problem and to get internal leverage to correct it.

The contract is also useful for addressing more serious or prolonged digressions from the agreed-upon process. As leader of the coaching process, you have the right to call for a meeting with client and sponsors in such situations to discuss and resolve threats to the overall success of the engagement. However, the need for such a measure is less likely if you have invested the time it takes to get all the parties to accept the contract before coaching starts.

Sample contracts are included as Exhibits 2, 3, and 4 in the supplementary material at the end of this book.

CASE ILLUSTRATION: CONTRACTING PROVIDES A SOLID FOUNDATION TO COACHING

Contracting gives both the coach and the organization time to consider process options and confirm all important details. While there may be pressure on the coach to engage quickly, there is always time to contract with key participants in the process. Sometimes this contracting phase is straightforward, as in the case described here. Other times, it reveals important history, obstacles, and other details that need to be considered when designing the engagement. In both instances, however, contracting serves as an opportunity for the key participants to begin collaborating on an important developmental project.

Richard, an executive coach, was contacted by Lorraine, the head of HR for a large professional services firm. He had been recommended by a colleague and had never worked with the firm before. During a phone conversation, Richard and Lorraine discussed how the chief administrative officer (CAO) was frustrated with his direct report, Craig, the chief information officer (CIO). The key goal of coaching turned out to be to help Craig embrace his current responsibilities. Recently promoted, he appeared to be doing more of his previous technical job instead of the thinking and planning that his new job required. After further discussion of the CIO's development need, the firm's prior use of coaching, and Richard's relevant coaching experience, Lorraine asked him to send her a proposal.

Richard was able to tailor his standard proposal to reflect the specifics of the case. In the modified proposal, he mentioned very generally what he understood about the organization's goal for the CIO (help Craig step up to his new level in the organization) and summarized the coaching process that he recommended: initial meetings with HR and the CAO; coaching meetings with Craig; 360-degree interviewing; feedback to Craig; development planning; a four-way meeting to get consensus on the plan; biweekly coaching sessions to support implementation of the plan; regular progress and process checks with Craig's manager as well as with HR; and follow-up support to be structured later. The proposal also included information about confidentiality, fees, and Richard's usual invoicing practice.

Richard e-mailed this document to Lorraine, inviting her questions and requesting that she initial the document and send it back if everything was acceptable. She did this with the understanding that Richard should set up an initial appointment with Craig to do a "chemistry check" and get Craig's okay to proceed. During that appointment, Richard introduced himself, asked about Craig's sense of areas for development, and reconfirmed the coaching process (steps and confidentiality guidelines). They also talked about Craig taking the lead on selecting 360-degree interviewees but also reviewing his list with his manager and HR, since the sponsors had indicated they wanted to be included in that decision process. The coaching then proceeded according to the contracted plan and resulted in both insights and behavior change for Craig.

Supervisor's Observations

While discussing and confirming the elements of the coaching process may not be the most complex part of coaching, it is an essential foundation to a successful engagement. Coaches often neglect important details, such as steps in the coaching process, data gathering, or confidentiality. In the case described here, the negotiations had moved along very quickly, and the sponsoring organization clearly wanted the coach to engage with the client without any delay. The coach was responsive to that urgency, but also took the time to make sure the HR sponsor had a written contract in hand and could confirm its acceptability before any coaching began. Contracts are not always shared with clients, but in this case, with a job potentially in jeopardy and pressure for a quick start, discussing the contract with the client (without reference to fees and invoicing) may facilitate progress.

Also, since the CAO seems to be the driving force behind the need for the coaching, the coach found it helpful to interview him very early in the process, get his feedback on the client's needs, and contract with him about the time and steps required for the coaching. This type of discussion helps to prevent gaps from emerging later in the process. The coach can also discuss with the manager the interdependency of client, coach, and sponsors and how each supports developmental progress.

Takeaways

- There are three parties to contracting, with overlapping interests: client, sponsoring organization (typically represented by the client's manager and HR), and you, the coach. All three parties can and should have a hand in shaping the contract.

- Whether written or oral, a contract comprises the recommended elements: steps in the coaching process, roles and responsibilities, data-gathering process, time frame, frequency of coaching meetings, confidentiality, and other details. It may also include a general statement about the goals of the coaching.

- Client-coach contracting is the initial part of establishing a working relationship, so the elements must be mutually agreed to. They are usually addressed orally, but a written contract can be shared with clients as well.

- Your Personal Model of coaching can help you determine the suitability of the case. If you become aware that anyone—the sponsoring organization or even the client—has process expectations that conflict with your model or appear to reduce the likelihood of success, you may need to negotiate these elements or consider not taking the case.

- Time spent in the contracting process can pay off by keeping the client, sponsors, and you aligned with an effective coaching process.

6

Sponsor and Stakeholder Involvement

E VEN IF THE CLIENT INITIATED CONTACT WITH YOU, IN AN EXECUTIVE COACH-
ING ENGAGEMENT, THERE ARE OTHER PARTICIPANTS WHO ARE STAKEHOLDERS
AND ESSENTIAL TO ITS SUCCESS. THESE PEOPLE INCLUDE YOUR CLIENT'S
immediate manager and, if appropriate, a Human Resource manager who
has an interest in, or some actual responsibility for, the client's organization.
We call these participants *sponsors* of the coaching. In larger organizations
there may be others in this sponsor group, such as a centralized coaching
coordinator or talent management professional. In most coaching situations,
sponsors have responsibility for evaluating your qualifications and approving your proposal to deliver coaching.

Engaging sponsors productively is a key difference between executive
coaching and other types of coaching in which the client contracts with you
directly. Establishing your relationship with sponsors at the same time that
you build and maintain a partnership with your client reflects both the definition and a key challenge of executive coaching. Sponsor involvement,
while often stipulated in the contract, has significant upside potential in supporting your client's development, so it is worth your effort to keep them
appropriately involved. During most coaching engagements, you are also

likely to interact with a wider stakeholder group around the client, such as peers and direct reports, especially when gathering information about your client.

In working with sponsors and other stakeholders, keep in mind that:

- Planning for the participation of sponsors and other stakeholders will make their involvement more useful and productive.

- The client, usually in conjunction with the sponsors, determines which other stakeholders to include in the process and how to approach them, relying on your guidance as the coach.

- The involvement of sponsors and stakeholders in the coaching process needs to be transparent to the client.

The Role of Sponsors in the Coaching Process

Coaching is just one of many elements in the ongoing relationship between the sponsors and the client. It is your responsibility to be sure that coaching does not replace any aspect of that relationship or get lost in the flow of usual work interactions. In fact, an implicit goal in your management of sponsors is that coaching improves relationships between client and sponsors and enhances their developmental collaboration.

Engagements that become frustrating or disappointing can often be traced back to the lack of sponsor involvement. When sponsor involvement in coaching is planned, there are fewer distractions in your relationship with your client, and you are better able to capitalize on sponsor intentions to support the effort. Without such planning, sponsors may feel the need to push for involvement or insert themselves at inappropriate times.

You can anticipate the sponsors' legitimate needs for input to the coaching process and interest in its progress by building sponsor touchpoints into the process. These touchpoints may have different schedules and content depending upon the type of coaching you are doing and the process you have contracted.

Touchpoints for Sponsors

Of all the participants in the coaching process, sponsors are involved over the longest period of time. There are six points at which they participate during a typical executive coaching engagement:

1. Before coaching in screening coaches
2. During the contracting of the coaching process
3. At the point that a development plan is drafted
4. As support during the implementation of the plan and for providing feedback and course corrections
5. At the conclusion of coaching
6. During post-coaching evaluation and client support

Touchpoint 1

Usually, a coach is brought into an organization because the sponsors have evaluated developmental options for the client and recommended coaching. Less frequently, the client may approach sponsors to initiate coaching. In both cases, sponsors usually set up criteria and screen coaches before any are introduced to clients, even if the organization already has a pool of qualified coaches. For most engagements, therefore, your first contact in a coaching engagement will be with sponsors as they screen coaches and discuss contracting details.

Touchpoint 2

As discussed in the previous chapter on contracting, sponsors are involved in all aspects of designing and approving plans for the coaching process. The key decisions they need to make in creating the contract have to do with the budget for the engagement, the time frame, how confidentiality will be maintained, and what assessments will be used and whom to sample in data-gathering. Clients are involved in some of these decisions, too.

Paying attention to how sponsors handle the contracting process may reveal information that will later be helpful in your coaching. You might note the speed at which the organization makes decisions, the organization's preferred arrangements with vendors, how much involvement the sponsors ask for, whether this is the first time the organization has used coaching, and what the sponsors know, or think they know, about the process. It is also very important to explore the sponsors' perspectives about client development needs. How they describe *felt needs* may inform your recommendations about assessment choices and how development goals are phrased.

Be careful about assuming that the sponsors know much about coaching, even when they talk authoritatively about it. Especially with the client's manager, it is safer to confirm all touchpoints, need for support, and how the coaching process will unfold rather than being disappointed later.

Touchpoint 3

After data gathering and giving feedback to the client, you and the client will distill themes from the feedback as a basis for drafting a development action plan. The development plan (described in detail in Chapter 11) typically lists between one and three developmental goals and ideas for on-the-job actions to help achieve those goals.

Obtaining sponsors' reactions to, and suggestions about, the development plan is an important part of most executive coaching. Not only can their suggestions strengthen the plan, but their input to it builds buy-in and support for the client's development. Involving the sponsors, particularly the client's manager at this point, demonstrates that the development plan is shared and provides an opportunity for collaboration, while indirectly supporting the confidentiality of all other content in the coaching relationship. It should be noted that while the Human Resources representative may get the engagement started, the client's manager more often takes the lead during the development plan discussion and subsequent implementation.

Sponsor involvement in development planning is frequently accomplished during a three- or four-way development planning meeting with coach, client, and sponsors. Other options for getting their involvement might have the client eliciting comments from the sponsors and bringing that information back to you. Whichever way it happens, sponsor buy-in to the development plan is essential to the success of coaching.

Touchpoint 4

Once you are assured that you have the sponsors' support for a development plan, you and the client can focus on its implementation. This is when sponsors can really enrich and empower the client's progress. With a well-founded and motivating development plan, the manager is in a much stronger position to provide feedback and managerial coaching to the client. The HR professional can do the same, often observing aspects of the client's behavior that the manager may not perceive. Following up with the manager and HR during this phase keeps them involved and provides useful feedback on progress to you and your client.

Touchpoint 5

Often at the conclusion of coaching, sponsors participate in a program review meeting. Also structured as a three- or four-way meeting, it reaffirms the key role of the sponsors in continuing to support the client's development once coaching comes to an official close, even if the coach will also provide predetermined follow-up support steps.

This is the point in coaching when you officially hand the client's development back to the sponsors and, particularly, to the client's manager. It is important for the closing meeting to highlight progress as well as those areas needing ongoing developmental attention and vigilance in maintaining the changes that have started during coaching. Coaching initiates a process of continuing development that sponsors are now expected to support. You may find yourself offering suggestions to the sponsors about how they can support the client's development. As in a relay, you are passing the baton to those who are continuing the long-distance event.

Touchpoint 6

Some coaching contracts anticipate the value of follow-up support, but more often it is discussed as coaching comes to a close. With sponsor approval, you and the client can decide the best way that you can support the client's ongoing development. This is also an appropriate time for you to ask for feedback from the sponsors about both their satisfaction with the overall process and their evaluation of its effectiveness.

Some organizations require that you provide sponsors with progress reports at key milestones in the engagement. Other organizations may ask for a jointly written report from you and the client after initial goal setting and then later with the development plan. These requests are meant to be helpful to the process in fostering accountability, although coaches and clients sometimes experience them as intrusive. In order to respond to those requests without unsettling the trust that you establish with clients, make your contacts with sponsors transparent to the client whenever they occur during the coaching process. In addition, whatever is conveyed in progress reports to sponsors can be prepared jointly by you and the client.

The Wider Group of Stakeholders

Beyond the sponsors, a wider group of stakeholders, comprised of colleagues who interact with the client, may be invited by the client to provide their perspective to inform the client's development plan. Stakeholders might include peers of the client, the client's direct reports, executives in a matrix relationship to the client, internal customers, and others. Their involvement with the coaching process is limited but useful, and it would have been incorporated into the contract with sponsors and your client. (How to tap their input is covered in Chapter 9.)

Some clients may involve stakeholders more than others. They may, for example, ask you to sit in on meetings to observe their interactions with stakeholders (sometimes referred to as *shadowing* the client), share all or part of their development plan with them, or encourage them to provide ongoing feedback about areas the client is working on. Other clients choose to have coaching and their development maintain a lower profile. The preference depends on several variables: the client's openness to feedback, the visibility of the development goals, the organization's culture about feedback, and the way that coaching is structured in that organization.

> Some coaches "shadow" clients by being present when the client makes a presentation, sitting in at staff or one-to-one meetings with direct reports and colleagues, or undertaking other, similar observing opportunities. The coach is like a shadow falling behind the client, staying in the background, hence the term. The client needs to introduce the coach to others but usually the coach does not interact with others or contribute to the meeting.
>
> Shadowing a client introduces a more public element into coaching than is usual when coach and client meet out of the sight of others. The client's organizational culture needs to support this more exposed use of coaching. Shadowing a client works best in organizational cultures where coaching is widely used, seen as positive, and colleagues are mutually supportive of their development.

You can influence the degree of stakeholder involvement, informed by your Personal Model of coaching. Your preferences about contact with stakeholders reflect your beliefs about how best to foster change. Some coaches make the involvement of stakeholders, both as contributors to development planning and as evaluators of progress, a central element of coaching. Other coaches place more weight on building deep and trusting relationships with clients, fostering self-insight, and learning. The question of stakeholder involvement deserves attention in how you shape your approach to coaching. Having a clear sense of the rationale for your preferred level of sponsor involvement will allow you to advocate for your approach during contracting.

CASE ILLUSTRATION: THE DISAPPEARING SPONSOR

This chapter addresses one of the public aspects of executive coaching: how to involve sponsors and stakeholders in the process. Not setting expectations about their involvement can create unnecessary obstacles and challenges for your coaching and the relationships between your client and the client's manager, such as a surprise demand from a manager who wants to know details of your conversations with your client. Sponsor involvement has the potential to be awkward at the least or may even undermine coaching if it is not managed. Ideally, the client's energy and enthusiasm for development will grow with the process. This is facilitated by having appropriate involvement by sponsors throughout the coaching. The following case illustrates some of the challenges of making that happen.

Rita engaged Sal, the coach, for a six-month coaching assignment for her direct report Marco. He had been promoted recently to the position of Director of Sales and Distribution for the company's Eastern Region. Rita described Marco as an outstanding district salesman and team leader. She believed that he was now ready to take on broader responsibilities and also increase his exposure within the company. She also believed that this would be a big step for Marco and that coaching would help him step into his new role and become the leader he was capable of being.

The coaching got off to a good start with Rita's active support. Very early on in the engagement, however, Sal began to understand a different side of Rita. Marco told Sal that Rita "never kept appointments" with him and scheduled team meetings that usually were postponed. Marco had heard about Rita's unpredictable schedule in his prior job, but he had been quite removed from regular contact with her. Now he was experiencing it firsthand and was feeling somewhat abandoned.

At first, Sal was surprised to hear this, since Rita had expressed a clear commitment to provide whatever support Marco needed. But Sal began to experience her lack of availability also. On several occasions, Sal called Rita and left messages, which Rita responded to, yet somehow was not able to actually schedule time to talk. Rita's initial enthusiasm for Marco's development and coaching was beginning to ring hollow to Sal. He could also see that Marco's enthusiasm was diminished by Rita's lack of availability. Sal was transparent about his calls to Rita; they were, after all, part of the coaching contract. When Marco asked about them, and Sal reported that conversations hadn't happened, it was easy to see Marco's disappointment. In addition, Sal was conflicted about showing his own irritation. He didn't want to set up a dynamic in which he joined with Marco to complain about Rita. Sal also didn't want to pester Rita or annoy her, even though he was increasingly frustrated. He would have gone directly to her office and scheduled time through her assistant, but this wasn't possible given the distance between headquarters and Marco's location.

Sal decided that disparaging Rita with Marco would not help either of them. In giving the situation some thought and discussing it with a trusted colleague, Sal realized that he was taking the situation too personally. Maybe Rita was unusually busy or she misunderstood how important her role was in the coaching process. Sal also admitted to himself that he might not have been as clear as he should have with Rita about the touchpoints. He realized that maybe he needed to try some different tactics for engaging with Rita.

Sal decided to speak with the HR contact and ask for help in getting on Rita's calendar. The HR sponsor provided a perspective by explaining that this was an especially busy time for Rita, but also provided Sal with the direct line for Rita's assistant. Sal was able to connect with Rita by scheduling time through the assistant. He also sent Rita an e-mail in advance of the call, writing it in an upbeat, positive tone and highlighting that he was looking forward to Rita's input to facilitate progress of the coaching. During that call, Sal made sure that Rita understood how important her involvement was and bracketed the time frame of the next touchpoint in the process. Both Marco and Sal were relieved to have that conversation behind them, and Sal felt more confident about Rita's accessibility in the future. They were also able to use this experience to give Marco a springboard in his own dealings with Rita: Be resourceful, not discouraged, in finding ways of getting what Marco needed from Rita.

Supervisor's Observations

In hindsight, it is easy to see that Rita and Sal were in different places about how best to involve sponsors in coaching. This can happen for many reasons: The coach's contracting may have assumed too much; the manager's expectations may have been wishful thinking; or unexpected pressures may have emerged. But when a manager does not follow through on a meeting time or on another commitment the manager made to the coaching, it is very apparent and unsettling to both coach and client. The coach is excited to be working with the client, and hopefully the client is excited too, but the manager may not realize how pivotal her involvement is to capitalizing on that enthusiasm. In fact, managers sometimes worry about interfering in the coaching and pull back too far. It is not unknown for a manager to be quite enthusiastic about engaging a coach and then disengage, perhaps relieved to have delegated development as if it is a task that the coach can do by himself or herself.

Keeping managers aligned with the progress of the coaching engagement is a key challenge in executive coaching. Their involvement is essential to creating a well-founded development plan, as well as demonstrating support for the client's development. Later in the coaching, the manager's involvement is equally important because once coaching is ended, then the manager again must assume a lead role in the client's development. Gaps in understanding can occur, and in this case, Sal's efforts to engage Rita were being watched by the client, most likely because Marco wanted to gauge his own challenges in getting more time and attention from her. This made it more important for Sal to succeed in a way that would be a model for Marco.

Sal made good choices here. First, he avoided publicizing his frustration, no matter how much it reflected the client's own experience with the boss. Second, he took responsibility for the lack of contact and thought creatively about what he could do differently. As a result, he started operating differently in terms of actually getting on her calendar and in mirroring her enthusiastic style and emphasizing her importance to the engagement. He also reached out to the HR sponsor to get some useful perspective and advice, viewing it as a challenge to be solved rather than personalizing the situation and becoming overtly frustrated. Sal's success in renewing Rita's involvement was both important to the coaching process and encouraging to Marco in his other dealings with her.

This is not to say the challenge won't happen again. Managers can be extremely busy; some schedules are truly impossible, and even high-priority items can get postponed without much explanation. It is natural to be puzzled or frustrated by a sponsor's lack of involvement; after all, the organization is paying for the coaching, so you would think the sponsors would do everything requested in support of it. But there are many ways in which good intentions can go astray, and coaches need to model optimism, resourcefulness, and accountability, especially when the client is tending toward powerlessness or blaming others. In all circumstances, you need to find ways of working with the situation as it presents itself, even when sponsors are not helping as they should.

Takeaways

- While your relationship with the client is your first priority, you are also accountable to the sponsors of the engagement.

- There are at least six touchpoints where you will want to anticipate and plan for sponsor participation.

- Other colleagues, such as peers and direct reports, are frequently important to the process as well, both as feedback providers and progress observers. We refer to them as *stakeholders* because they stand to benefit from the client's development.

- The stakeholders' involvement in the coaching process is much more limited than that of the sponsors. It is usually determined by the client, the sponsors, and your preferred coaching approach.

- Communications with sponsors and other stakeholders are most effective when kept transparent and done in partnership with the client.

- One of the more challenging parts of a coaching engagement is to keep the right amount of connectivity between sponsors and you as the coach. It is your responsibility to find ways of keeping to the contracted process and engaging with them, even when schedules are truly challenging.

- Your dealings with sponsors serve as a model to your client beyond the coaching engagement.

- Responding to sponsor absence with optimism and resourcefulness can foster those same qualities in clients dealing with disappointment.

CHAPTER

7

Building Early
Relationships with Clients

A S IN OTHER HELPING PROFESSIONS, THE QUALITY OF THE RELATIONSHIP
BETWEEN YOU, AS COACH, AND YOUR CLIENT IS A MORE IMPORTANT DETER-
MINANT OF POSITIVE OUTCOMES THAN ANY OTHER VARIABLE UNDER YOUR
control.[1] Creating and sustaining a safe but engaging relationship with clients
is the cornerstone of a successful coaching process. Coaches who rely on a
formulaic process or favored instruments are under-leveraging the potential
power of that relationship. Clients who feel that you are truly *seeing* them will
be much more engaged and open. Your particular style of relating to clients
is grounded in your Personal Model, but there are several general points to
guide you, especially in early sessions.

> **Trust** ... based on client safety and clear confidentiality guidelines
> **Honesty** ... based on your observations and fostering client openness
> **Caring** ... based on your empathy and connection with the client
> **Credibility** ... based on your professionalism and command of the process

Throughout the entire engagement, it is vital to maintain trust, honesty,
caring, and credibility. These characteristics are even more critical in the
early stages when anxiety may be high and progress is just beginning.

Although contracting establishes the foundation for these characteristics, clients need to be reassured in early sessions about confidentiality and other process elements. Your behavior during sessions conveys that reassurance. Clients are very observant about your communication and interpersonal skills. You are a high-profile role model for clients, so how you handle yourself needs to be intentional. Being open and genuine without being unfocused and reactive is a tricky balance. You need to know your own strengths and vulnerabilities in achieving that balance even when the client's and your own anxieties are pulling you in other directions.

Thorough preparation for sessions can help you manage your anxiety and present the credible image you want. Assuming that you check and organize your notes as soon as possible after a session, find a time to review them and plan an agenda for the next session (e.g., immediately after the last session, after your thoughts settle, or just before the next session). As you review your notes, reflect on themes that can be carried forward or that you want to explore with your client. Make note of your thoughts and build a flexible agenda for the next session. Identify session goals, both for you and for the client. Your goals may highlight ways you want to manage the interaction, whereas your client's goals would focus on progress toward development insights and actions. For example, you may target a goal of staying more focused on key issues and not getting sidetracked, whereas for your client, the session should produce at least one possible development theme.

You can also record your reactions to the client's characteristics and behaviors, both those that attract you and those that you find off-putting. When you encounter something that is off-putting, counterbalance a sense of distance with stronger empathy, to show you understand what the client might be experiencing. Those characteristics may be temporary nervous responses to the unknowns of a coaching relationship. If these tension points continue beyond early sessions or are echoed in others' descriptions of your client, observing them may contribute to your ability to form hypotheses and provide feedback later.

Your hypotheses do not need to be used in early sessions, but without at least capturing them, you will not be able to use them later. For example, a client's initial handshake and early demeanor seemed to convey lack of interest to his coach. In fact, it became apparent later that the client was deeply interested in his own development and was unaware of the mixed signals he was sending. How the client's cues played out in his wider relationships became a key focus of his coaching.

Paradoxically, thorough preparation allows you to relax and tune into what the client is saying and feeling. Conscious preparation, encompassing session agendas, goals, and reactions to client characteristics, provides a foundation for you to be present and responsive to the client instead of struggling to remember what you wanted to cover. As in all interactions, preparation does not guarantee that important topics will be covered, but it certainly helps you be ready when issues emerge.

What happens during coaching sessions is the intersection of many factors, including your preferred coaching style, the process you have designed, the client's personality, and the organization's agenda. In early sessions the interplay of these elements is still fluid. Clients may be unsure of how to use coaching and bring their day-to-day challenges to you as they might to a consultant. Clarifying your coaching role and the process may be necessary. Hopefully, you can redirect what a client brings to early sessions toward discovery and development versus advice and recommendations. This is part of educating the client about how to get the most from coaching, but it can be challenging when the client has a pressing problem and wants help. Translating that urgency into a topic that fits under a coaching framework draws on your resourcefulness.

Session agendas need to allow for responsiveness to the client but also instill a feeling of progress. At the start, ask clients how they feel, inquire about their actions and thoughts since the last coaching session, and ask them to tell you what they would like to cover. This sets a pattern that clients can depend on, as well as confirming that the agenda is a shared responsibility. You might ask any one of several questions: What have you been thinking about or tried since we last met? What hasn't worked out as well as you would have liked? What topic would you like to go back to? What would be a useful place to start today? Or you may choose a question that reflects a focus within your Personal Model. For instance: "What has gone well this week?" or "What insights have emerged?"

Steps to guide you through the initial coaching session are shown in Figure 7-1.

Figure 7-1. Guidelines for the first coaching session

➤ Introduce yourself fully and provide a general overview about the coaching process and confidentiality guidelines (i.e., the contract). *Bring your biographical sketch and contact information even if available from HR or online.*

➤ Start where the client wants to start. *Consider broad questions and the client's need for clarity and reassurance.*

➤ Always think about relationship building and partnership. *First impressions are important; be engaged, genuine, and patient.*

➤ Gather initial information about the client's career and performance story; use your facilitation skills. *There is great value in just feeling heard; don't try to do too much too fast.*

➤ Assess how much short-term pressure the client is under to change or grow. *This pressure may be organizationally driven, internal to the client, or both.*

    a. If pressure is high, explore the causes and mobilize the process more quickly.

    b. If pressure is low, you can take more time for insight and learning.

➤ Think about, and possibly suggest, a "doable" development goal or two, consistent with the contracting details of the engagement. *You are beginning to set expectations for the coaching relationship.*

➤ If needed, clarify the balance of responsibility between you and the client. *Show your commitment to the client's emerging goals but within the boundaries of what you can do in your role as coach.*

➤ At the end of the first coaching session:

    a. You and/or the client summarize in simple terms what has been covered; highlight emerging goals and other insights.

    b. Reconfirm process expectations and mutual commitments.

    c. Ask for reactions to the session and coaching in general.

    d. Schedule session two and beyond, if possible.

As the client responds to your interest, your comments and nonverbal cues convey what you feel is productive to discuss. Your facilitation of what the client presents, assuming it is within the boundaries of executive coaching, enhances the relationship and builds a bond that is both motivating and reassuring. By uncovering insights, making linkages between points, and expressing ideas that might be pivotal, you are assuring your clients that they are being truly heard. This is the basis for moving the agenda forward, toward the articulation of important development themes.

Another important step in building a productive relationship is thinking about a client from several different perspectives. Some coaches may be attuned to career issues, others to leadership issues, and still others to emotional variables in a client's life. Your preferred perspective—whether it is cognitive, career, behavioral, emotional, or something else—is reflected in your Personal Model. Even though you have a preferred lens, it is useful to expand your focus and learn to use multiple lenses in viewing the client. Refining your understanding of the client involves familiarizing yourself with a range of theories about adult change and growth (summarized in Chapter 3) that have been applied to coaching. Generating alternative hypotheses can expand your understanding of specific clients and make you a more versatile coach in general.

Clients are very observant about your adherence to the confidentiality commitments you have made. Pay special attention to the transparency of your contacts with sponsors and others in the organization. Even casual or unexpected interactions, such as bumping into your client's manager in the building lobby or being observed talking to a colleague of your client, should be noted and described to your client to prevent any misunderstanding should it be mentioned to the client.

Making sure that coaching appointments have the highest priority on your calendar models what you expect from clients and will reduce postponement or rescheduling. Not moving a scheduled appointment with a client, except in an emergency, demonstrates that commitment. You must align your behavior with what you have told the client about the coaching process in order to foster trust, which in turn encourages openness. (For additional suggestions about structuring sessions, see Figure 7-2.)

Figure 7-2. Session structure

Suggestions for structuring ongoing coaching sessions (standard active coaching sessions rather than unique sessions, such as a feedback or development planning meeting):

➤ Greetings, reactions to last session; ideas that resonated

➤ Client's current feelings and stress level

➤ Client's goals or agenda items for the session

➤ Coach's agenda items

➤ Debrief on-the-job action plans implemented or other homework activities

➤ Consider progress and topics from the development plan

➤ Discuss and contract for actions aimed at development progress

➤ Reflect on learning, motivation, and situational variables; encourage feedback-seeking behavior

➤ Confirm phase of the coaching engagement and next session

Questions helpful in moving through the session structure:

➤ What interactions have you had since we last met that you were pleased with?

➤ What's a recent situation that presented an opportunity for you to try something new and how did it go?

➤ What are your goals for this session?

➤ What ideas from the last session have been helpful?

➤ What barriers and obstacles to development exist?

➤ How difficult were the changes attempted?

➤ What challenges are coming up?

When you encounter client behaviors that are negative, demanding, critical, defeatist, or defensive, it is possible that the client is acting out of fear of change or loss of what is familiar. Although these behaviors are sometimes labeled *resistance to change,* it is more helpful to reframe them and refer to them as *reluctance to change.* This semantic distinction makes a big difference in your coaching posture. Explaining client behavior as reluctance is more likely to prompt your curiosity about the reason for the hesitation. As you convey acceptance instead of judgment of your client's feelings, you are providing your client with needed support for any fears the client may have.

It is key for you to be patient in appreciating and understanding your client's reactions to the organization's felt needs. Changes that may appear obviously appropriate to you, or to the organization, may not be clear to the client in the early stages of coaching. Even clients who are creating negative work environments through their behavior may reject the need for change. They need time to consider their impact and explore other approaches to their work. Coaching can facilitate that by providing a safe environment for exploring how change might feel to them.

Your patience in responding to a client's reluctance also conveys positivity and hope. Clients who are wary and hesitant often feel locked into behavior patterns that they know are not ideal, but they are unaware of other options. Organizations can be politicized and conflicted, adding to a client's hesitant reactions to coaching. Exploring the client's hesitations and the organizational constraints while reinforcing your own trustworthiness can begin to move difficult clients in productive directions. (Additional material on reluctance is presented in Chapter 14.)

Theories of intentional change are also helpful in dealing with reluctant clients.[2] According to these theories, there are several natural, preliminary steps that must be accomplished before people commit to plans for making changes in their lives. Pre-contemplation, contemplation, and determination must precede action that makes change happen. Helping clients move from each step to the next can be quite challenging. Some clients may have already had feedback and are contemplating the changes that coaching will support. For other clients, lack of feedback and their own hesitation may put them in a pre-contemplation stage where any suggestion of change is a new and unsettling idea. Applying these stages to your clients' state of mind can help you anticipate what you need to do to help them make progress.

With those clients, moving them from pre-contemplation to action uses a process known as *motivational interviewing*.[3] It relies on broad, open questions to explore with the client both current conditions and what change might bring. Motivational interviewing embodies a patient, client-centered process of movement toward change. The questions that motivational interviewing employs are useful in a range of coaching situations: What does change mean to you? What are the pros and cons of change in your situation? What would you need to give up to make a change? What are the upsides and downsides of the status quo? What past attempts at change have worked and why? For hesitant and reluctant clients, these types of questions can make change less threatening so that they can take a step toward considering it.

CASE ILLUSTRATION: TRUSTING THE PROCESS IN EARLY COACHING

An important element of building relationships involves keeping your coaching hat on, even if the client is pulling you into a more consultative stance. While this may be a challenge in the moment, the greater good of your working relationship depends on your staying the course in your role as coach. The following case illustrates the kinds of challenges that can come up in the early stages of relationship building.

Sarah, the coach, and Brenda, the client, had started their coaching relationship a month earlier. They had discussed several preliminary goals and getting feedback from Brenda's colleagues. But at the start of their third appointment, Brenda asked for help on an especially difficult project that would draw upon several lines of business in the consulting firm she worked for. This project would be a hybrid, and even writing the proposal would raise client management and delivery issues. It was a pressing challenge: She had been assigned to pull together a proposal for an existing client that was unusual in that most projects were categorized and controlled by a particular practice.

After listening to Brenda's description of the challenge, Sarah was a bit conflicted. On the one hand, she thought, "I should meet Brenda where she is and encourage her to bring challenges to our coaching sessions." She certainly could come up with ideas for Brenda, and the topic was appropriate because teamwork and collaboration had already surfaced as likely developmental themes. But on the other hand, Sarah was aware of the downside—by moving into consulting mode, she would not be modeling the coaching process that she had described to Brenda, and it could derail the progress they had already made toward identifying development goals.

Sarah decided that it was very important at this early stage of coaching to refuse to simply answer Brenda's immediate need about this pressured situation. If she didn't, she would be setting an expectation of solving future challenges, too. This was a precedent she did not want to set. So, anticipating Brenda's frustration, she decided to push the challenge back to Brenda. This way she would convey both confidence in Brenda's ability to meet her own challenges and also establish how they should work together.

In fact, Brenda was disappointed about not getting Sarah's immediate suggestions and even implied that Sarah was holding back on expertise when Brenda really needed it. But Sarah held to her decision. She asked Brenda to summarize the key issues about the client's need and the internal challenges, asked follow-up questions, and restated frequently. As the opportunities and obstacles emerged, Sarah asked Brenda to think about identifying leverage points with stakeholders, how best to include them, and what her role should be.

As Brenda formulated ideas and progress was made, Sarah took the conversation in a slightly different direction. She suggested that having made productive use of this challenge, they could continue using it toward Brenda's development. Since collaboration skills had been emerging as a likely development area for Brenda, Sarah suggested that this project would be a useful forum for applying new skills and furthering Brenda's development objectives.

Supervisor's Observations

Early in coaching relationships, clients may challenge coaches in various ways: to give them direct advice, to intervene on their behalf, to feel sorry for them, to join them in their victim status, and the like. They may not be consciously aware that these are challenges to the coaching relationship and may believe that the coach is supposed to help them in whatever way would be useful or supportive. Coaches, however, need to gently but firmly establish a helping relationship consistent with the coaching role that is focused on facilitating discovery. This is especially important in the early stages of coaching. Newer coaches may feel the pressure of the client's expectations and give in to providing answers and advice, since they may not be as secure in their roles as they will become later. They need to be able to risk the client's frustration and anger at not being given the help that is asked for.

Sarah was able to tolerate that risk and partner with the client to help her in a different way, by becoming Brenda's facilitator rather than consultant. Faced with this kind of difficult decision, there is the potential for the coach to be fraught with fears about the client's anger or even rejection. As helping professionals, coaches sometimes *overlearn* their mission and fail to differentiate what clients actually need from what they ask for. Sarah was able to stay on course with Brenda at this early stage of coaching. She also found a way to tie the specific challenge back into the client's likely development need, further cementing her position of supporting Brenda's growth but not reducing Brenda's responsibility for progress.

Furthermore, coaches often assume that clients see the development potential in the challenges that present themselves, but it is always useful to point them out. Most of the time, clients won't notice the developmental value that could be obtained from a new challenge because they are immersed in just getting the work done. An important part of the coach's role in helping the client develop is to look past the actual work pressures and demands and see opportunities for learning and growth.

Finally, at a later session, Sarah could further affirm her coaching role by referring back to this very exchange as an example of the push and pull that is inherent in coaching. It is a tangible example of the coach-client partnership, and making it overt may help the client understand how to work with the coach to get the help that is needed. While she might have done all that in the session when it happened, time doesn't always allow for a complete discussion. Nothing is sacrificed, and a time lag may even be beneficial, allowing the coach to go back to reflect on a lesson and, in a subsequent session, to highlight that learning with the client.

Takeaways

- A productive coaching relationship is based on contracting that sets the ground rules and eases client concerns about the process and confidentiality.

- How you prepare for sessions and behave during them are important elements of establishing the trust, reliability, and authenticity necessary for an effective coaching relationship.

- A safe place where conversation can flow is created when you demonstrate your full interest. Use focused listening skills and show support for the client with open questions and reflective responses.

- It is important throughout coaching, but especially in the early stages of relationship building, to focus on facilitation and discovery instead of providing answers or advice. How you manage yourself models the type of relationship you want to have with clients.

- Some tension with your client is typical, but as you stay on track in your coaching role, it benefits the client in the longer term.

- Redefining client opposition or lack of cooperation as reluctance (as opposed to outright resistance) will stimulate your curiosity about what is important to your clients and what they need to protect; trying to understand works better than applying pressure.

- Some clients will not have even contemplated the need for changes in their behavior; consider using the techniques of motivational interviewing to help move them toward change.

8

Goal Evolution

A S THE COACHING RELATIONSHIP WITH YOUR CLIENT STRENGTHENS, DEVELOPMENT AREAS BECOME CLEARER AND ACTIONABLE GOALS EMERGE. THIS PROCESS OF GOAL EVOLUTION, WHICH WAS DESCRIBED BRIEFLY IN Chapter 4, begins with general needs and progresses to development objectives that become part of a well-founded action plan. While subtle, this process adds value to your client's development by facilitating the identification of goals that both resonate for your client and incorporate the organization's viewpoint.

Development goals need to be shaped, not imposed, and tied to the reality of the client's context. One of the pivotal moments in any coaching engagement happens when the client realizes, "That's what I should be working on!" These *aha!* moments occur after you and the client have bonded in a professional alliance and are in alignment regarding the client's challenges. Merely reiterating organizational descriptions of what the client needs to work on will not generate insight or commitment.

As development goals evolve, keep in mind these important considerations:

⊙ While the time frame contracted in a coaching engagement needs to be respected, goal evolution should not be unduly rushed, since it is one of the key benefits of coaching.

- By the conclusion of goal evolution, development objectives have been informed by a variety of perspectives—client, coach, sponsors, and often other colleagues.

- Typically, the emergence of goals occurs in stages, although they are always open to fine-tuning and action planning.

You may encounter organizational policies that are not sensitive to the time needed to allow resonant goals to evolve. For instance, you may be expected to define coaching goals as early in the process as possible. Indeed, protocols for coaching often assume that the coach will define developmental objectives by the end of the first session and sometimes even before coaching starts! This requirement offers the benefit of establishing a focus for coaching from the beginning but compromise clarity, depth, and sense of client ownership. Both the coaching process, which usually generates data about the client, and the dynamics of creating a coach-client working alliance are needed to effect a clear articulation and buy-in of goals. When it comes to establishing an appropriate time frame for goal setting, you can compromise by articulating very general goals initially with the expectation of more specific ones later.

In addition, you can educate sponsors about the evolution of goals within the coaching process. They will gain an appreciation of the value of goal evolution if it is presented as a key contributor to successful coaching outcomes. One way to explain it is by describing the three typical phases, as shown in Figure 8-1.

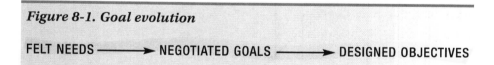

Figure 8-1. Goal evolution

FELT NEEDS ⟶ NEGOTIATED GOALS ⟶ DESIGNED OBJECTIVES

Felt needs are the goals that the organizational sponsors and/or client articulate when you are first contacted. These needs are often described with general labels such as *executive presence, influence on others*, or *better delegation.* Alternatively, behaviors that sponsors would like the client to eliminate can be felt needs, such as *control outbursts, be less pushy,* or *stop micro-managing*. These descriptions may provide some guidance in the early stages of coaching, but they rarely offer enough clarity to focus developmental efforts. If clients found such descriptions useful, coaching would not be needed, since these articulations have been available long before you arrived. An important reason coaching is initiated is that these descriptions have not generated productive action.

In point of fact, felt needs are only useful as points of departure and as very general standards for what the coaching might accomplish. After you and the client discuss them and explore the client's history, you can look at whatever prior feedback is available and examine the client's self-perceptions. Then you and the client will be in a better position to articulate more clearly what the client would like to accomplish through coaching. These statements are called *negotiated goals*.

The term *negotiated* doesn't refer to the way adversaries arrive at agreement, but to the way a ship enters a channel or a race car driver handles a curve on the track. Although still not as clear as they might be, negotiated goals are more specific and more meaningful for the client than felt needs. They move the process, and the relationship, in a productive direction. As a result of participating in their articulation, clients have an increased commitment to working on them. Useful insights, action ideas, and even behavioral progress can occur based on negotiated goals. *Empower my staff more and let go of some control*, or *Recognize challenging situations before I get into them and have strategies to control my reactions*, are two examples of negotiated goals that suggest areas to explore and where to focus assessment choices while still allowing more specificity or even other themes to emerge.

Negotiated goals provide a productive focus for you and the client while other necessary processes are being completed. One of the most valuable processes is the application of structured assessments of the client. Coaching often includes informational interviewing of stakeholders, sometimes called *360-degree interviewing*. Other assessment methods can also be used to foster insight about the client (covered in Chapter 9). The next goal evolution milestone, *designed objectives*, is usually reached only after assessment results and other data are analyzed, summarized, and discussed with the client.

Designed objectives are key to creating a development plan that includes on-the-job action ideas. Most of the time, they are refinements of negotiated goals, but they may diverge from goals that were previously identified. Extrapolating from the two aforementioned examples of negotiated goals, the designed objectives based on them might be, *Become a more empowering leader and stretch the skills of my team*, and *Expand my influencing style to be more positive and inspiring*. These statements are aspirational and optimistic, expressing a vision for the client's future leadership style. Unlike objectives that may have been suggested by others, these designed development objectives are jointly created by you and the client, built on earlier insights by a thorough data-gathering process. Because they have been co-created using multiple perspectives, designed objectives have greater potential to motivate the client and generate willingness to devote precious discretionary time to their achievement.

A final task in this evolution is for you to consider the connection between the original felt needs, especially those expressed by the sponsors, and the final designed objectives. Most of the time, there is a clear conceptual link, and it is obvious that general or negatively expressed felt needs have evolved into clear, actionable, and positive statements. Clients will readily see the similarities, but those connections are not as apparent to sponsors, who were not privy to the process that supported the evolution. When you get to the point of discussing designed objectives with sponsors, you may need to make those connections more obvious so that sponsors will understand that their felt needs have been incorporated into the development plan, although the language has changed in ways to better support the client's development.

Designed objectives represent an important and tangible work product of coaching. Adding action ideas to move the client toward those objectives yields a development action plan that can serve as an excellent basis for a development discussion between client and sponsors. Producing a development action plan (covered in Chapter 11) demonstrates progress in coaching and invites support for the client's growth.

Although the evolution of goals from felt needs to negotiated goals to designed objectives may take four to eight weeks or even more elapsed time from the start of coaching, it is time well invested. Coaches can use the three stages of goal evolution to pace themselves, trusting that a well-founded process, not unduly truncated by organization pressures or administrative requirements, will yield progress and an action plan that the client truly owns.

CASE ILLUSTRATION: GOAL EVOLUTION REFLECTS A PRODUCTIVE COACHING PROCESS

Understanding typical coaching processes and anticipating steps allows coaches to make choices with greater confidence. Even if those choices have some degree of risk, choices do need to be made and clients need guidance from coaches about how best to make them. The following case illustrates how understanding the goal evolution process is essential in choosing paths to productive action with clients.

Howard, a vice president of IT in a financial services organization, was introduced to Ankit, a coach who had worked with the firm in the past. Howard's manager had articulated a felt need for coaching in order to reduce Howard's reliance on micromanaging. His manager described to Ankit that Howard's overly controlling management style was an impediment to considering him for a promotion to managing director. Howard agreed that he needed to back off and empower his direct reports more, but he was unsure how to relinquish control and still maintain his high standards on so many critical projects.

Early in the coaching relationship, it became clear to Ankit that Howard had a long history of being clear and exacting about projects. He had talent in breaking down complex goals into tasks that others could execute. These project skills had served him well, and he had a very positive reputation among his internal clients for both understanding their needs and delivering IT solutions. It was also clear from their discussions, however, that the promotion to managing director would change the nature of Howard's challenges. Both the scope of the work and the level of his direct reports would be elevated. A particularly enlightening question that Ankit asked Howard was, "How would you describe the leadership style that you, in your current role, would find motivating?" Howard's reflections on this question had led him to embrace that he needed to make changes, even though the specifics were unclear.

Through their early conversations, Howard and Ankit evolved a negotiated goal and fleshed out some of the details of how to achieve it. Howard definitely needed to empower his direct reports with more responsibility for project management, including client relationships and overcoming obstacles. In order to meet this objective, however, he realized that he needed to shift some of his focus toward building more robust partnerships with the members of his team. He needed to get to know them better, including their interests and aspirations, so that he could raise the bar on their accountabilities in handling broader aspects of projects. They described this change in terms of building partnerships for better empowerment. Howard would need to take some risks to accomplish this objective, but he began to embrace that these were risks worth taking.

Howard and Ankit continued to explore and apply a negotiated goal of greater empowerment and, at the same time, Ankit conducted a series of informational interviews of Howard's direct reports and other colleagues. The results were both confirmatory and useful. From all perspectives, Howard was clearly a strong contributor, set a high standard, and had the best intentions in his drive for project progress. Yet there was clear agreement that he was distant, formal, and often judgmental—he was all business. Ankit found that how Howard communicated was an impediment; he needed to listen more carefully, have a less autocratic style, and enter into brainstorming discussions without judging. This was a very consistent theme across the interviews that Ankit conducted, but considering Howard's self-assessment and the sponsors' felt needs, Ankit decided to keep the focus on Howard's management of direct reports and put the peer relationship issues aside at this point in the coaching.

Based on this feedback, Howard and Ankit articulated a designed objective that had a different emphasis than the negotiated goal: Build more complete relationships with direct reports to support greater empowerment. The action ideas cascaded directly from this objective, informed by the feedback results. As they shaped these points into a development plan, Ankit could see

Howard's commitment to the plan increase and looked forward to the discussion of the plan with Howard and his manager. Ankit also knew that, given Howard's style, the changes wouldn't happen overnight, and some changes would be quite difficult for him to make. Ankit was confident, however, that making these changes would indeed resolve questions about Howard's readiness for the promotion.

Supervisor's Observations

Ankit knew that goal evolution is integral to building a productive coaching relationship and to creating a development plan that channels the client's motivation. By conceptualizing a felt need, moving to a negotiated goal, and then evolving into designed objectives and a development action plan, Ankit was able to work productively with Howard. At the same time, he understood that sponsors may not immediately see the connection between their felt needs and the designed objectives emerging from coaching. Ankit was willing to have his work exposed to that scrutiny and, at the appropriate time, support Howard in explaining those connections to sponsors in order to achieve their support of the development plan.

Moving from an early focus that initiated the coaching to evolving specific, actionable objectives is rarely a linear process. It can be a challenge for a coach to assist the client in getting greater clarity on what is important, while also identifying what might evolve into a motivating development plan. Ankit, while sensing a larger issue, engaged Howard in multiple conversations about his management style and need for change. This process allowed a clear focus, anchored by felt needs at the same time that it encouraged a wider discussion about what change would actually look like. Howard was able to reflect and gain awareness of what he needed to do differently. By embracing this process, Ankit was able to give Howard the time and support he needed to create a development action plan for his most pressing needs.

Ankit was also making a very important decision about what to focus on in coaching. Goal evolution and data gathering clearly highlighted where to start. At the same time, Ankit knew that even designed objectives can evolve further and, in Howard's case, that such additional change is likely.

Howard's interpersonal style extends beyond his relationships with his direct reports. Data gathering revealed unproductive distance with peers and other colleagues as well. Ankit, however, decided to keep the focus on empowerment issues at this point, staying as close as possible to felt needs and Howard's motivation for his promotion. As they make progress on the development plan, Ankit can choose the right time to suggest a wider focus for change. Even well-articulated goals can evolve as they are addressed. As clients experience success with new behaviors, they gain the confidence to tackle other areas of development.

Takeaways

- Clients and sponsors may be unsure how best to articulate goals and select the most useful ones; it is your role as coach to help resolve those questions as a natural part of the coaching process.

- Case-specific coaching goals that are targeted and customized to the individual evolve as a result of data generated by the coaching process and the dynamics of the coach-client partnership.

- *Felt needs* are the initial wishes articulated by organizational sponsors and sometimes by clients.

- Useful *negotiated goals* evolve from an exploration of the client's history, feedback, and self-perceptions and increase the client's focus and energy, even though they may still be somewhat tentative.

- *Designed objectives* are shaped from negotiated goals that are informed by data gathered during coaching. They almost always relate conceptually to the original felt needs and are specific and actionable, providing the foundation for a development plan that mobilizes progress.

- As coach, you are simultaneously focused on those client goals reflecting current needs and on being open to incorporate new directions as they emerge, even after the development plan is implemented.

CHAPTER 9

Assessment and Information Gathering

D
ATA FROM ASSESSMENTS AND OTHER SOURCES ADDS TO THE DISCUSSION ABOUT CLIENT DEVELOPMENT AND IS USEFUL IN EXPANDING ON YOUR CLIENT'S SELF-INSIGHT AND YOUR OWN IMPRESSIONS. THIS NEW DATA includes the results of informational interviewing of your client's colleagues as well as the results from standardized questionnaires or other assessment tools. These additional perspectives can help your client move from negotiated goals to designed objectives.

When approaching this aspect of the coaching process, consider the following points:

- Decisions about what types of data to collect are shaped by multiple factors, such as the circumstances of the case, negotiated goals, the organization's prior use of particular methods, your own preferences for certain assessments, your Personal Model, and your client's interest in feedback.

- Using several data-gathering methods can be especially helpful if the client has limited self-insight or is really unsure about what improvements or changes to work on.

⊙ Assessment methods differ with respect to how visible they are to the rest of the organization (e.g., assessment questionnaires versus 360-degree interviewing of colleagues), which may also be a consideration in selecting assessment methods.

Types of Data

There are two broad categories of data that can be collected for use in coaching: quantitative (i.e., scorable, standardized) and qualitative (i.e., subjective, descriptive). Data of both types can be very helpful in building your working relationship with clients and in suggesting insights. When you use multiple assessment methods, it is useful to interpret assessment results both separately and collectively. In other words, the total picture of a client using assessment results is often greater than the sum of the separate assessment parts.

Quantitative Data

Quantitative data come from standardized instruments that describe the client using various dimensional terms, often based on conceptualizations of personality, interpersonal dynamics, communication style, and leadership competencies. Quantitative data can be collected both through self-report assessments and multirater (360-degree) instruments.

Self-Report Assessments. These assessments are completed by the client, usually online, and then scored by the publisher of the questionnaire. Results, profiles, and narratives based on the client's scores are sent to the coach for interpretation and for sharing with the client, almost always in conjunction with a feedback discussion. The most common categories of self-report questionnaires used in coaching include:

1. Personality Assessments (e.g., I6PF and California Psychological Inventory)
2. Motivational/Values Instruments (e.g., Hogan Values Scale)
3. Communication Preference Indicators (e.g., MBTI and DiSC)

4. Interpersonal-Style Measures (e.g., FIRO-B)

5. Learning Preferences (e.g., Learning Styles Inventory)

⊙ *Multirater Assessments.* Multirater surveys, also called *360-degree questionnaires*, capture perceptions of the client and colleagues on a wide range of skills and leadership dimensions. The colleagues typically include manager(s), peers, direct reports, and potentially other groups such as internal customers. These surveys became popular in the 1990s as a means of providing developmental feedback. (For some of the more widely used 360-degree instruments see Figure 9-1.) They have continued to grow in application and complexity and have become so widely used that it is not unusual to find a prospective coaching client with the results of such a survey on hand.

Figure 9-1. Popular 360-degree feedback instruments

Examples of widely used 360-degree tools include

CCL's *Benchmarks*

PDI's *Profilor*

Clark Wilson's *Management Practices*

Management Research Group's *Leadership Effectiveness Analysis*

Denison's *Leadership Development Survey*

Many large organizations have customized these instruments or created their own, reflecting a competency model that the organization has embraced. There are also numerous computerized survey engines that can be used to create a 360-degree feedback tool from start to finish.

The client and as many as eight to twelve colleagues, representing different perspectives, complete the questionnaire online. Peer, direct report, and other group data are averaged for anonymity. Many standardized 360-degree questionnaires include norms so that clients can benchmark their scores against an external reference point of how managers are typically rated. The profiled results are provided to you, the coach, in preparation for a feedback discussion. These surveys focus on soft-skills areas that have become recognized as keys to leadership success and derailment avoidance. Capturing the perceptions of colleagues on these skills areas is compelling input to a coaching process and a development plan.

Early innovators in using 360-degree questionnaires conducted research on managerial jobs to determine objectively the competencies required; those competencies were further divided into key behaviors that were used to create the items to be rated. Different classes of jobs have different competencies, and so corresponding questionnaires were created: for middle managers, for executives, for sales, for individual contributors, and so on. There are also 360-degree questionnaires linked to particular leadership concepts such as conflict resolution and emotional intelligence.

As the use of these questionnaires has expanded, they have become a standard part of both feedback and leadership development processes. Multirater assessments are also sometimes used to aid in performance ratings for compensation and in bonus determination, although their use for these applications may distort their developmental meaning. In other words, if you have access to 360-degree feedback for your client, ask why it was collected and how it is used in the organization because it may not have as much developmental value as one used exclusively for that purpose.

Most often, 360-degree questionnaires use a five- or seven-point scale of effectiveness or frequency on each of the skill questions, with higher scores better than lower ones. There may be anywhere from a few dozen questions to over a hundred, depending on the complexity of the underlying model. Most questionnaires also ask the rater to identify the most important skills for job success. Open-ended, write-in questions yielding qualitative feedback are often included, using prompts such as, "In your own words, list the manager's key strengths and development needs."

Coaches, trainers, facilitators, as well as management and executive development professionals, all need experience in using 360-degree feedback tools. Interpreting the results to get to a well-founded development action plan is a frequent activity of all these professionals. You don't have to be an expert in the psychometrics of such tools in order to use them effectively. Some of these tools require training and certification, but supervised experience is always recommended before using a specific survey with clients.

Many coaches working at the executive level prefer informational interviewing to multirater surveys. (Informational interviewing is a qualitative method discussed further in the next section.) For short-program coaching or at middle management levels, however, 360-degree questionnaires are more consistently used because they are more efficient in terms of professional time and cost. In addition, they provide comprehensive skills coverage and quantitative ratings so that the relative size of a particular strength or gap is indicated. Also, it is easy for the sample of colleagues included to be larger than with time-intensive interviews.

With regard to quantitative methods overall, both self-report and multi-rater, you may want to identify questionnaires popular among the coaches and Human Resource professionals you know as the starting point for your own toolkit of measures. Certification courses, manuals, user guides, and guidance from other coaches are all helpful as you begin to use questionnaires with clients. Adding additional measures is a lifelong activity for coaches as new conceptualizations and questionnaires become of interest. Building a foundation of how to learn about and use assessment methods facilitates that growth as you encounter new tools and apply them to client challenges.

Qualitative Data

Qualitative data come from perceptions that others have about the client as well as from your own impressions. There are many types of qualitative data available to you in your coaching work. Your own observations of the client in sessions and in the office environment, along with descriptive documents such as performance appraisals, can provide helpful qualitative data. Your *shadowing* of the client in actual meetings, when properly set up, can also yield useful information about client behavior. In executive coaching, however, the most frequently used qualitative data-collection method is informational interviewing of the client's colleagues. Figure 9-2 is an example of how a coach might initiate an informational interview with a client's professional colleagues.

Figure 9-2. Introduction to the informational interview

SAMPLE INTRODUCTION for an INFORMATIONAL INTERVIEW (as input to a transition coaching engagement)

Coach: I'm Susan Spence, an executive coach working with Brad Winter as he transitions into his new position as Director. What is your understanding as to why we are meeting?

Colleague: Brad asked me to participate in this meeting about his development. That's really all I know.

Coach: Yes, we are focusing on his development, particularly areas of strength that he can further leverage and any gaps going into his new job. Because leadership doesn't happen in a vacuum, we agreed it would be beneficial to obtain the perspective of those with whom he works. I will be summarizing in my own words what I hear from all those interviewed into themes to be shared with him. I will not be attributing remarks to any individual. I may ask follow-up questions. Examples are useful so I thoroughly understand your point of view, but those examples will not be shared with Brad. Any questions about why we are talking or the process we will use?

Colleague: No, it is clear now. What do you want to know?

Coach: You can start by describing the context in which you and Brad interact; for example, how long and in what capacities you have worked with Brad? Then I'd like to hear about your observations of what Brad does well as a leader. I am also interested in areas you consider opportunities for him to develop, especially in terms of this job. Finally, I would welcome any specific suggestions you have about what Brad should start or stop doing now. Any questions before we proceed?

In early interactions, clients will share their self-perceptions, and you will form impressions of them. Tapping into others' perceptions of the client builds on that foundation and provides context that will be useful to you in development planning. The goal of informational interviewing is similar to other assessment methods: to gain a broader and deeper understanding of a client more quickly and efficiently than could be done just through dialogue with the client. Based on the ease of application and the usefulness of the data, informational interviewing has become a standard element in supporting movement from relationship building toward insight and designed objectives.

Like all aspects of the coaching process, the specifics of arranging and conducting interviews require transparency and planning, especially with the client. Here are the recommended steps in arranging informational interviews:

1. Contract, or confirm earlier contracting, about the specifics of the informational interviewing process.

2. Discuss whom to interview and have your client gain the sponsors' support for the respondent list. Typically, this list includes the client's sponsors, direct reports, a sample of peers, and other colleagues who work or have worked with the client for at least six months. The total is usually eight to twelve people, but the number could go higher to include key stakeholders.

3. Support the client in finding a comfortable way to inform respondents about the process, request their participation, and set expectations for you to contact each person. (This is often completed via e-mail.)

4. Collaborate with the client about what his or her topics of interest are, what questions you should use, and what you should listen for in the answers. Be sure to consider your own preferred questions as well.

5. Confirm with the client the confidentiality of respondent information. Generally, results are shared only with the client and only as themes. Manager information/feedback can be used more directly or even verbatim, although this should be confirmed with the manager.

6. Discuss client follow-up, such as thanking the participants or later sharing with them the development themes that become part of a development action plan.

7. Consider the logistics of the interviews (where, when, how long).

8. Establish a general but consistent structure for the interviews, con-

sidering what you will say about yourself and the process and the questions you will ask; budget appropriate time and make sure respondents know what to expect.

9. Consider asking sponsors special questions about the client's career, advancement potential, goals of coaching, and similar topics that only they would have information about.

10. Conduct the interviews (by phone and/or in person).

11. Analyze the contents of your interview notes.

12. Distill key points about the client's strengths and development areas, looking within groups (e.g., direct reports) and across groups, focusing on specific questions that were of interest to the client.

13. Prepare a written summary to be shared with the client highlighting strengths, development areas, and other useful information.

14. Plan and conduct your feedback conversation.

Becoming both familiar with, and facile in, using a range of qualitative and quantitative assessment methods is an important component of your growth as a coach. The qualitative methods especially will draw on your well-developed questioning and listening skills and will be useful in most engagements.

CASE ILLUSTRATION: HIGH-POTENTIAL COACHING USING INFORMATIONAL INTERVIEWING

While coaches often need to contract for their choice of assessment methods at the start of coaching, some organizations standardize assessment processes, often in conjunction with leadership development efforts that have classroom, coaching, and action learning elements. This makes the coaching contracting much easier but sometimes introduces other challenges for the coach in conforming to the organization's process.

Following a leadership development program, Henry, the coach, was assigned to work with Marty to help create and implement Marty's development action plan. This follow-up coaching was standardized in that it was provided to all participants in the program using informational interviews with six to eight colleagues. Self-report assessment results that had been used during the leadership program were also available as part of the coaching engagement. This structure made for a smooth transition from the program into coaching without any risk of stigma and with the clear support of others in the organization. However, the organization used 360-degree questionnaires as part of the performance management process, and so the coaches were asked not to refer to the informational interview as a "360 process." Instead, it was called "developmental feedback" and included a list of consistent open-ended questions (e.g., strengths, development areas, job challenges, recommendations for success) to be asked of respondents.

Like most participants in the program, Marty was thrilled to be seen as part of the future bench strength of the organization. Still, Henry was sensitive to the exposure that such a process brings with it. During their first meeting, he carefully explained to Marty the structure of the coaching and the "development feedback" interview process. He confirmed that data he gathered from the interviews would be held in confidence and he would prepare a thematic summary for Marty. Henry and Marty would use this summary, along with other assessment results coming from the leadership program, to create a development action plan. The coaching process also included a three-way meeting with Marty's manager, Yolanda, to review that plan and four follow-up coaching sessions to get the plan off to a solid start.

Henry conducted a thorough interview of Marty, making sure to ask him the same questions that were to be included in the development feedback process. They also discussed Marty's experience during the leadership program and Marty's ideas about possible development goals. Henry asked Marty to list six to eight colleagues, including Yolanda, who would provide feedback, and he encouraged Marty to get Yolanda's suggestions for the list, too. Ideally, creating the list was the first step in facilitating Marty's and Yolanda's collaboration about his development. Henry also provided Marty with a standard e-mail request that the coaching program had created for participants to signal to others in the organization that the coach would be calling for feedback.

A standard practice is to interview the client's manager first and then continue with remaining interviews in whatever order is convenient. Henry made an in-person appointment with Yolanda and used the first few minutes to contract with her about the process and the three-way meeting that would occur after a development plan was drafted. He then asked her the questions; the other seven interviews flowed similarly, minus the process contracting. Each interview required approximately forty-five minutes.

Henry had significant experience summarizing informational interviews, and he readily organized what he had heard into strength and development categories. However, he found that Yolanda's data had a unique element that he felt was important to share. While in this particular program even manager feedback was intended to be anonymous, Henry felt that feedback from Marty's manager was different from that of other colleagues. Additionally, he knew from what Marty had told him that Marty's relationship with Yolanda had been difficult but seemed to be improving. Holding back or merging Yolanda's unique views may blur information important to Marty. After consulting with an experienced coaching colleague, Henry decided to err on the side of caution and get Yolanda's permission to use her feedback more directly. Henry also made a mental note to set aside time during the three-way meeting to explore Yolanda's feedback in reference to Marty's development plan.

Yolanda agreed that Henry could quote her if that would be useful, however, he decided to use his own words to summarize her viewpoint and present that information, with attribution, as part of the overall summary of development feedback data. Henry was confident that handling Yolanda's feedback in this way, along with themes from the other interviews, kept the spirit of how the data was intended to be used, and he felt prepared for the feedback discussion with Marty.

Supervisor's Observations

Prestructured coaching processes reduce the need for contracting with clients and sponsors, but challenges remain. Coaches sometimes mistakenly assume that because the coaching *protocol* has been set up in advance, everyone is familiar with and comfortable about what will happen. In fact, clients can have many reactions, including trepidation, distrust, excitement, or even disinterest, that need to be heard and explored.

Henry wisely did not assume that Marty had clear information about the coaching process and made sure to have a thorough conversation with him about the data gathering that would be taking place. Doing so builds the connection between coach and client, even though process changes are unlikely. In this case, Henry did a good job both of explaining the data gathering and of differentiating it from similar, but nondevelopmental, processes that the organization used.

In addition, even in prestructured processes, special challenges can arise. Henry believed that merging Yolanda's point of view in with the others would lose important information. Even though Yolanda may have expected that her information would be used more directly than that of others, Henry did not make that assumption. He wisely sought counsel from a trusted colleague about how to balance the general requirement for confidential feedback with the need to share Yolanda's specific concerns. He also found his own way to use her information directly, choosing not to quote her even though she gave him permission to do that. He also used the fact that a three-way meeting was a standard part of the process to make sure that Marty and Yolanda would have an opportunity to explore her point of view along with the draft development plan.

Takeaways

- Decisions about the types of information and the timing of data collection in coaching depend upon many factors tied to client, context, and your preferred coaching process.

- The goals of data collection include expanding your understanding of the client, the client's own desire for self-awareness, and the need to explore how the client is perceived and experienced in the work context.

- Both qualitative and quantitative assessment results can also be used to pique clients' interest in development by providing new perspectives that are seen as credible.

- A consideration in collecting qualitative information from colleagues is how public the coaching should be, as determined by you, the client, and the sponsors.

- Involving colleagues using a 360-degree survey or informational interviews adds complexity but can be very beneficial in terms of capturing perceptions of the client, surfacing action ideas for on-the-job development, and gaining wider support for the client's growth.

- It is important to select questions and focal topics for use in your informational interviewing and to include your client in identifying them.

- Selecting respondents can be a milestone since it includes the client's manager and can reveal your client's comfort in seeking feedback.

- Ideally, data enriches your discussion with clients and provides new ideas and perspectives while building your working relationship in the journey toward a well-founded and motivating development plan.

CHAPTER

10

Feedback:
What and How

W HILE APPROACHES TO EXECUTIVE COACHING DIFFER, THEY ALMOST
ALWAYS INCLUDE INFORMATION GATHERING ABOUT THE CLIENT AND THE
RELATED RESPONSIBILITIES OF INTERPRETING RESULTS AND PROVIDING
feedback. As you prepare to do this, it is important to bear in mind that:

- Interpreting the results of self-report questionnaires, 360-degree surveys, informational interviews, and other assessment methods is a core challenge of coaching.

- Offering useful feedback from those sources relies on your ability to extract meaning from the results; it becomes even more valuable if you can also consider the client's priorities and context.

- Feedback is meant to facilitate the client's self-insight and motivation toward growth by sharing views from different angles and perspectives.

- Confidentiality of feedback is important so that clients will feel more open to respond and willing to consider even critical, challenging results.

Feedback that is tailored to the client's needs and interests is much more likely to be accepted and then incorporated into development action plans. In other words, regardless of the rigor and research base of the feedback source, it is useful only insofar as it facilitates self-insight and motivates professional growth. Even the most sophisticated and valid tool is a means of fostering insights that resonate with your client. The tools and measures themselves should be in the foreground of the conversation only long enough to be understood.

The goals of feedback differ depending on the type of coaching you are doing. Some coaching engagements are quite short, only a session or two, and just involve interpretation of a 360-degree survey and a self-report instrument. These types of engagements are referred to as *feedback coaching* or *development plan coaching*. (See Figure 3-2, The Coaching Continuum, in Chapter 3.) They are aimed at achieving modest gains in self-insight and suggesting areas to consider for development. More typical three- to six-month coaching engagements often use comprehensive assessment methods, and so the feedback comes from both quantitative and qualitative sources, such as informational interviews. Those feedback sessions draw on both your interpretive and client-relationship skills in highlighting results that are particularly relevant for development.

In the usual coaching engagement, you will also be expected to compare the negotiated goals that emerged in your earlier coaching sessions with assessment-based feedback so as to arrive at designed objectives and development action plans. Often, the connections among the feedback, objectives, and plans fall into place as you discuss the feedback; other times, you will need to point out connections, linkages, and possible interpretations. When multiple measures are being used, integrating all of them can be complex. Your guidance is the essential factor in transforming assessment results into client insights and agendas for change.

> All feedback is not created equal. Even when it is judged by the client to be accurate, we must ask: *Does it matter to the client's managerial or leadership effectiveness?*

Feedback of Quantitative Assessments

Clients, even those eager for feedback, are usually apprehensive about receiving the results of standardized assessments; numbers and graphs can be intimidating. That is why feedback is best explored in the context of a trusted relationship. Even if the coaching engagement is short and does not allow much time for relationship building, it is important for you to be sensitive to your client's potential anxiety and create a safe environment in which to look at results.

Facilitating feedback based on quantitative measures that yield dimensional scores is a unique challenge since numerical results sometimes carry more impact than is warranted. Indeed, to balance that impact, narrative reports often accompany the dimensional scores that are provided from quantitative instrument feedback. Some test publishers use lengthy computer-generated reports to turn scores into descriptions or even developmental recommendations. However, as the coach, you are in a position to help your client make sense of scores, graphs, and narrative reports and decide what in that material has developmental relevance.

It is important that you are familiar enough with the measures you are using to explain scales and scores, sharing examples as needed. You also need to help the client understand any inconsistent results and unusual score combinations. These interpretive skills draw on your experience with the instruments and knowledge of the possible patterns. Giving feedback from standardized questions sometimes requires you to explain specialized terms unique to those instruments; at other times it is more simply offering your descriptions of how the client's behavior might be represented by the dimensional scores in the results.

Coaches usually develop their own flow in discussing quantitative feedback. For example, loosely scripted explanations of the rationale and premise of a questionnaire and how the results are displayed can be a useful preamble to giving the client the results. Some coaches also like to arrange the discussion so that those tests which are likely to be most interesting to the client are discussed first. You might experiment with different introductions and flows to arrive at what feels right to you. If you have the opportunity to do a number of development plan or feedback coaching engagements, having a consistent flow makes it easier for you to prepare and facilitate these interactions.

Feedback of Qualitative Information

The use of informational, or 360-degree, interviews by coaches is pervasive, but there is a wide variation in how coaches conduct feedback from them. For example, some coaches use verbatim comments, some rely on written summaries, some prefer oral feedback discussions, and some structure the feedback by competency or perspective (e.g., from direct reports, from peers, and from other stakeholders). Regardless of what you choose to do, when you combine the results of interviews with assessment scores, extracting interesting themes and suggestions may be all that is necessary, since there are often many points to interpret. Remembering that feedback is a precursor to a development plan, you can highlight those themes, in effect confirming negotiated goals as well as pointing out results that require further consideration.

Just as results associated with quantitative tools, analyzing feedback from informational interviews draws on your interpretive skills. In addition, summarizing interview feedback also draws on your ability to express yourself and capture themes in writing. A two-step process is customary in preparing interview-based feedback: (1) analyzing the content of the interviews, and (2) writing a summary of that analysis that can be given to the client directly and/or used as a guide to the feedback discussion.

While there is no rigid formula for the first step, distilling strengths and development needs from your interview notes well before your feedback discussion is the usual approach. This effort will make the feedback meeting much more efficient and also will reduce the risk of revealing a source because you will not be using your interview notes directly during the meeting. If colleagues are promised confidentiality of their comments, as they usually are, it is the coach's responsibility to uphold that commitment rigorously. The use of direct quotes or situational examples, when they add important information, needs to be handled carefully. Using these comments needs to be contracted with interviewees or should be avoided. Paraphrasing an interviewee's intent or putting sentiments in your own words is fine and consistent with your task of summarizing themes. Comments from the client's manager can be used more directly in situations where that adds essential information. On balance, however, most coaches prefer to interpret all feedback instead of sharing it verbatim, confirming to the client that a rigorous process has been used to extract themes from the interview notes. The decision about how directly to use interview data also is guided by your Personal Model in how best to motivate change.

In terms of the second step, coaches usually design a written summary format that is clear and comprehensive. This document is often the most impactful of all the feedback provided, so crafting the summary is important. There are no hard-and-fast rules about writing a summary of informational interviews, but there are options and choices you can make. The objective of the written feedback summary is to help clients reflect on and absorb the key points as a precursor to development planning. Since you want to capture a complete picture of the client, consider sharing strength themes first, followed by possible development areas that came out of your interviews. These themes can then be discussed with respect to the development areas already under consideration, whether felt needs or negotiated goals. This approach sets up a discussion about what themes may end up in the development plan and which ones may be less clear or important for the client's development.

> Regardless of the style of feedback report you choose—narrative, bulleted, verbatim, thematic, by perspective—it is preferable to arrange extra meeting time, present the report in person, and walk the client through the report in detail while maintaining a posture of discovery. Remind yourself and your client that perceptions are based upon observations: Perceptions are not facts. Perceptions are altered as changed behaviors are observed. *Intention cannot be observed*

When interview results vary based on perspective (i.e., respondent groupings, such as peers or direct reports), you can show those differences as clustered themes, as long as you have sufficient numbers in each category so that no feedback can be tied back to any particular person. Usually the requirement is three or more respondents per perspective. The client's manager is a special case since this person usually does not require strict confidentiality. Still, you may choose to weight the manager's feedback more heavily in the summary and weave it in to broader themes rather than call it out as a separate perspective. In general, bullet points are used rather than narrative paragraphs. Note: Exhibits 5 and 6 are examples of two different styles of interview feedback reports.

Integrating Feedback Sources

When there are both quantitative and qualitative feedback sources, your goal is to help the client look across all the results and identify themes; there is no need to utilize every score or feedback element. You, as coach, are the filter by which clients will avoid being overwhelmed by feedback. You can help your client understand that all feedback is not created equal. Feedback can be true and yet irrelevant to the client's life. Current priorities, organizational context, and career plans are key moderators of the value of even accurate feedback.

A different lens

In that respect, feedback is better thought of as a view through a different lens or a new perspective worth discussing, rather than as information that is right or accurate. That is why it is best shared in the context of a confidential discussion. The goal of a feedback meeting is to foster discovery and insight. To reinforce that feedback is neither right nor wrong; it is best to use terms such as *descriptive, clear, useful, interesting, thought-provoking,* or *confusing, inconsistent, vague,* and the like. This way you help the client keep a balanced perspective about the feedback rather than feel compelled to use all of it. As mentioned previously, a written feedback summary of interviews is an important addition to a feedback discussion. When a written summary complements results from standardized assessments, it often generates themes that can serve as a framework for development planning.

The complete feedback picture may take the form of a packet of findings reflecting results from both quantitative and qualitative assessments. This material reduces the need for the client to take notes during the feedback discussion, although clients can be encouraged to make margin notes and capture other emerging insights, just as you will also be doing. Since the interview data is often very compelling, that written summary is essential in providing the client with a means to review and reflect upon the themes after a feedback meeting. It also provides the coach with a written record of what was covered in the feedback discussion.

A feedback discussion is one of the most pivotal moments in coaching. The client's eyes are opened to input and perspectives that may never have been considered before. The feedback discussion may produce significant shifts in the client's insights and contain opportunities for breakthroughs. As the coach, you can capitalize on these opportunities by helping clients make productive use of all the sources of feedback that are available.

Delivery of feedback is best thought of as part of an ongoing conversation about development, not an event to be checked off a list. It requires patience and process skills, not to mention in-depth experience with the tools and the results they provide. Clients may ask for time to consider the feedback, to integrate it into their own thinking, to make sense of it, and to link it to possible action. You want to be sensitive to these natural processes while still encouraging movement on the coaching engagement and development action planning. At its core, the feedback discussion should help the client answer just two questions: How useful is this description of you? What, if anything, do you want to do about it?

CASE ILLUSTRATION: FACILITATING RATHER THAN TELLING

Feedback facilitates insight, but predicting where that insight will come from isn't easy. Even when coaches are very familiar with assessment measures and there is a tight time frame on the coaching engagement, it is important for the feedback discussion to emphasize facilitation rather than the coach's own recommendations. There may be a time for coaches to share their conclusions, but the emphasis is more usefully placed on clarifying results and helping clients reach their own interpretations.

Max was a novice coach who felt fortunate to be part of a large-scale coaching intervention aimed at middle managers in a consumer-goods firm. Each participant in the program received four coaching sessions. The first two sessions focused on feedback from leadership assessments that had already been administered, as well as discussion of the client's emerging development goals. After the second session, Max interviewed six colleagues whom the client and his manager had previously agreed would provide useful perspectives about the client's development. Max would then summarize the data for a feedback discussion during the third session. Optionally, the client could bring in other materials, such as performance reviews, for discussion. The fourth session would be used to pull all this material together into a development action plan that the client would discuss later with his manager.

One of Max's clients in this process was Eric. He was an up-and-coming young executive, moving from a purely professional role into leadership responsibilities. During the first and second sessions, Max facilitated Eric's understanding of the leadership assessments. Using the information, Eric was able to identify several areas where he could improve, such as being a better feedback provider and coach to his team and achieving a better work/life balance. Max felt that these sessions provided a productive start toward devising a development action plan with Eric.

Max conducted the six informational interviews, including one with Eric's manager, and summarized the results. However, as Max was preparing for the feedback meeting, he was aware of several sensibilities to consider. With only a single feedback session, growth areas would need to be prioritized. And even though Eric was a bright young man and eager to develop, Max was also aware that Eric had a healthy ego and hadn't had much feedback before. While the assessment feedback had gone well, Max was concerned about Eric's openness to the feedback from colleagues, especially when several problem areas were highlighted.

Max settled on two developmental themes: helping Eric understand that he needed a wider repertoire of people management skills than his very direct style, and explaining how time management and delegation skills could contribute to more quality time at home. These themes were well supported by the interview results, but some of the findings of the leadership assessments were not as clear.

Max struggled with how to integrate all the pieces into conclusions for Eric. In the end, he decided he was working too hard to reach conclusions for Eric and instead would be more helpful if he presented Eric with a comprehensive summary of all the data and let him determine the final interpretations. So, in addition to the interview summary, Max prepared summary points for the other measures but decided not to share his recommendations until he and Eric had reviewed all the results. Although Max ran the risk of confusing Eric, given the limitations of a single session, the approach he decided to use also set the expectation that Eric needed to prioritize what should be on his own development plan. Max was confident that he could help Eric extract what was most important for him, even if it differed from Max's preferred interpretation.

Supervisor's Observations

Providing feedback can be very helpful in both shorter and longer coaching engagements. However, with piles of interview notes and other information it is easy for a coach to slip into overkill and share everything without much interpretation. On the other hand, when coaching time is limited, there is a tendency to describe results too broadly, hoping they resonate with the client. In framing feedback, it is important for you to consider several variables, including how much time is available in the engagement, the goals and interests of the client, and the client's openness and curiosity.

It is best to connect feedback to what is likely to be important to the client. In this case, Eric was concerned about how his management style was perceived and how to better balance his work and personal life. Any larger themes of Eric's personal ambitions and his sensitivity to criticism would need more time than this engagement provided. Still, very useful coaching could be accomplished within the constraints of the engagement, and Max effectively focused on Eric determining what was important from the data.

`Max, like most coaches, needed to choose between the clarity of the conclusions and client buy-in, based on the client's own interpretation. He chose the latter approach, which demonstrated his commitment to the coaching process, even under time constraints. There are no guarantees as to how things will turn out, but generally it is better to build on the momentum that is there and see if the client is interested in exploring other points. The two themes that Max identified would certainly have been important for Eric to work on, but Max was willing to let them go if Eric's interpretation and priorities went in a different direction. The specific conclusions may be less important than the quality of the coach-client working relationship, which is needed to produce a compelling and actionable development plan. Whichever way the conclusions went, Max and Eric would have a working relationship to support the preparation of a practical, actionable development plan.

Takeaways

- Because clients are usually apprehensive about discussing feedback, it is best explored in the context of a confidential, trusting relationship.

- The goals of feedback differ depending on the type of coaching you are doing.

- Shorter coaching engagements may be limited to facilitating interpretation of quantitative instruments or 360-degree feedback surveys.

- More comprehensive coaching may use feedback from both quantitative and qualitative sources.

- Quantitative instrument feedback is provided in dimensional scores, often accompanied by a standardized report.

- The coach's job is to help the client make sense of scores, charts, and standardized narrative reports and decide what specific information in that material has developmental relevance.

- It is essential to spend time analyzing and summarizing feedback from informational interviews prior to offering it to your client, since this kind of data can carry great weight and significantly impact the client.

- When there are both quantitative and qualitative feedback sources, you can help the client identify the most useful themes across both.

- Feedback is often a pivotal moment in coaching when the client's eyes are opened to new perspectives; it is best approached as a discussion of what is useful in the data rather than what is right or wrong.

CHAPTER

11

Development Planning

D EVELOPMENT PLANNING REPRESENTS A MILESTONE IN THE COACHING PROCESS BECAUSE:

- It begins the formal transition from discovery to implementation.
- It bridges the private and public elements of coaching.
- It links today's developmental actions with future aspirations.

Development planning embodies key principles of adult learning. It is anchored in client self-insight, so it is designed to fit the individual in the context of that person's work challenges. It extrapolates from awareness to clear, positive development goals, supported by specific behavioral action ideas. Lastly, development action planning assumes that growth is iterative; actions are followed by reflection, feedback, adjustment, and more action to yield progress. All of these points reflect ways in which adults learn best.

Ideally, development plans are the natural outgrowth of the earlier stages of coaching. Goal evolution, discussed in Chapter 8, describes an important aspect of that process. Clients value and feel ownership of development plans that have incorporated their self-discovery and situational reality. Needs that were felt but only vaguely expressed now have clear articulation; new paths forward have been identified. These steps help to optimize client commitment and motivation toward change.

Development planning begins with the negotiated goals that you and your client have articulated. Through the feedback steps in your coaching process, designed objectives will emerge, constituting the headlines on the client's development plan. On-the-job implementation ideas, based on discussion and brainstorming with your client, are natural next steps in helping the client make progress toward objectives. Those ideas for action in development plans are identified in the spirit of the expression: *A plan is a basis for change.* The actions tied to designed objectives are subject to revision as the client tries out new approaches and works with you to evaluate results. Even as actions may be changed, discarded, or added, designed objectives remain, anchoring the overall developmental effort

Once the designed objectives are clear to you and your client, and action ideas are emerging, it is time to begin creating a written plan. This process can happen during and between coaching conversations and via e-mails aimed at drafting this tangible work product of coaching. Who begins the process of drafting development plans, whether you or the client, is a decision that may reflect your approach to coaching or practical considerations about moving the process along. Also, development plans are written with the expectation that they will be shared with sponsors, so they need to be clear to those who have not been part of the process of creating them. Help your client step into the sponsor's shoes and make the objectives and actions as clear as possible.

Formats for development plans can vary based on the client's specific situation. Typical sections, however, include a brief statement about the process that has yielded the plan, client strengths, and each designed objective, followed by the action ideas to make progress toward that objective. There are many variations on these standard sections, including implementation details; resources, obstacles, and time frames for action; situational factors that may help or hinder progress; and examples of what to do and what to avoid doing as change takes hold. The particular structure of development plans that you help to create is an opportunity for your creativity to be responsive to the needs of specific clients and their organizational settings. (In the supplementary material at the end of this book, Exhibit 7, Exhibit 8, and Exhibit 9 provide sample development plans using different formats.)

Here are some questions to help you make sure the plan is robust:

- To what extent does the plan provide a balanced picture of the client, showing strengths as well as developmental areas?
- How well do the designed objectives capture the client's aspirations for being a more effective manager and leader?
- What is the conceptual overlap between the original felt needs and the designed objectives in the plan?
- To what extent are the objectives broader than the action ideas so that they will remain valid even if some actions are discarded?
- How manageable is the plan in the short term given your client's workload and other constraints?
- If there are ambitious and longer-range aspects of the objectives, how might they be implemented in stages?

Once development plans are drafted, sharing them with sponsors usually occurs during three- or four-way meetings devoted to achieving consensus on objectives and actions. At a development planning meeting, your client can present the plan for reactions and suggestions. Not every coach feels the need to be present at all development planning meetings, and this choice may be an aspect of your Personal Model.

Your participation can be very useful, however, because it provides you with information about the client's relationship with her manager and that manager's support for the client's development. (Note: The Human Resource sponsor may or may not be present during development planning meetings, depending on the organization's culture and structure, although the plan would generally be shared with that person, present or not.) Your presence also is a clear reminder to the manager that this plan reflects the work of the coaching process. Furthermore, it is simply easier for you to hear reactions and suggestions directly, instead of having them conveyed to you via your client. Finally, as a participant in the discussion, you can ask questions that would be difficult for your client to ask, such as, "In what ways will you support this development plan?" and "What might get in the way of implementing these changes, and how can we prevent that from happening?"

If you do participate in a development planning meeting, your role is that of facilitator. It is your client's meeting and your objective is to encourage direct dialogue between client and manager. You can provide perspective about the coaching process and prompt issues that need to be discussed. It is the client's responsibility to present the plan and foster reactions to it. This is particularly important for the client's ownership of the plan and its implementation after coaching is concluded.

A typical development planning meeting might flow as follows:

1. The coach states the goal of the meeting and provides an overview of the process that has led to this draft development plan.

2. The client presents the plan to the manager (and HR sponsor, if present), going section by section to ensure understanding and encouraging questions and suggestions about development actions.

3. The client highlights the process of arriving at designed objectives and links them to the original felt needs.

4. The coach can foster the manager's participation, if necessary, by asking for reactions and additional ideas about goals and actions.

5. After the entire plan has been discussed and suggestions made, the coach can raise broader questions about ongoing support and feedback.

6. The parties thank one another, and the coach confirms the next steps in the coaching process, noting that subsequent contacts will use the plan as a basis for discussion.

7. Coach and client debrief the meeting.

If the plan has been revised, the client can provide the revised plan to the manager within a short time after the meeting.

Figure 11-1. Benefits of Development Planning Meetings

- Observe developmental alignment between the client and manager
- Elevate the profile of development in the organization, especially if HR participates
- Model a developmental process and create well-founded development plan
- Confirm that manager and client can have development conversations
- Estimate the overall length of the coaching engagement and consider next steps
- Gain overt support for development from the manager and thus increase the client's motivation to implement the plan
- Anticipate the close of coaching, at which time the plan will be in the hands of the manager and others supporting the client's ongoing development

---

While the payoffs of Development Planning Meetings can be high (see Figure 11-1), there are also *risks.* These include:

1. The client's manager may demonstrate an evident lack of interest, negativity, or shift in the needs originally stated.

2. The client's performance in presenting the plan may be poor (e.g., talking too much, appearing overtly anxious or disorganized).

3. The manager or the HR sponsor may raise negative feedback about the client that had not been offered earlier in the process.

4. Issues may surface that were not previously raised by any of the parties, including new political realities, job changes, or other organizational events that can impact the execution of the client's plan.

It is important for you, as coach, to be mindful of these risks and be clear about the alignment between the client and the client's manager before proceeding with this meeting. Coaches often make preparation for the development planning meeting a topic for the session preceding it. You or the client under your guidance can share an agenda and the development plan document in advance with the sponsors and answer any questions they may have about the meeting.

If significant time has passed between the manager's input and the meeting, it may be advisable for you to reach out to the sponsors and ask for feedback about the client's progress and any new issues that have emerged. It is better to delay the meeting and address concerns rather than be blindsided by negative feedback during the meeting. After the meeting, it is also helpful to debrief with your client. Congratulations are in order, and it is natural for the client to ask you for feedback. In addition, you can prompt reflection by asking: "How did it go?" What messages should be taken away? What adjustments to the plan are necessary? You or the client can also follow up with the sponsors to ask for feedback about the meeting itself and any other thoughts they have about the client's plan.

The development planning phase of the engagement focuses on your responsibility to link the initial work of coaching (relationship building, identifying negotiated goals, gathering data, and giving feedback) with more public and formal aspects of development. The private elements of coaching—everything you have learned in your coaching conversations—meet the public aspects of what the organization expects the client to do in furthering his development. The art of coaching shows in your ability both to partner with the client privately at the same time that you are guided by input from coaching sponsors and other stakeholders.

The development planning phase also represents an opportunity for direct collaboration among the client, the sponsors, and you. During the coaching engagement, sponsors—and the client's manager in particular—can be very helpful in supporting change. While the development plan is never finished in any absolute sense and needs to remain amenable to adjustment, it provides a guide that gets everyone on the same page in supporting the client's development.

Having a development plan also makes for a smoother handoff of the client's development back to the sponsors at the conclusion of coaching. Although a development planning meeting may occur as early as the first quarter in a six-month coaching timeline, it actually anticipates the conclusion of coaching when the client's manager will again be in the foreground of the client's development. You can consider reconvening for a program review meeting near the close of coaching and use the development plan to acknowledge progress and note areas needing more developmental attention after coaching concludes.

CASE ILLUSTRATION: DEVELOPMENT PLANNING IN ACTION

Development planning is the culmination of the earlier stages of coaching. By design, sponsors are not aware of the discussions that have occurred between you and your client, but a development plan is one way they will judge progress and positive return on their coaching investment. It is also exciting for your client to see efforts in the coaching process yield tangible results toward growth and development. Here is one coach's experience in making development planning a gratifying stage for all in the coaching process.

Brian, the coach, had met with Joy five times as part of their coaching engagement. They had worked through the stages of relationship building, Joy's self-assessment, and obtaining input from her manager, John. Based on all that work, they determined that Joy's immediate development goals were likely to be focused on her behavior as a leader. She was new to the executive level and felt unsure about how to both engage and motivate her multilayered staff. She and Brian had agreed that feedback from peers and direct reports would be useful. Brian had conducted twelve informational interviews. The feedback was quite enlightening and helped Brian and Joy isolate a key objective for her development, with many specific action ideas to support her movement toward it. Based on that feedback, they worked together to draft a development action plan for her continued growth as a leader.

The draft development plan highlighted Joy's strengths, which she need-ed to continue leveraging. In the feedback, Joy was described as being:

1. *An extraordinarily caring leader; someone people like working for*
2. *Committed to doing the right thing for the company*
3. *Results-oriented; thorough and dependable*
4. *Highly collaborative with peers*
5. *Well networked across the organization, but not at upper levels*
6. *Someone whose work and life are well integrated*

The plan also articulated Joy's key leadership challenge and action steps for making progress on it:

Developmental Goal: More fully embrace my leadership persona in all its elements.
> *Action Ideas:*

1. *In team settings, counterbalance my natural reticence with more candid sharing of my leadership values and priorities.*
2. *Because leadership is a performance art, my activities as a leader don't always have to align with my natural preferences.*
3. *Share more of my career to date and the trajectory of where the team might go together.*
4. *Pick the times when it is necessary to show more of my command presence; many on my team need to have clearer marching orders.*
5. *Don't assume my motivational profile is the same as others. People need me to show more active interest: follow up and acknowledge their efforts.*
6. *Seek out more opportunities to be exposed to other executives and especially senior leaders. Ask John for support and access.*
7. *Be more assertive in meetings with my peers and in John's staff meetings. Collaboration is fine, but I compromise too much.*

Brian and Joy worked on the development plan in a coaching session and then exchanged drafts via e-mail until both were satisfied that it was clear and engaging. They also agreed that Brian would facilitate a three-way development planning meeting with Joy and her manager John, and they scheduled it for the following week. During that meeting, Joy took the lead, and John added several suggestions to the development action plan. For example, he encouraged her to try out her career story and future vision with him before using it with the team. He was very encouraging of her contact with other senior leaders of the firm and offered to set up some of those meetings. John also responded to Brian's question about what might derail the plan by noting that there was a likely acquisition in the next six months that would make Joy's organization bigger, but this pending change could also be a good opportunity for Joy to demonstrate her leadership.

Brian and Joy debriefed the development planning meeting and both felt that it had gone well. Brian committed to following up with John in the next day or two to get his candid view, and Joy felt that she would follow up with him in the normal course of events. She was surprised to hear about the possible acquisition and wondered what other news John might be holding close to his vest. Still, she was glad that he supported her development plan, and she made a mental note to question him more and be a bit less accepting of whatever he chose to tell her. Brian thought Joy had done a good job in the development planning meeting and it was a strong start to the implementation phase of coaching.

Supervisor's Observations

As an experienced coach, Brian understood the importance of this development planning phase of coaching. His client's insight that leadership is a performance art parallels his own understanding of the performance aspects to coaching. Creating a rich process that culminates in a well-founded, resonant development plan demonstrates to client and sponsors that development is possible.

In addition, the duet of coaching became a trio during the development planning meeting; this was only possible because of solid preparation. Brian orchestrated the preliminary steps and the meeting itself so that Joy and her manager could really focus on her development and his role in supporting it. As a result, new information on a pending business acquisition emerged in a safe setting, which allowed Brian and Joy to incorporate this information into her development plan. In fact, based on what happened during the meeting, Joy might choose to take more risks with John. This would become more likely because Brian was a witness to their interaction and his support for her changes. Brian also realized that this action was aligned with other steps for strengthening Joy's leadership presence. Applying it to John offered another opportunity for her growth, but it also expanded the possibilities in their ongoing work relationship.

Takeaways

- Moving into the development planning phase of coaching is a milestone in the process and is the juncture between the private and public aspects of coaching.

- A written draft of a development plan containing both designed objectives and actions reflects a productive collaboration between you and the client.

- Designed objectives on the development plan look forward to the client's aspirations while the action ideas ground those goals in the here and now.

- The spirit behind the development planning process is that application, reflection, and adjustment will keep actions focused on the objectives.

- Development plans are often shared with the client's manager and possibly the HR sponsor during meetings devoted to achieving consensus and involving them in the client's development.

12

Encouraging Dialogue and Stories

COACHES ACHIEVE RESULTS BY FACILITATING CLIENT DISCOVERY. RATHER THAN PROVIDING SOLUTIONS, COACHES HELP CLIENTS USE CHALLENGES AS A PLATFORM FOR GROWTH. THIS PROCESS RELIES HEAVILY ON A COACH'S listening and communication skills. Although every coach has preferred ways of encouraging clients to self-reflect, all coaches use skills aimed at facilitating the client's story and stimulating dialogue around it.

There are many facilitation skills you can apply to your coaching:

- Open-ended questions, such as those that ask *what* and *how*, or ask the client to *explain, elaborate*, or *describe*

- Supportive/positive comments, such as *That's interesting; I understand; Tell me more;* or *That's a real achievement.*

- Restatements of information, such as *You believe that your biggest strength is ...* and, *What I hear you saying is ...*

- Summary statements at transition points, such as *Before we close today, let's summarize what we have covered ...* and, *The theme that I am taking away is ...*

- Reflection of feelings, such as *You sound disappointed about what's happened ...* and, *I can hear the energy in your voice.*

- Nonverbal signals of attention and interest, such as making eye contact, leaning in toward the client, and using positive, encouraging facial expressions

Experienced coaches employ these and other facilitation skills the way an artist selects from a wide-ranging palette of colors to best reflect a particular subject. It takes practice and self-awareness to apply these skills naturally and effectively. In early sessions, you can use facilitation skills to explore events in the client's education and work history, formative experiences, achievements, setbacks, transitions, and milestones. These events are used as a basis for highlighting your client's skills, personal characteristics, strengths, gaps, interests, and values. With your help, patterns will emerge, triggering both follow-up questions and insights. This process strengthens the coach-client bond as the client experiences your help and interest.

Broad questions, such as *Describe your leadership experiences*, or *Which organizational values are most important to you?* tend to prompt answers that often lead to client stories. Here is an example of how a story can begin to reveal a client's personality:

> At the first meeting in Fredericka's office, Ethan, the coach, looked around and noticed windows on three sides of her office, which overlooked a river and the city beyond. It was bright and airy, not what he had imagined. On her large dark mahogany desk sat dozens of playful trinkets and family photographs. These surprised him because they appeared out of character from what he had heard about Fredericka.
>
> Ethan introduced himself and provided a brief overview of his coaching experience. He told her that every time he meets a new client, he feels as if he is walking into a movie late, well after it had begun. This made him want to catch up on what he had missed. So, he suggested that she might bring him up to date on her movie.
>
> Ethan listened as Fredericka began her story. She described her family first and the history of the whimsical trinkets on her desk. She told him

that each one came from a satisfied client or from one of her four children. She mentioned that she knew she was a bit "rough on the outside" and she expected that they would focus on that in their coaching.

"But," she offered, "I'm more bark than bite." Then she smiled. She went on to suggest that maybe her upbringing had something to do with her demeanor. This admission surprised Ethan, but he remained attentive, aware that he was sensing both serious and playful currents from listening to her and seeing her office. She continued, "I grew up as an adopted child in a household that expected boys to achieve while the girls were to stay at home. The only problem was that I was always raising my hand in school, getting top grades, went to college on scholarship, and finished with honors. I wasn't supposed to do all that."

As Fredericka talked, she toyed with a trinket and looked out the window. Ethan was attentive and leaned toward her to encourage her to continue telling the story. She said that she had learned to break out of the stereotype where girls were not expected to achieve by moving into roles that her upbringing had told her were "reserved for boys." "I always felt that I shouldn't be so smart because that wasn't what was expected in my family; but I couldn't help myself." At that point she paused reflectively as if hearing herself in a different way. Then she said, "I don't try to be mean. I just want to get things done."

Ethan sensed that even this brief piece of Fredericka's story was an important start to their work together.

Stories are the descriptions of our life events that define who we are. They contain factual information but, more important, they include explanations and rationales for our experiences, both positive experiences and those that are disappointing. As such, they are subjective interpretations of past events. After multiple tellings, they may take on aspects of myth. They illustrate organizing principles for how we live, and often are used to justify the choices that we make.

Some stories may be short yet pivotal anecdotes about past events; others are longer, involving plot elements, challenges, and characters. Each story has the potential to tell you how your client sees life inside and outside the organizational context. While most stories show clients in a positive light, they can also illustrate difficult lessons, setbacks, and disappointments. Your questions about stories can help clients identify the meaning that they take from them and perhaps even rewrite lessons that have outlived their usefulness.

> **"A personal myth is an act of imagination that is a patterned integration of our remembered past, perceived present, and anticipated future."**
> —Dan McAdams[1]

Usually clients are heroes of their own stories, but not always. As protagonists in their own stories, clients depict themselves as actively shaping life events. If a client tells passive stories in which things happen to him or his stories lack a hero, he may feel like a victim. Such a posture needs to be addressed, explored, and hopefully changed because no progress can happen when the client is a passive recipient of the world's actions. Think about what this client is saying in telling his story:

> Wherever I have been, I've had managers who don't appreciate my special talents. I'm a great technology person and have demonstrated that I understand systems and how to imagine, design, and get new projects completed on time. I keep having bosses whose job I can do better than they can. My current manager is no different. I find myself going around him to get what I need. Also, I deserve a promotion and it's clear he won't help me. Why is this always happening to me?

Clients' roles in their stories and interpretations of meaning can act as springboards toward deeper and richer understanding. Stories can reveal alignment or conflict across a client's positions as well as indicate life priorities. Keep your focus on what the story is saying about a client and try not to get unnecessarily involved with factual content.

As you listen to a client's story, you may see an opportunity to highlight an area for development. These opportunities often are revealed through an unresolved question, a dilemma, a frustration, a challenge, or an aspiration. Deciding whether to use a story to suggest a development goal requires understanding the client's interests and context. For example, hearing a story about a leadership lesson or a career mentor may provide fruitful material with a newly promoted manager that you are coaching (e.g., *What parallels do you hear between that story and your new challenges?).* In contrast, you may choose not to seek further meaning from a story about that manager's technical skills. Stories also may reveal life lessons that are limiting or counterproductive. These stories can be questioned to explore the possibility of alternative interpretations (e.g., *What are the opportunities in your current context to explore a different resolution to that story?).*

Here's another client story to consider:

> I was always a good student and my parents put a lot of value on education, even though we moved around a lot. I came to see that my good grades were the way I got recognition. I always wanted to be at the top of the class even though my social interactions suffered. I am singularly focused on doing my best, whatever it takes. To this day I maintain the highest standards and apply the same to others. I don't understand when some of my staff members try to just get by. It gets frustrating because I won't accept that in myself.

As you facilitate client stories, reexamination often takes place without much prompting. In the context of a coaching relationship, clients hear their stories with greater self-awareness and open-mindedness. Your act of listening can foster new insights as the client hears, occasionally for the first time, elements of the story that are negative, passive, positive, or empowered. These can be very revealing *aha!* moments as your client recognizes that a familiar story contains insights applicable to current challenges.

Some stories, even from work experiences, can be deeply felt and upsetting to revisit. They may include disappointing career outcomes, unfairness, rejection, blame, stress, and other painful on-the-job events. The extent to which a client can disclose such troubling stories is a positive indicator of the bond between you. In telling such a story, your client is sharing a very trying time and is therefore less alone with it. Difficult feelings can be experienced and eased. Trust is strengthened when those stories are shared with you, whether or not they have direct relevance to the developmental agenda. The coaching challenge is to find the middle ground between tapping deeply emotional experiences that you are not trained to deal with versus avoidance of difficult subjects. Examine your own reactions to painful stories to be sure that you appropriately support their telling.

Listen to a client's leadership story:

> Leadership is about having a big picture and getting others to do what you want. It's important to surround yourself with bright, talented managers who will execute on your vision. I hire smart people who want to succeed and play by my rules and whom I can trust. That way I can assure good results. It's what has gotten me to the executive suite. [Long pause.] Wow, you know, that sounds kind of arrogant. I don't know if I would want to work for me! Where does that leave me as a leader?

Clients often have repeated stories that are almost automatic in response to specific questions. The emergence of less rehearsed, more ambiguous stories is an indication of a client's growing trust in you and the coaching relationship. Accepting the earlier stories is fine as long as the subsequent stories get more of your coaching time and attention. For example, if your client tells an early story about being at the losing end of various endeavors, you may choose not to explore it. Later in the coaching, the client may reveal a story about an unresolved quandary or disappointment that may get your full facilitative attention. You have considerable latitude in deciding what to do with a story based on what will help your client move toward productive self-reflection and insight.

As you listen to stories, meaning can be conveyed through description of events as well as your client's nonverbal signs. When those appear to be incongruent, there is an opening to better understand your client (e.g., *You don't sound very pleased about that promotion.*). Supportive comments and restatements can sharpen gaps between content and behavioral cues (e.g., *Help me understand your mixed feelings about that.*). Summary questions bring a pause that may prompt the client to reconsider interpretations (e.g., *What new meaning did you hear in that story?*).

Coaching a client in a more senior leadership role brings a stronger emphasis on storytelling. Stories with a clear message told well are essential tools for leaders at the top of organizational units. As a coach, you may want to listen for the qualities of those stories that convey leadership style, values, vision, and motivational ideas. Aspects of leadership stories can provide insight into your client as well as illustrate opportunities for leadership development. In some cases, telling more impactful and inspiring stories becomes part of a client's developmental objectives. (More information on this point is provided in Chapter 15, Coaching for Leadership.)

While emphasizing client stories, coaches may occasionally tell a story from their own lives to illustrate a point, pique curiosity, or ease a particularly difficult moment. If they are done with the right intention at the right moment, coach-generated stories can help a client see a point differently or feel less alone. Also, stories tend to beget stories. When a client listens to you telling a story, associations, memories, and other ideas are triggered that otherwise might not have occurred. Those stories, however, should be told very selectively and only in the service of client needs, never your own enjoyment of an audience. Here's an example of how a coach might interject a personal story to make a point with a client:

> That reminds me of a story. Years ago before I was a coach, I was appointed as director of a large group. I believed I was up to the task, but I was concerned about being the boss of people with whom I had worked as a colleague for a long time and who were much more expert in their areas than I was. I thought of myself as a collaborative person and saw the new position as needing me to be more overtly in charge of the work of others. Through discussions with my mentor, I realized that I didn't have to radically change my preferred leadership style, but I did need to add some pieces to it. There was a lot I had to learn about working at a higher organizational level, but my leadership values still applied. That was both reassuring and challenging.

As you continue your development as a coach, regularly evaluate your effectiveness in fostering dialogue and client stories. Self-assessment can be aided by asking for feedback and suggestions from case supervisors and colleagues. Both verbal and nonverbal facilitation skills need to be scrutinized. Some coaches regularly record sessions for their own reflection and learning (with the client's permission, of course). These recordings are valuable in highlighting opportunities for better facilitation of client stories. Part of your ongoing development as a coach is striving to improve listening and story exploration skills.

CASE ILLUSTRATION: THE STORY OF "POOR ME"

While stories that clients convey are usually engaging and revealing, sometimes they are not. Clients can use stories to deny responsibility, prove themselves superior to others, or criticize others. Such stories are diagnostic and useful in a different way. They hold up a screen that obscures the client's characteristics and may reflect defensiveness or lack of trust. Nonetheless, a range of facilitation methods can be used to leverage stories meant to deflect attention, as the following case illustrates.

After three coaching sessions with Rick, the CFO of a large insurance company, Rachel had heard many of his stories, and they all had the same messages: Life just wasn't fair, and the company was filled with "inept incompetents."

In response to Rachel's questions about his work life, Rick's answers tended to be, "I am the only one that pulls through," or "They brought me in to get things done, but all I get is grief." Rachel began to think that Rick was always sharing "poor me" stories, and she was becoming frustrated with how to make the dialogue more productive.

Rick's approach to work also included an officious style that valued closure over everything else, including understanding processes and building relationships with others. Changing Rick's style was the felt need described by Rick's sponsors, but he was not buying into their view. When he made overly general statements blaming others for performance problems, Rachel tried to challenge him using pure logic: "Are you sure that no one else ever makes a positive contribution?" Rick just brushed aside these challenges. Rachel also tried to engage his stake in the situation by asking, "What might you do to improve what's happening?" or "What's your best shot at making a difference?"

These questions didn't make much progress, either. Rachel needed different tactics. In discussing the challenges of "victim posture" clients with her supervisor, Rachel hit on several new ideas. First, she would stop responding with logic and start responding empathetically. She would reflect feelings that she assumed were part of Rick's experience and try to draw out the emo-

tional aspects of his stories. She felt that if she could get him to acknowledge the feelings behind the frustration and anger, such as fear or a sense of isolation, she might be able to connect his stories with a need for change. She also realized that she could use her own frustration positively. While this tactic could be confrontational, she felt that it might be necessary to react to Rick as others must, with remarks such as "Rick, when you tell a 'poor me' story, I stop listening." Or even more pointedly, "Rick, if it's all about them, I can't help you." Rachel decided to try these approaches in the first half of the next session to see if he could actually tell a story that was about himself, without blaming others.

Supervisor's Observations

There are all kinds of stories that clients will share. One of your jobs as a coach is to use facilitation skills to convey sincere interest so that clients feel safe going beneath the surface facts. It is possible that Rick's stories have an underlying purpose that is more self-protective than exploratory. In such situations, coaches have to be careful not to let their own frustration and negative judgment color their reactions. It is important for them to recognize when this is happening, as Rachel did when she began thinking about the *poor me* label she was using for her client.

Once that challenge is identified, you have choices about how to use your awareness. Given the sessions that had passed, Rachel believed that Rick's approach to coaching was not going to change based on time, no matter how attentive she was to him. So creating more trust and safety didn't appear to be the best approach at this point. Instead, she decided to try something different—first, by facilitating the underlying feelings, and second, by making use of her own natural reactions. This *use of self* can be powerful in coaching, especially when you translate your frustration into *I messages* and observations.

As a coach, your self-awareness of your own reactions to a client's story is key to making choices about how to respond. It is not uncommon to get caught up in a client's story and forget to step back and think about its meaning, the client's objective in telling it, and how you feel as you listen to it. If you focus too much on the content of the story, you will overlook more important questions for the client to consider. When you use what you observe in the client as the story is told, what you feel in response to the story, and the message the client is conveying, then you can facilitate a different story experience. Your goal is to help generate insights and ideas that the facts alone will not prompt. The extent to which your clients respond with growing interest in your questions and observations about their stories is usually an indicator of their readiness for coaching.

Takeaways

- To foster client self-reflection and insight, coaches use skills that facilitate dialogue, such as open-ended questions, supportive comments, summary statements, reflection of feeling, and positive nonverbal cues.

- The use of broader, self-reflective questions is a facilitation skill that has particular value since these types of questions tend to prompt client stories.

- Telling a story often suggests new meaning and messages to the client.

- Client disclosure of troubling or upsetting stories creates bonds and trust with you.

- When coaching leaders, you need to tap into your client's stories, not only to understand them, but also to assess the impact their stories have on the people they are leading.

- When clients tell stories that deflect inquiry and serve to maintain the status quo, facilitation skills can help in getting to deeper meaning.

- In some cases, you may choose to tell a story from your own experience that illustrates a leadership principle or a developmental struggle.

CHAPTER

13

Strengthening the Partnership

THERE ARE MANY CONSIDERATIONS AND CHALLENGES IN AN EXECUTIVE COACH-
ING ENGAGEMENT. SPONSOR ROLES, CONTRACTING, GOAL EVOLUTION, DATA
GATHERING, AND DEVELOPMENT PLANNING ARE ESSENTIAL ELEMENTS FOR
successful outcomes. At the same time, there are factors operating at the
interpersonal level that are equally important but can get overshadowed by
the more visible aspects of coaching. One of the less obvious but critical factors is the coach-client partnership.

To summarize from Chapter 7, the quality of the relationship you are able
to build and sustain with your client is the most important factor that you
have control over when it comes to influencing positive outcomes.[1] Trust,
honesty, caring, and credibility should characterize relationships you establish with your clients. Your ability to foster these qualities depends upon:

- Modeling the communication and interpersonal skills conducive to a
  productive relationship.

- Awareness of how to adjust your behavior to strengthen the partnership

- Avoiding responses that may distance you from clients

Clients and coaching situations that trigger your fears, frustrations, or anger can be especially challenging. For example, clients who do not follow through on committed tasks, clients who work at a different pace than you do, or sponsors who offer support but are unavailable—all these situations can be very frustrating. You may feel angry, misled, or even irrelevant. These are natural reactions, but expressing them spontaneously is not useful and can damage a fragile relationship. Even when your reactions are related directly to how the client treats you, such as canceling appointments on short notice, the ability to contain, consider, and productively channel those reactions is an important skill for you to develop. Self-management, which is part of the concept of *containment* (illustrated in Figure 13-1), involves noting your reactions as objectively as you can, reframing them as data that may be used later, or quieting yourself meditatively so that you can listen to the client more closely.

Your time in the coaching role and the accumulation of experiences with different types of clients will help this self-awareness and self-discipline happen. Also supporting this growth is reflection and discussion with trusted colleagues or case supervisors about the difficult moments you have experi-

Figure 13-1. Containment equation

Containment = Confidentiality + Coaching Practices + Self-Management + Supervision

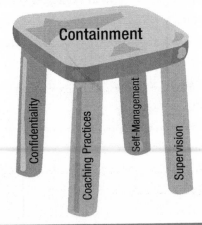

enced with your clients. Turning those encounters into learning experiences contributes to your skill in tolerating and modulating your reactivity to your clients, sponsors, and other organizational contacts you may have.

As you become better able to look honestly at the quality of your relationships with clients, you may discover areas for improvement. You may feel stuck, lose your focus, talk too much, give advice too quickly, work too hard, or evidence other less-than-ideal behaviors or feelings. These reflect insecurities and skill gaps that you need to address more productively. You may decide to prepare for sessions with greater self-awareness or consciously calm and balance your interpersonal posture. You may seek counsel from more experienced coaches about these challenges or scan the coaching literature for ideas. The point is that you cannot tune into the client's emotional state if you are confused and unsettled in your own feelings.

> **Make choices that enhance the quality of the coaching relationship. Consider: your pacing, client feedback readiness, work context pressures, stage in the coaching process, and behavioral traction with the client.**

Once you gain an awareness of your reactions to clients and are better able to sort out your own emotions, your intuition becomes very useful. For example, you might notice that you feel unsure or unsettled with a client. On reflection, you realize it is because the client is sending mixed facial cues, such as smiling when angry or frowning when thinking about an issue. Furthermore, you hypothesize that the client's direct reports may experience the same confusion. This hypothesis becomes something you listen for during the informational interviews. Alternatively, you may decide to share that observation with your client based on your intuition that it could be important to his or her development.

Deciding if and when to use your observations, feelings, and intuitions with a client, which can be thought of as *use of self*, is an important skill for coaches. *Use of self* is a key component of building an open and trusting relationship with clients (also discussed in Chapter 2), but its very subjectivity makes it challenging to learn. As you gain coaching experience, you will gain confidence about noticing and valuing your own reactions to clients. Refining that skill involves becoming an astute observer of client words, behaviors, and nonverbal signals, noticing your reactions to these characteristics, and allowing those sometimes discrete elements to coalesce into an observation, intuition, or hypothesis. Although your skill at doing this will grow over time, it is never too early to begin reflecting about, and describing, your perceptions about clients.

If you choose to share an observation or reaction with a client, examine your words for any hint of negative judgment. Deconstruct your observation to get as close as possible to your own experience of the client and be descriptive of the client's behavior. For example, saying, "I have noticed that you seem uneasy when we talk about Bill," is better than saying, "Why are you uncomfortable when we discuss Bill?" As the coach, phrasing feedback as an *I* message makes it more neutral, immediate, and inviting.

It is important to bring immediacy to those moments and speak directly to your client without apology or lengthy explanations. Invite discussion of possible parallels between your observations and broader issues or challenges that your client is facing. As you take prudent risks with sharing honest and interesting *use of self* observations about clients, your partnership with them strengthens.

To augment your *use of self* with clients, here are a few suggestions:

- Become more confident about the usefulness of your own personal and emotional reactions to clients and sponsors.
- Be able to empathize with a wide array of different personalities and backgrounds, even if your life experiences are very different.
- Tune into what is going on in your own emotional reactions during an otherwise intellectual conversation with a client.
- Improve your verbal facility to channel your reactions into observations about your client and their situation; be willing to be controversial.
- Practice narrating your feelings and reactions in your journal, with a supervisor, and with a trusted colleague. Distill those feelings and reactions into messages that may be useful in coaching.

⊙ When you feel stuck or lost with a client, reflect on what the client is saying or doing that has diminished your control or confidence; then consider what to do to rectify the situation.

As you experiment with these suggestions and make choices about how best to connect with your clients, you can be confident that whatever contributes to the quality of your relationships has the highest probability of paying off in terms of coaching outcomes.

CASE ILLUSTRATION: PRAISE CAN INTERFERE WITH A RELATIONSHIP

Coaches often find themselves caught between their natural human reactions and what they feel are the responsibilities of the coaching role. Especially when you are put off by something the client has done or said, there is ambiguity about what you should do in response. You could do nothing and continue with coaching, but if your reactions are getting in the way of a productive relationship or they are reflective of others' experience of the client, you need to find ways to share those reactions with the client. Some of the most pivotal coaching moments happen when you are able to use your reactions wisely and sensitively to provide *in-the-moment feedback* to your client. This case shows how one coach handled that challenge.

Hani, an organization development professional, had received training to provide internal coaching services in her organization. She was very excited about the one-on-one activity of coaching and more directly using her interpersonal skill set. In one of her first engagements, she contracted with Elliot, a new managing director, to help him step up to the demands of his new level. He had gotten feedback about empowering his direct reports and setting higher performance expectations. Also, he'd been told he needed to improve his strategic thinking and longer-range planning skills

Hani knew that Elliot had worked his way up in the organization during his eight years with the company from supervisor to manager and now to managing director. She learned from Elliot that he had enjoyed his managerial work and was considered an excellent developer of people. He also felt that he was a good team player and supported his peers as they worked toward organizational objectives. Elliot reported that he did not see himself as ambitious or competitive, but did see himself as very committed. After his recent promotion, he realized he was taking on broad responsibility for areas completely new to him, and so he had requested a coach to help him with the transition.

Hani and Elliot met several times. They were moving toward drafting a transition plan that would have developmental elements for Elliot. He seemed very open to the process and eager to apply what he was learning. In fact, after each session, Elliot repeatedly thanked Hani for "giving so many good suggestions." While Elliot's gratitude appeared to be sincere, Hani felt put off. She was intentionally avoiding giving Elliot suggestions, consistent with her training as a coach and her Personal Model. If he was experiencing what she said as suggestions, maybe she was doing something wrong. She reexamined how she was listening to his stories and exploring his ideas. Yet his effusive thanks continued to grate on her. She saw herself as a journey partner, not the expert at what was best for her client. Hani knew she needed to address her feelings in some way and yet hesitated; it felt risky.

Internal coaches at Hani's company were provided with case support by an outside, experienced coach supervisor. Hani and her supervisor quickly determined that her own reactions to Elliot were getting in the way of her listening because she experienced Elliot's frequent thanks as ingratiating. Hani wondered if others might have the same reaction to Elliot. She also wondered if being so nice was preventing him from empowering others because he might have to deal with performance shortfalls.

Hani resolved to use her own reactions more directly with Elliot, although she didn't want him to feel criticized for being appreciative. Still, she believed that this was useful data for Elliot to have, and so she rehearsed several ways of phrasing her feedback.

At the end of the next session Elliot once again thanked her by saying, "Hani, your ideas are great; I wish I had you with me all the time." Hani paused before responding, "It feels good to be thanked, but if I were with you all the time, who would actually be making your decisions?" Elliot was listening, so she went on: "We spent time discussing your situation and coming up with ideas, but I don't see myself as needing to be with you to help you run your department." Elliot was quiet and thoughtful. He agreed that she was right and would think about why he said what he did.

Hani didn't have to prompt Elliot at the beginning of their next meeting.

He was excited to share that her comment had made him think about other situations when others had expressed discomfort about being thanked. This topic had come up recently with his direct reports because he was asking them to do more, but thanking them so effusively was confusing. He and Hani agreed that this apparently habitual behavior was not supportive of his new role. They continued their discussion to understand its unintended but negative impact on others and what he could do to modify his behavior. They also contracted for Hani to gather early perceptions of Elliot from direct reports to see how they would describe his leadership style. This time when Elliot said "thanks!" for the session, it felt genuine and appropriate.

Supervisor's Observations

Strengthening a coaching relationship requires the coach to notice and understand reactions to a client's behavior and then to determine if it might be useful to share them. This is not as easy as it sounds because our reactions can sometimes be confusing. Hani had mixed feelings about being praised for something that she believed she shouldn't be doing in the first place. Rather than trying to ignore her reaction, she made it a topic for discussion with her supervisor. She then began to consider the meaning of her feelings, and several interesting hypotheses emerged. She concluded that the client's behavior might extend beyond the coaching relationship and that her reaction to it could be useful.

A coaching relationship has the unusual potential to take those reactions seriously and put them on the table for discussion. Very few other relationships in life support that level of attention and honesty. Most clients will experience these *use of self* moments as indicating true caring and deepening the coach-client partnership.

Use of self can seem very challenging to a newer coach, but it is eminently learnable. It does require self-reflection to understand your reactions, but as you get better at figuring out those reactions, you can use them more quickly. While using a reaction spontaneously can have great impact, a client's patterns tend to repeat themselves, so other opportunities are likely to arise. Although you can't always be sure where sharing your reactions will lead, tapping into them will enhance the relationship and self-discovery for the client.

Takeaways

- The quality of the coach-client relationship is the most important ingredient under the coach's control in the client's progress and change.

- It is important to monitor and manage your conduct in order to be experienced as a caring and receptive partner as well as a model of effective communication and interpersonal characteristics.

- Your reactions to the client are an important source of information and insight, but it is important to distinguish your reactions about the client from those that come from your own concerns or insecurities.

- There are a variety of choices about what to do with your useful reactions to the client. Deciding if and how to use your reactions is a coaching skill called *use of self*.

- *Use of self* involves taking risks, but it can be learned. Even experienced coaches can deepen their ability to self-monitor and capitalize on tuning into the impact clients have on you.

- If you choose to share an observation or reaction, deconstruct it and be descriptive of the client's behavior. Then invite dialogue to explore its meaning for the client.

Using the Partnership to Motivate Change

A S YOUR RELATIONSHIPS WITH CLIENTS STRENGTHEN DURING COACHING ENGAGEMENTS, THEY STILL REMAIN IN FLUX. DIFFERENT CHALLENGES EMERGE REQUIRING ADJUSTMENTS IN YOUR APPROACH. JUST AS A GROWING tree can support more weight as it ages, the coach-client partnership needs to be able to handle more intensity and pressure as the engagement progresses.

Keep in mind that:

- The support you provide during the early stages of coaching will shift toward expectations for behavioral change as coaching progresses.

- As clients try new behaviors, you can set expectations for reflection and fine-tuning.

- Your encouragement will help clients surface obstacles and use coaching as a forum for problem solving over time.

- You and your clients can begin to ask for feedback from managers and other stakeholders as implementation of the development plan occurs.

A natural shift of responsibility occurs during the course of a successful coaching engagement. In the early stages of coaching, you are more responsible for leading a process that yields insight and developmental plans. Later on, it is up to your client to take more responsibility for developmental progress. A useful indication of the success of the coach-client relationship is a lessening of your role and a corresponding increase in your client's commitment and activity level.

Having earned your client's trust in the earlier stages of coaching, you are in a position to encourage, even urge, action on the challenges in the development plan. Your support, acceptance, and ideas remain valuable, but probably your expectations have increased that your client can accomplish developmental tasks even if they are difficult. At the same time that you empathize with those challenges, you convey confidence that the client can engender positive change. Clients need your optimism and support, along with focus and discipline, to take the necessary risks inherent in implementing the behavior changes in the development plan.

The reality is that there will be setbacks as well as successes. Progress does not follow a straight ascending line. Your openness to client discouragement provides a safe context to explore challenges, make adjustments, and get back on track. Being able to openly discuss disappointments motivates clients to stay focused on development objectives even though actions may not be yielding the intended results. Most clients will want to please you with reports of progress, but a strong relationship supports the open sharing of discouragement as well. It provides both the safety to admit the need for help and the collaborative structure to arrive at better options. If your coaching partnership is to foster change, mistakes and misfires are as much opportunities for learning as are successes.

A common challenge in coaching is associated with the mixed feelings most clients have about change. Even change that is designed by your client and aimed in a clearly positive direction will trigger concerns and doubts: *Have we figured out the right things to focus on? Will others support me in doing things differently? Is the effort to change worth the risk?* As clients depart from familiar patterns, they know there are no guarantees of success, so doubts are close to the surface.

Compounding those concerns, some clients may associate change with the loss of predictability, even if the original situation had been quite problematic; familiarity is a powerful force. The loss of what is known may be emotionally evocative, connected with other losses in the client's life. While we cannot always predict these responses to change, as professionals we need to understand and accept emotional reactions that are stronger than we might have expected, even when they are associated with ineffective behaviors and backsliding on commitments.

In view of the risks inherent in change, it is not surprising that clients are hesitant at various points in change efforts, even when they are making progress. A coach might think, *Why isn't he doing what we agreed to?* or *Why is she moving so slowly to implement the plan?* As was mentioned in Chapter 7, labeling lack of follow-through or delay as *resistance* reflects a negative judgment that does not support openness and joint problem solving. Since change is difficult and caution is appropriate, client hesitation is to be expected and accepted with curiosity rather than a negative label. Figure 14-1 offers suggestions on how to reframe *resistance.*

Reluctance to change can appear in the guise of a legitimate obstacle over which your client has little or no control. You may hear the client make statements such as, "I'm too busy to see you this month," "I didn't get a chance to try that new behavior we discussed," or "I thought you were going to send me the development plan draft." All these claims may be true at a rational level, but they reflect feelings of reluctance.

You cannot see those inner vicissitudes, but you can respond to their outer manifestations. Although clients seeking praise may report progress, you can demonstrate acceptance of reluctance by encouraging dialogue about doubts, difficulties, and perceptions of risk. Accepting the legitimacy of your client's mixed feelings, even as you support the need for change, prompts exploration and understanding along with renewed commitment.

Encouraging openness when reluctance surfaces helps you find out more about what matters most to your client. In fact, the stronger the reluctance is in terms of avoidance, excuses, and inactivity, the greater importance you can assume the old behavior has. This awareness can suggest that you explore considerations weighing on your client about the real costs and benefits of behavior change. It is important for clients to feel safe in the coaching relationship to benefit from your questions about the fears and risks.

Figure 14-1. Reframing resistance

- ➤ Reframe *resistance* as *reluctance* to view it as a natural response to change and uncertainty.

- ➤ Exploring reluctance can reveal strongly held beliefs and values.

- ➤ Reluctance can be triggered by feelings of *loss* or *disappointment*, which need to be acknowledged.

- ➤ Change involves risk; imagine worst-case and positive outcomes.

- ➤ Change is iterative, a series of experiments rather than right answers.

- ➤ Reduce barriers by reframing success as learning, becoming rather than perfection.

- ➤ Even with the best of intentions, advice implies a negative judgment, which can trigger reluctance.

- ➤ Reluctance may also indicate deficiencies in the plan or goal; explore alternatives.

Some clients may credit you with more power and authority than you feel you have. They may convey admiration, submissiveness, frustration, or resentment, verbally and nonverbally, toward you. When clients project strong feelings onto a helping professional it is called *transference*. It is a central element of psychodynamic approaches to therapy originally described by Freud, but as a concept, it can be applied to any professional relationship. For practitioners trained to understand and use transference reactions, it can provide leverage in facilitating insight and growth. You need to recognize the presence of transference when it happens, but that may be all you choose to do. This awareness can help you keep your focus even if a client is reacting to you in ways that feel more extreme than warranted. Sometimes these reactions can be discussed with clients through use of self to bring more attention and understanding to them. If such reactions threaten to derail your relationship with a client, seek out counsel from a coaching supervisor, possibly one who has clinical training.

Another leverage point that should be used sparingly is your description of how similar challenges were handled by others. No one likes to be compared to someone else or lumped into general categories of people with problems. When you tell the success stories of others, especially if they were your clients, there are risks to your current relationship. Even well-intended comparisons can imply that others have the correct answers or that they were somehow better or stronger. A client may even misconstrue an example as if it conveys your recommendation about what the client should do.

Occasionally, however, a client will find the success stories of others useful. For example, telling a client about another manager's successful passage from being too hands-on to empowering the team, or about the behaviors used by a naturally reticent leader to become more visible and interpersonally engaged, can legitimize the challenges of making these changes and provide specific ideas. Such stories convey that your client is not alone and that change efforts yield results.

CASE ILLUSTRATION: TOUGH TALK LATER IN COACHING

Healthy growth in the coach-client partnership supports a shift of responsibility from coach to client. When such a shift occurs, coaches are freer in what they can do to foster client progress, especially when that progress plateaus. Of course, leveraging the partnership involves a professional judgment that contains some risk, but the coach in this case has decided to take it.

Martha had been coaching Jim for about three months. Jim is a thirty-eight-year-old director of marketing for a large consumer-goods manufacturer. He worked his way up in the field from sales to supervisor and then to district sales manager before being promoted about a year earlier to his current position at headquarters (HQ). Jim was very successful in his prior field roles, applying his energy, outgoing style, and competitive spirit in leading his teams toward positive results. However, as he and Martha determined, those skills weren't as effective in his new job at HQ. Data gathering had revealed that there seemed to be a "fit" problem: His strong presence, assertiveness, and directness did not endear him to his HQ colleagues, who were more evenly paced, measured, and diplomatic. Some of his coworkers described Jim as "walking over people" and abrasive or even combative.

While Jim felt defensive about the feedback and resented the suggestion that everyone had to have a similar style at HQ, he did like his job. Being in marketing was allowing him to have a larger impact on the overall business, and he was learning a lot about analytical tools and marketing programs. Still, he recognized that his rocky relationships with several colleagues were getting in the way of his success. He found coaching useful in charting these unfamiliar waters.

Martha and Jim drafted a development plan. It challenged Jim to be more sensitive to his general interpersonal impact on others and to use a more collaborative style when working on teams. However, from progress checks that Martha did with sponsors, it appeared to her that Jim wasn't applying the new behaviors that were in the plan. And when they discussed his implementation of the plan, he described distractions or unusual circumstances that seemed to have gotten in the way of trying new behaviors.

Martha decided that her relationship with Jim was strong enough to sustain a more challenging posture from her. At their next session, she put her concerns on the table: "Jim, from what I am hearing, your progress has lost some momentum." Being no wallflower, Jim disputed this claim and asserted that he felt he was making positive changes. Martha confronted him with a summary of her progress checks that showed others were not seeing much difference and hadn't changed their perceptions of Jim. She drove the point home with an analogy: "Just as in your marketing work, having a plan is less than half the battle; implementation can make or break even the best ideas." This seemed to get Jim's attention. Martha turned the conversation to what was getting in the way of his making the changes they had planned. He admitted these changes were more difficult than he imagined and that he wasn't really putting in the effort to try them out. Martha challenged him fur-

ther by adding, "The question I have for you is, since when has a goal's difficulty stopped you before?" She observed his posture change as he reacted to her challenge.

He and Martha continued the dialogue, highlighting several specific changes he could apply in the coming week and how he might partner with someone to get immediate feedback about how he did. She knew there were no guarantees, but she felt that Jim's commitment was stronger, and she was confident that progress would help to reinforce the changes.

Supervisor's Observations

By the second half of a typical coaching engagement, coaches have established a working partnership with clients. Trust has deepened, and clients are actively engaged in making changes. This shift gives the coach a lot of leverage to be more assertive and to hold clients to commitments. So, it is important that Martha was able to use that leverage directly. On the continuum from being supportive, on one hand, to challenging the client on the other, both are important competencies for coaches so that they can respond effectively to the varying needs that clients have. Martha was able to move along that continuum by drawing on several other factors in the coaching relationship. She had consciously thought through the risks and potential gains in changing her posture with Jim. She was confident that the relationship would support more challenge. Finally, she knew Jim well in terms of his emotional stability and motivational structure so that she could both push and pull him toward the plan that he had committed to. She may not have been consciously aware of all these factors, but clearly her intuition tapped into them.

As is true with many forms of power, however, *push* works best when used very sparingly. If Martha decided to continue pushing Jim to implement change, then there are other issues that she would have needed to address. Martha might prepare for implementation by imagining herself in Jim's place and thus tune into what else he needs. She may decide that even goal-driven Jim is a bit out of his element at HQ. He may need more time in his role to gain confidence and get more of a *team feel* in his relationships with peers, or build other hidden but important support systems. Martha has shown that she can be as direct as she needs to be, but she also will need to keep her empathy tuned into what Jim might need, beyond the specifics of the development plan.

Takeaways

- ◎ All change is difficult. You can support your client by being positive and hopeful even at times when your client is discouraged.

- ◎ *Reluctance*, instead of *resistance*, is a more useful label for client hesitation and concerns about change because it tends to open up dialogue and helps you focus on the issues behind the reluctance that you can address.

- ◎ When you have earned the trust of a client, you may shift to a more assertive and expectant posture to support your client's approach to challenges that have been agreed to.

- ◎ As you leverage your maturing relationship with your client, it is important for you to remain connected emotionally to your client's developmental experiences.

- ◎ When clients are looking for ways to deal with long-standing or frustrating issues in themselves or in their context, an occasional story of another's success can be motivational.

15

Coaching for Leadership

L EADERSHIP IS EXERCISED BY PEOPLE AT ALMOST EVERY LEVEL OF THE ORGANI-
ZATIONAL HIERARCHY. THAT IS WHY THE TOPIC OF LEADERSHIP IS OFTEN A
FOCUS IN COACHING. MOST COACHES SEEK TO DEVELOP A KEEN UNDERSTAND-
ING of leadership concepts and practices, as well as an appreciation for the
special challenges and quandaries that leaders face. Some coaches become
expert on the subject and use it as the foundation of their Personal Models of
coaching. The majority, however, use their own professional and consulting
experiences, augmented by reading and courses, to integrate leadership concepts, guidelines, and challenges into a broader coaching practice.

Understanding the demands of leadership in today's organizations is
essential. Although it can be challenging, many coaches without much organizational experience do absorb leadership vocabulary, learn to appreciate
organizational challenges, refine their grasp of leadership options, and thus
grow more confident about using their leadership insights in coaching
leaders.

From your own experiences in organizations—as a leader, follower, consultant, volunteer, or observer—you probably have developed a wealth of
ideas about leadership. Depending on the type of experience you have had,

you might have made observations about formal authority and structure, dealings between staff groups and internal customers, power versus influencing, the challenges of leading physically dispersed locations, connections between leadership development and organizational objectives, organizational culture, and many other topics. These observations may have led you to consider broad questions about leadership: What does it mean to be an effective leader? How do leaders balance ambition and humility? Who are your role models for leadership effectiveness? What skills do leaders need to conduct the important interactions they have with others, such as building teams, running meetings, encouraging diversity, resolving differences, providing feedback, and so forth? The more you are a thoughtful student of organizational dynamics and leadership, the more able you will be to work with a real-life organizational leader who is struggling with similar questions.

> **Broadly speaking, coaches are called upon to work with leaders on their self-management, interpersonal effectiveness, and leadership impact.**

At the same time, your clients will have their own ideas about leadership. Exploring their leadership principles, assumptions, and values is often a fruitful line of inquiry. A leader's development may be narrowed by fixed beliefs about leadership, such as *Leaders must drive people forward*, or *Leaders should be above politics*. You can help clients by engaging them in questioning their leadership assumptions and identifying ways they emerge in behavior.

Leadership Challenges

Leading others is a very complex human endeavor. Leaders need confidence and self-esteem if they are to provide consistent direction and withstand scrutiny and criticism. On the other hand, excessive confidence has been shown to be a significant problem in isolating leaders from needed feedback and learning. Finding a balance between confident decisiveness and open humility is a key challenge for leaders.

In some situations it is also difficult to maintain the distinction between leadership and management. Leadership is a broader topic than management and is associated with vision, strategy, inspiration, challenge, and charisma. Management, on the other hand, may be thought of as the implementation of what leaders initiate. Managerial skills, such as contracting for performance, delegating, and providing feedback, may be subsumed under the leadership umbrella. Development goals may be tied to both managerial skills and leadership topics, often in the same client, regardless of level or title.

Another issue for leaders is decision making. Organizations are dynamic, and leading them requires making many decisions. There will be winners and losers as leaders make decisions that support some people but not others. While it is important for followers to feel that these decisions have a basis in logic and fairness, leaders cannot please everyone. In garnering support for the decisions they make, leaders must use informal alliances, positional power, and clear reasoning. Leaders who depend too much on pure logic or positional power will lose support from constituents. As an executive coach, you can counterbalance this tendency by helping leaders use a wide range of skills in conveying decisions.

Leaders frequently need to initiate change and make decisions with limited information; decisiveness is key and may be more important than finding the perfect answer. These decisions, especially when they affect people's careers, are difficult on many levels—analytical, political, and emotional. In addition, these decisions sometimes cause leaders to isolate themselves to avoid being petitioned by those affected. You can help leaders make more balanced, tough decisions by facilitating a full exploration of the options, showing them that there is no commitment in listening to constituents, and providing support when they are feeling the weight of their impact on their employees.

Leaders also need to become comfortable with the exposure that leadership roles involve. Small actions and casual comments can have impacts beyond what the leader intends or is even aware of. Examples include who the leader says "hello" to in the morning, who is included in meetings and memos, where the leader eats lunch, or whose jokes the leader laughs at. Successful leaders need to learn to live in a fishbowl and find ways of tuning into how their words and actions are being perceived while maintaining the ability to think independently. You can provide an honest perspective about how leaders' actions might be misperceived and help leaders build awareness of the alignment, or lack of it, between their intentions and how their actions might be perceived by others.

Leadership roles often require the performance of various symbolic tasks and appearances to reach as many employees as possible. These activities require much time and energy without clear or immediate payback. Thus, leaders also need to be skilled communicators and presenters, able to translate complex situations into readily understood explanations. Depending on the leader, these activities may be challenging and engaging or boring and frustrating. You can help leaders accept their mixed feelings about these activities and tolerate them better by helping them understand their importance to others in the organization.

It has been said that ultimately leadership cannot be taught but it can be learned. In facilitating that learning, you can stay attuned to four issues that come up repeatedly in coaching leaders:

1. The choice to lead
2. Stories that leaders tell themselves and others
3. Organizational influencing and politics
4. Polarities that drive the leader's style choices

Choice to Lead

As described previously, management and leadership are conceptually different, but in practice they overlap. Every manager's job has some leadership elements, even if on a small scale. However, as managers begin to advance through the managerial ranks, their responsibilities as leaders may be downplayed. As a result, managers may find themselves in roles with significant leadership demands without having consciously chosen to become leaders.[1] They may have been promoted without really appreciating the demands of being a leader, or they may have been following advancement and financial incentives without fully considering their actual interests and other trade-offs.

In the context of a trusted coaching relationship, you may want to explore your client's choice to lead. It is possible such a choice has never been considered. Questioning your clients about their real interest in leadership challenges, aspirations to higher levels of leadership, and strengths and gaps for leadership activities may both deepen their understanding of leadership and confirm their true interest in the role. On the other hand, your queries may reveal a lack of connection to leadership demands and unspoken concerns about trade-offs in being a leader. These issues may be a hidden drag on your clients' energy. Either way, conversation about the choice to lead can yield useful insights.

Leadership Stories

As discussed in Chapter 12, eliciting a client's career story is a way to foster dialogue and build a productive coaching relationship. In coaching leaders, however, stories take on even more importance.[2] Leaders rely on the stories they tell themselves about how and why they have achieved what they have. Those stories clarify their values and confirm lessons learned. They also reveal the client's implicit beliefs about leadership, which may need to be explored and expanded.

Leaders also tell stories to their followers to engage and inspire them. Some have said that successful leadership depends on the ability to tell compelling stories. As experienced sounding boards, coaches can help leaders explore the power of their stories, especially those they tell others. Coaches can help leaders evaluate key questions about stories, such as: How engaging is the vision described in the story? How clear is the message about what needs to happen? How well does the story strengthen leader-follower connections? How strongly does the story motivate followers to be part of the organization's future? You can use these prompts to increase a leader's impact through both delivery and content improvements.

Organizational Influencing and Politics

Stories are especially helpful to the formal part of leadership in painting a picture of the organization's future. Equally important are the stories that leaders use in the informal processes of persuasion: seeking support among influential followers; creating opportunities for informal discussion; giving some topics prominence over others; taking advantage of interactions that happen in the hallway, during lunch, or during travel or other occasions that can give a leader significant leverage. These informal influencing activities can be referred to as *organizational politics*, although the term carries a negative connotation for some clients. Clients who have been on the losing side of influencing a decision or who have been outmaneuvered by others may have rejected politics as an influencing tool, which is unfortunate. You can help those clients understand that politics do not need to be negative and are a fact of organizational life; avoiding them weakens leaders by reducing the number of tools they have to exert influence. While some clients may equate politics with underhanded or destructive behavior, you can help them identify the natural and essential elements of informal influencing that organizational politics embody.

Leadership Polarities and Choices

While there are many lists of leadership competencies, using polarities illustrates leadership skills more accurately than lists do. Every behavioral or stylistic choice that a leader makes tends to limit another choice that exists on the other end of the same continuum. For example, leaders who choose to encourage harmony cannot at the same moment foster overt debate.

Another implication of this idea is that too much of a particular leadership dimension can be counterproductive. As such, more is not necessarily better. Making informed choices requires leaders to have well-tuned situational judgment so that they can choose the side of the polarity, as well as the amount, that is needed at a particular moment.[3] Taking the idea further, leaders who are more skilled and comfortable at one end of a polarity may tend to overuse that skill and miss opportunities for using its opposite. For example, leaders who are very comfortable with operating environments and making tactical decisions may rely on these skills too much as they advance in an organization's hierarchy, resulting in the lack of empowerment of others. Limitations due to overuse can be significant gaps for leaders that you, as the executive coach, can help them overcome.

> Examples of other leadership polarities include: interpersonal closeness versus distance, pride versus humility, approachability versus toughness, and empowering versus directing. Leaders need to be able to range across these continua and make conscious choices about which skill to use and how strongly to apply it.

You can help to bring these four leadership challenges to the forefront of your client's awareness through asking questions and encouraging discussion. To the extent that you can anticipate these topics and leverage your ability to explore them, your leader-clients are likely to have more insights about likely developmental issues and what skills or behaviors they might need to work on in coaching.

Coaching Senior Leaders

Leadership issues for senior level, or *C-suite* executives (such as the chief executive officer, chief financial officer, chief operating officer, chief marketing officer) require a modified approach to coaching—a change of style that allows you to be in sync with the pressures of being at the top of an organizational hierarchy.

Senior leaders generally do not get to their positions because they are reflective or even conceptual. Moreover, they probably do not want to give up whatever set of skills and behaviors got them to their current level. Thus, when building credibility with senior-level managers, you may want to avoid too much introspection, abstraction, or critiquing past habits. The willingness to do these things may come in time but requires patience as your credibility is tested more than at lower organizational levels. When working with senior leaders, it is even more important for you to do your homework about the client's organization and background, as well as about the broad topic of leadership at the top of organizations.

The use of psychometrics and standardized 360-degree questionnaires is generally less frequent at senior levels of the organization. The statistical norms are less meaningful, and clients are likely to find less value in being labeled using dimensional language. Unless the assessments are tied to a developmental program that senior leaders attend, they generally prefer that you do qualitative data gathering. In addition to doing informational interviewing to gather data about these clients, you may also be able to contract to shadow them during actual meetings, and some coaches emphasize it in their Personal Models. Because shadowing involves your direct observation of the senior leader in action, during daily activities or important meetings or presentations, it presents an opportunity for you to provide immediate feedback that can be a powerful intervention. Shadowing requires that the client be completely open with others about your presence and the coaching process.

Senior leaders are likely to treat all outside professionals as consultants. Unfortunately, they may lump you into that same category. As a result, they expect you to be prepared, even though they may not be. They may also expect you to be unusually flexible about scheduling and changing appointments. In addition, they may seek to change your contracted work if it suits their needs or interests. So-called *mission creep* can occur as your coaching relationship morphs into recruiting, team building, and even career counseling. You need to know your own boundaries and how much you can flex them in order to be prepared for senior leaders who have expectations that are not part of your usual coaching relationships.

As confident as senior leaders can appear, they often really need and value a journey partner. Their executive roles can be isolating and lonely, at the same time that they are heady and privileged. Coaching can help meet their emotional needs for connection, honesty, and support in ways that their collegial relationships may not. Senior leaders appreciate the contrast to their thinking that your observations and ideas represent. In fact, senior leaders may contract with you to be a sounding board for their thinking and not be that interested in data gathering or development plans. Such a relationship can be very useful to senior leaders as long as it focuses on a leader's development and does not become consulting on HR or organizational decisions.

Finally, C-suite executives may or may not want their Human Resources VP involved in their coaching. Be careful not to assume that involvement as you might with coaching at lower levels. Instead, contract with the leader about how to include HR, if at all. Looking in the other organizational direction, you may want to explore if there are board directors who have a role in the senior leader's development and contract for their involvement as sponsors or stakeholders in the coaching engagement.

CASE ILLUSTRATION: NICE GUYS SOMETIMES GET THE TOP JOB

While stereotypes abound, senior leaders are not always confident, polished, and politically astute. Those qualities are certainly valuable, but there are many ways to be a leader and still achieve great things. All leaders bring to their roles both strengths and deficiencies. Organizational culture plays a role in the type of leadership style that will be effective in each situation. In the case that follows, the senior leader's professional and personal characteristics had served him well, and they are likely to be essential to him in the future, but only with the coach's help in making adjustments and building confidence about leadership at the top.

Marsha, an executive coach, was asked by her HR contact, Eric, to meet with the COO, Tom, who was interested in working with a coach. Eric told Marsha that he would not have his usual involvement in the engagement and that Tom had his own budget for development. Marsha had substantial prior experience coaching in the organization, but she had never met Tom. She did know that he was respected for his technical expertise, was generally liked, and had been asked to head up a new business venture for the company.

Marsha did not know what to expect at their first meeting, but they quickly clicked and began getting into the serious issues that were troubling Tom.

First, there was the issue of Tom's boss, the CEO. He had made it clear to Tom that he believed Tom needed a stronger leadership presence. Tom didn't disagree with this assessment, but from a practical standpoint, he didn't know what he actually should do differently and even if he did, whether he was capable of being a different type of leader. Marsha's follow-up questions and explorations during the next two coaching sessions revealed Tom's story. He was proud of his engineering background and enjoyed applying its discipline even to nonengineering problems. In the current job, however, there was never enough information, and the time frames were too short to allow the usual analytical rigor that he preferred. In some cases, he even was unsure if he had identified all the essential variables, let alone get thorough information about them. He also had strong inclinations to be cooperative with others and a supportive team member.

Now he was head of the team, and the climate was not to his liking. There was internal competition for his support, and he sensed some crosscurrents among people who might actually gain something by his failure. He also admitted that the job was draining him. He couldn't seem to stay ahead of the demands and sincerely didn't know if he could satisfy all the internal clients, his own staff, and his boss. Finally, during earlier assessments, he had learned that he preferred an introverted style. He could be effective leading people, usually on technical challenges, but he needed his private time, too. He wondered aloud whether he was cut out for the constant exposure, demands, and political forces at his current level in the organization.

Tom seemed to find some benefit in unburdening himself to Marsha; trust had developed. However, they both agreed that they needed some additional data. Since standardized assessments had not helped Tom evaluate his suitability for leadership, Marsha chose a qualitative approach, opting to interview Tom's boss and eight other colleagues. This process even included getting Eric's perspective on the situation. After completing the interviews and summarizing the themes, Marsha discovered that Tom was doing better than either he or his boss thought. He was well regarded for his integrity, intelligence, dedication, and experience. His unforgiving standards for himself did not really show up in what others were experiencing. People recognized that this new venture was a major challenge for all concerned, and they offered suggestions. However, they all believed that Tom had a good chance of making it succeed. They also suggested that Tom's boss had unrealistic expectations for progress. Marsha confirmed that competition and politics surrounded Tom's role; the company's recent and rapid growth had created a scramble for resources and influence.

Marsha and Tom discussed the situational variables, his strengths, and his new challenges thoroughly. There were several outcomes from this discussion. First, they agreed that Tom had some equity as a leader in the organization and that it would buy him some time to adjust to the new role. They labeled it his "learning to lead" agenda and decided that they would use it to shape immediate and short-term leadership challenges that Tom would need to learn to deal with. They would also include Tom's boss in some of that discussion. Second, they would take seriously, but hold in abeyance, decisions about whether Tom really wanted to be a leader at his current level. Third, they would identify the truly exciting challenges that the position offered and bring out more of the upside of them, while still being cognizant of the demands on Tom. Finally, they contracted for biweekly coaching sessions for a longer course than the usual six-month engagement, estimating that it would probably take closer to a year to provide Tom with both the learning and interpersonal support that he would need.

Supervisor's Observations

Coaching senior leaders is a challenge that requires both significant skill and flexibility. Executives expect you to step into their situations quickly and make positive contributions based on very limited information. They also expect you to take the lead on devising a coaching process that meets their needs.

Marsha appears to be handling the situation with Tom well. She created a safe place for Tom to deal with his uncertainties, and she was able to contain them without denying their importance. She used his story well to build insight about both strengths and possible gaps. Using qualitative data-gathering methods provided valuable input and, more important, room to maneuver.

There are several scripts in Tom's thinking that they will need to revisit several times and hopefully rewrite, such as his need to lead through being technically correct and his belief that conflict is bad and to be avoided. In addition, she will find it helpful to remember that clients sometimes confuse the results of quantitative and other standardized tests with truth; introversion is a preference, not a dictate. It will help Tom to be reminded that there are many very effective leaders who are introverted. Leadership is about behavior, not traits, and Tom has choices, which Marsha can help him make, especially as he develops his own sense of what effective leadership means for him.

They have made a good start on their coaching relationship and Tom's development, but there is much work to do. In addition to a substantial leadership learning agenda, tailored to Tom's particular style and situation, he may need help managing his boss's expectations. The boss probably has a very different leadership style, and Tom needs the confidence to differentiate the boss's approach from his own. Tom also needs help accepting some of the trade-offs in being a senior leader, such as constant visibility, balancing personal and professional priorities, empowering others but also holding them accountable, and wanting to be a nice person but making decisions that some people won't like.

Assuming the coaching succeeds in the medium term, more advanced topics will increase in importance. Tom could then work on being more political in building alliances within the culture and setting a vision for his unit that ties in with the larger organization. Ultimately, the success of Marsha's coaching supports the success of the company, truly showing the action learning aspects of senior leadership coaching.

Takeaways

- While not every coach is an expert on leadership, it is important for you to have familiarity with leadership definitions, concepts, and models.

- There are key challenges in being a leader that coaches need to grasp: exposure, difficult decisions, symbolic activities, and constant communication demands are examples.

- Leadership and management are different but overlapping concepts; coaches often work on both.

- Four issues that come up repeatedly in coaching leaders are the choice to lead; stories that leaders tell themselves and others; organizational influencing and politics; and the polarities that drive the leader's style choices.

- Senior leaders are apt to treat coaches as consultants, so *mission creep* needs to be monitored. Most leaders, however, really value a coach's observations and perspectives as a counterbalance to the isolation of their executive roles.

16

Differences

F OR MOST PEOPLE, SIMILARITIES, EVEN SUPERFICIAL ONES, MAKE INTERPERSON-
AL CONNECTIONS EASIER. WE TEND TO FEEL SAFER WITH WHAT IS FAMILIAR.
ON THE OTHER HAND, DIFFERENCES, BOTH OBVIOUS AND SUBTLE, CAN BE VERY
enlightening to explore. This is particularly true in coaching. Differences
between your clients and their colleagues with regard to background, preferences, interpersonal style, and other variables often figure into the development challenges of your clients. Differences between the coach and the client
also can be relevant to the progress made in coaching. It is important to help
clients avoid overemphasizing similarities while ignoring relevant differences.

Traditional diversity categories that organizations use for various inclusion initiatives include:

- ⊙ Ethnicity/Race
- ⊙ Gender
- ⊙ Religion
- ⊙ National Origin
- ⊙ Disability Status
- ⊙ Sexual Orientation

These categories, however, are actually a subset of the much larger group of differences; there are many other ways in which your clients can differ from their colleagues or we, as coaches, may differ from our clients. For example:

- Age
- Education (both level and field of study)
- Work Experience
- Interests
- Problem-Solving Style
- Interpersonal Style
- Income/Status

Since coaches work at the level of the individual, it is important for you to consider the possible impact of *all* relevant differences that may exist between you and your client and within your client's work world. If you focus only on the usual diversity categories you may miss important challenges facing the client.

Coach-Client Differences

You and your clients are likely to differ on one or more observable characteristics. Some clients may comment indirectly on your characteristics as compared to their own (e.g., "This business attracts a very young employee population," or "Maybe you can help me understand the women on my team"). Most will not. Instead, it is up to you to observe differences, especially during initial coaching meetings, and consider the implications of those differences. How do you feel about differences between yourself and the client? How might those differences inform or distract from the focus of the coaching? What are the big differences? What are the small ones? To the extent that observable coach-client differences may have implications for coaching, the responsibility is yours to put them on the table and discuss them with your client.

For example, you may decide it is important to ask minority clients how they feel about working with you if you are a nonminority coach, or how an older client feels about working with a younger coach. First, you must notice differences to consider the relevance of pointing them out and discussing their implications for your coaching relationship. If you feel that the difference may be of concern to your client, tactfully inviting discussion about it would be consistent with your coaching role.

Among the less visible differences that coaches need to be aware of are those involving preferred learning, interpersonal, and problem-solving styles. For example, your clients may be more concrete or short term in their thinking than you are. Differences such as these may generalize to issues in the client's work context (e.g., a very logical manager leading creative direct reports). Even when such differences do not emerge directly, coaches usually take responsibility for tailoring their approaches to suit their clients' preferences. For example, when coaching a client who is very fast-paced, you might shorten your explanations, emphasize quick wins, and deal with immediate pressures. On the other hand, this adjustment would not be helpful with a client who thinks in more strategical and longer-range terms.

Both differences and similarities between coach and client can occasionally influence how clients are matched with coaches. A client may select a coach based on a preference for a similar age or industry background. On the other hand, clients sometimes seek a coach who is different from themselves when a point of difference has implications for their learning. For example, a client might want to learn to improve relationships with a particular age group or race and may choose someone from that group for the coach role. In these cases, coach-client diversity becomes especially compelling when there is a direct application to the client's work effectiveness. A discussion of differences between coach and client can be an honest, safe forum for the client to explore issues and obstacles in working with differences affecting professional performance.

The Coach's Responsibility

It is important to heighten your self-awareness and insight about the possible effects of differences in your relationships. We, as coaches, tend to believe that we are more accepting than we really are, or we gloss over differences by latching onto superficial similarities with clients, just as most people do. Feeling discomfort about differences or the reverse—experiencing an excessive pull toward collegiality with clients—are indications that it would be helpful for you to explore those reactions with a mentor or case supervisor. Even when the similarities or differences between you and the client have contributed to the sponsor or client choosing you as a coach, the differences may be worthy of discussion.

Use Figure 16-1 to become more self-aware about your reactions to differences.

Figure 16-1. Self-assessment about differences

MYSELF:

> What do I notice about myself when I feel different?

> What do I see when I encounter differences between myself and others, and between others among themselves?

> In my past, if my difference was celebrated, how did that occur and what do I remember most about its celebration?

> What is my first impression when I encounter someone different? What is my first customary response?

> How do I make a distinction between something new and something different?

> Are there some differences around which I feel more comfort/discomfort? Which ones?

> What happens inside me when I encounter people whose values are not only different but in opposition to mine?

> How important are my values and biases when differences show up?

> How do I know I am judging? What do I see, hear, feel, do?

> How do I know I am observing? What do I see, hear, feel, do?

Continues on page 170

Figure 16-1. Self-assessment about differences (continued)

MY COACHING

- ➤ In what categories do I notice differences between myself and clients?
- ➤ What do I consider in the context of coaching to determine if differences matter?
- ➤ How important is it to notice differences?
- ➤ How do I decide to openly acknowledge a difference or not?
- ➤ When was there a time where I handled difference well and what did I do?

Differences in the Workplace

In the course of discussing felt needs, clients may point out differences they have noticed at work. These may run the gamut from traditional differences of age, gender, race, nationality, religion, and sexual orientation to some differences that are less common, such as organizational and cultural differences within a newly merged company. These differences could occur between your client and specific individuals or between departments and teams.

Your client may want help with how to address differences that may be triggering tensions among individuals or subgroups. Coaching is an excellent forum for the clients to consider the implications of the many differences that may exist in their organization. You are empowered to raise questions about those differences, especially if you believe that the client would be a more effective leader with more overt attention paid to them. While you are not a diversity consultant, raising your client's awareness about difference issues within the organization may fit directly into the client's development plan.

Coaching to Support Diversity Initiatives

Despite a significant increase in acceptance of differences and an emphasis on inclusion in corporate cultures, minorities, women, and other diversity groups experience obstacles to advancement. Many organizations are sensitive to the career aspirations of these groups and others who are underrepresented in managerial and executive ranks. To address these issues, most large organizations have introduced diversity or inclusion initiatives, mentoring programs, and employee support/affinity groups. It is not uncommon for them to engage coaches to accelerate the managerial and leadership skill development of minority employees and to create more acceptance and openness among majority employees. Some coaches, whether minorities themselves or not, have chosen in their Personal Models of coaching to specialize in these types of engagements. In addition to their expertise in matters of inclusion and expanding opportunities, these coaches need to possess a capacity to tolerate and manage tense interpersonal situations.

Figure 16-2 presents a decision guide to help coaches determine whether to bring a differences issue into coaching discussions.

CASE ILLUSTRATION: OBVIOUS SIMILARITIES, BUT IT'S THE SUBTLE DIFFERENCES THAT MATTER

There are often differences between coach and client. Interestingly, obvious differences are sometimes less important than the more subtle ones: the client whose regional American accent you find off-putting or the client who is disappointed that you don't play golf. You need to know your biases and personal triggers, and be able to manage them so they do not interfere with your job of creating and facilitating a safe environment for change. As a result, it is impossible to know for sure what differences will affect you or the client, even when there are obvious similarities. This is illustrated in the case that follows.

An external coach of Hispanic origin, Andrew, had a regular contract to work with high potentials in a client organization as part of an ongoing leadership development program. Matches between coach and client were made randomly. Through this process, Andrew was assigned to work with a client named Jean-Claude, and they set up an initial meeting. The HR coordinator knew both of them, and while they had been assigned to work together by chance, she assumed that since they both had immigrated to the United States from other countries, they would have much in common.

Figure 16-2. Differences decision tree

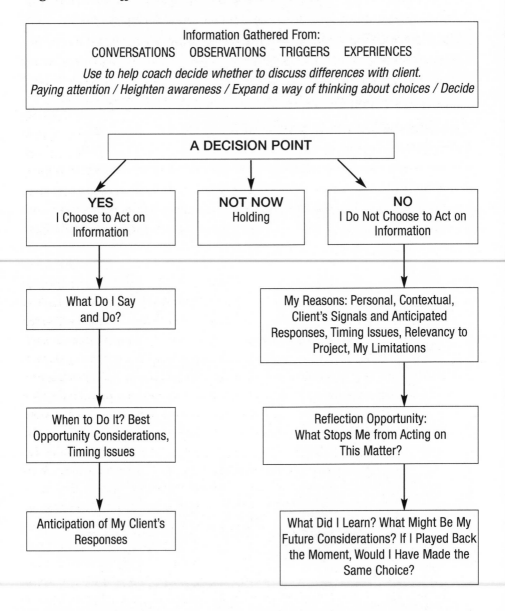

During the initial session, Andrew conducted his usual contracting con-versation, just to be sure everyone had the same expectations. He then moved into learning about Jean-Claude's education and professional back-ground. Andrew learned that Jean-Claude was born and raised in Haiti, had come to the United States for college, and had become a U.S. citizen. He still had many family members in Haiti. Andrew realized early in the meeting that he and Jean-Claude had several notable similarities: Both had immigrant parents, coincidentally from the same island (Hispaniola, which is divided between the Dominican Republic and Haiti), neither spoke English in their childhoods, and both had African-American heritage. However, Andrew real-ized immediately that this created a challenge for him. He didn't want to overemphasize their similarities, even though notable, because they were superficial. On the other hand, he and the client couldn't ignore them, both because they were so apparent and because ethnic background could figure into Jean-Claude's professional history.

Andrew decided to deal with this challenge by noting the similarities and asking Jean-Claude for his reactions. In their first meeting, this strategy worked well. They didn't dwell on the coincidence of the apparent similarities and were able to have a very productive conversation about Jean-Claude's professional history, his self-assessed strengths and gaps, and his career aspi-rations; in other words, for Andrew, this was a typical initial coaching session.

Between the first and second sessions, Andrew spoke with his case super-visor and reflected on his session with Jean-Claude. He concluded that the ethnic and cultural overlap between himself and Jean-Claude needed more exploration. At the start of the second session, Andrew asked Jean-Claude for his reaction to their similarities. This opened up a new perspective for Andrew. It turned out that Jean-Claude was much more aware of their differ-ences than their obvious similarities. He was concerned because they came from very different cultures; even though on the same island, their countries of origin are culturally distant. Similarly, they were divided by an obvious lan-guage difference, but more important to Jean-Claude, Andrew's English was clearer and less accented than his. On the other hand, Andrew had a more varied professional career here in the United States than Jean-Claude, which impressed Jean-Claude but also made him a bit envious. Finally, Jean-Claude questioned whether the organization had reduced them to superficial pro-

> *files in an effort to match them. This bothered him because coach-client matching was supposed to be random.*
>
> *Andrew felt as if his eyes had been opened to Jean-Claude's reality, and he thanked him for his honesty. It was immediately apparent to Andrew that having their differences on the table might facilitate the discussion of Jean-Claude's development. Andrew also acknowledged the importance of Jean-Claude's question about whether they had been profiled.*
>
> *They didn't specifically work on these issues, but Jean-Claude seemed genuinely relieved to have been able to open up about his concerns. Andrew was very glad he had reopened the topic, confirming that assumptions about similarities and differences are often erroneous. They need to be explored to build trust and to avoid misunderstandings that might surface later.*

Supervisor's Observations

The irony here is apparent and worth repeating: Obvious similarities may be distractions to more important differences. While Andrew and Jean-Claude have a surprising number of similarities, it is the more subtle differences that the client was focused on. Andrew wisely did not overemphasize the importance of the similarities, which could have been off-putting for the client who was more sensitive to an entirely different set of variables. Stressing similarities (rather than differences) or exaggerating them to get close to clients are common mistakes coaches make when they feel uncomfortable or nervous.

With sensitivity, Andrew did not try to use common histories but instead gave the client room to explore his reactions to Andrew's background. Doing so not only allowed new information to emerge, it modeled risk taking and openness as part of the coaching relationship. If these issues come up again—for example, if they came up in the client's work relationships—there is now readiness to discuss them further.

Andrew will need to stay attuned to the need to discuss both their similarities and differences. In particular, the client's question about the matching process implies a tension that Andrew will need to continue to tolerate and discuss. That question may also make Andrew wonder whether he is viewed by the organization as specializing in minority clients. Like the client, he has mixed feelings about being tracked toward certain engagements. This is something that he may need to discuss and try to resolve with his human resources contact, without revealing anything about his discussions with the client.

Takeaways

- There are many possible differences between you and clients and between clients and colleagues that go beyond the traditional diversity categories of ethnicity, gender, religion, national origin, and sexual orientation. Clients may want help bridging whatever difference issues they are facing.

- Deciding if and when to point out differences between you and a client should be based on questions or concerns that you believe the client may have; tact and timing are essential, but it is better to raise it directly than avoid it.

- It is important for you to develop self-awareness and insight into the possible effects of differences on your reactions to clients; your tolerance of tension about differences can serve as a model for clients.

- Similarities and differences between you and a possible client occasionally can be a factor in making the coach-client match.

- Coaches, whether minorities themselves or not, may choose to specialize in engagements that support diversity initiatives and develop expertise in inclusion programs.

Closure

C LOSURE, OR ENDING THE COACHING ENGAGEMENT, IS NOT SIMPLY A CESSA-
TION OF THE PROCESS; IT IS AN IMPORTANT AND DISTINCT PHASE. IF
APPROACHED WITH ATTENTIVENESS AND CARE, IT WILL ANCHOR THE
continued development of your client on the basis of the work that you have
done together.

Closure is multidimensional and involves all participants in the coaching
process:

- At its most basic level, it is about what you, the coach, do to prepare
  your client and sponsors for the end of active coaching and to capitalize on future learning opportunities.

- For your client, it can be an opportunity to evaluate a range of issues:
  What has been accomplished? What areas need continued focus and
  attention? What new challenges may emerge as growth continues?

- Sponsors likely also have opinions about what has been accomplished and what needs more attention. Their role in your client's
  development becomes more important as coaching ends.

Development themes and other insights from the coaching process often are reiterated during the ending phase. There is a natural desire to reflect on and review key learning points that have helped your client during the process. Your closure steps can build on that tendency as well as highlight any new insights that emerge. At the same time, you may encounter awkward reactions from your client, including discomfort, humor, and avoidance. Accepting these reactions, while at the same time making closure steps clear, will support a powerful and positive ending to the coaching.

Good endings have important characteristics:

- Expectancy of closure (anticipated and planned; not abrupt)
- Opportunity for reflection and discussion
- Acknowledgment of both closed/resolved and open/unresolved items
- Consideration of future support and relationships
- Celebration of achievements
- Acceptance of feelings of loss

Anticipating Closure

A productive closure process depends on what you do to anticipate and plan for the end of coaching. Usually coaching has an expected time frame that is part of the original contracting. While that time frame may not be rigidly binding, it conveys the notion that coaching is an intervention or a jumpstart and therefore of limited duration. Because of the engagement's temporary nature, it is important to acknowledge its transience at a relatively early stage in the process. Every beginning anticipates an endpoint, and it is never too early for you to openly refer to that eventuality. Doing so helps to mitigate what might be a more difficult discussion if it came up late in coaching. It also conveys an appropriate challenge to your client to make the most of coaching so that development will have momentum as the formal coaching process concludes.

> In your own life, you should take particular care with endings, for their color will forever tinge your memory of the entire relationship and your willingness to re-enter it.
>
> —Martin Seligman, *Authentic Happiness*[1]

For most people, endings can be emotionally evocative. They create both obvious and subtle reminders of endings of other relationships, both personal and professional, some of which might have been quite difficult. Strictly speaking, the coaching engagement is ending, but your relationship with your client continues in a different form. You and your client are moving into a phase without the regularity that characterizes active coaching. Depending on how you structure the next phase, with supportive contact scheduled or only provided on an *as needed* basis, your client may feel nervous, isolated, or even abandoned. Client reactions depend on past experiences of endings. Providing opportunities for these reactions to be discussed can help your client move forward to acknowledge and accept the feelings that are triggered. Waiting until the end of coaching to introduce closure does not provide adequate time to reflect on these feelings and responses to closure.

A complicating factor in closure is determining the right schedule for ending the coaching process. Even with contracts that stipulate a specific time frame of three or six months, the actual last coaching appointment would need to be labeled. By openly referring to an end session during the coaching process, and noting progress as milestones are achieved and passed, you are empowered to suggest a final appointment date. For most clients, this date will be an endpoint consistent with the original contract stipulations. For others, however, additional coaching may be warranted as you anticipate the final session. How much value a formal extension of the process will add is a difficult judgment to make, but you do need to have an opinion about it. Clients may express an interest in continuing and they may ask for your recommendation. Anticipating closure will help you prepare for that question and for the discussion with your client about how to proceed.

In those situations when you and your client agree that an extension of the coaching would be useful, you need to be aligned with your client about how to support the recommendation with sponsors. Usually, the rationale is based on what a particular client needs in order to capitalize on the work the client has already done in coaching. It might relate to the challenges of sustaining the particular behavioral changes in the development plan, the need for more opportunities for the client to practice new behaviors, organizational changes that slowed progress, or anticipated changes the client wants help navigating. After analyzing these or related elements, you and your client will be prepared to propose a possible extension to the sponsors so that everyone can decide together how best to design the structure of the extended coaching. This extension of the coaching engagement would constitute recontracting. As such, it benefits from specifying the process as well as the goals, if they are different from those in the original engagement.

Assuming that an extension is not needed, it is important to set a final session date well in advance. In fact, the ending of the coaching engagement may have a penultimate session that looks backward, while the final session is reserved for looking ahead. While these plans can shift by mutual consent, it is important to avoid letting the final session be a surprise either to the client or to you. Targeting a final session makes the ending tangible and prompts discussion of both plans and feelings about them. With the date set, ending and related issues can be regular topics during the coaching sessions that lead up to the final session.

Providing several coaching sessions to discuss closure is typical. You can use this time to ask your client to reflect on a number of issues:

- What has your client learned during the coaching engagement?
- What worked and what could have worked better?
- What was accomplished, and what items are still open?
- What experiences has the client internalized?
- What issues will the client continue to work on in the short, middle, and long term?
- How will the client continue to focus on development in the future?

- What learning resources are available for the client to access in the future to support growth?

- How can the manager and HR sponsor support the client's future developmental opportunities?

- What role, if any, will the coach play in the client's future?

- How will the ending of the coaching engagement be clearly noted for the client, stakeholders, and coach?

An important consideration is your client's future willingness to ask for feedback and help. Hopefully, coaching has removed some of the hesitation to seek help. Your clients can become more successful learners after coaching if, during the closure process, you reflect on how they learn when they get stuck, and how they continue growth. Using ideas from these considerations, you can use the concluding phase of coaching to help the organization support the future development of their employee, your client.

Part of that support involves you. Whether ending within the expected time frame or not, you need to consider what type of follow-up support would be useful with each client you work with (including the frequency and type of contact). Some coaches meet with clients quarterly for a session or two, schedule phone calls, or just rely on ever-present e-mail communications. Although you will have your own perspectives, your client's follow-up needs and how to address them should be discussed with your clients and appropriate sponsors so that a consensus can be reached about the support that you can provide after regular coaching meetings have concluded.

Another element that is sometimes planned to mark the end of coaching is a meeting that involves you, the client, the client's manager, and sometimes the HR representative. This *program review meeting* mirrors the development planning meeting (discussed in Chapter 11) in the earlier stages of coaching. The goal is to acknowledge progress openly, encourage the continuity of changes that have been made, and anticipate future support that would be useful to your client. Part of that discussion could also involve contracting how to structure an extension (if that has been agreed to) or how to provide appropriate follow-up support to the client. Whether you propose this meeting or it is built into the process, it can be a useful conclusion to coaching and formally re-engage the manager-client developmental partnership.

Endings demand self-management from you, demonstrating an example for your client to follow. Both of you may find some discomfort when thinking about ending the coaching engagement and what shape the relationship might take in the future. It is important to discuss endings to allow concerns about setbacks and obstacles to surface so that they can be discussed. Addressing these issues supports your client's resilience and energizes the strategies the client has used to stay active and focused in challenging situations. Accepting ambiguity, uncertainty, and unexpected emotion is important in all phases of coaching, but especially important during the ending phase.

Ending coaching is also an opportunity for you to reflect on your own experience. Everyone has feelings about endings; therefore, your self-awareness and self-monitoring are important so that any fears or concerns you are having are not inadvertently projected onto your client's particular experience of closure. Among other ways these emotions may influence your behavior is to cause you to try to forestall the ending. While the appeal of staying actively involved with the client is natural, it is both inconsistent with the typical coaching contract and may inadvertently convey a lack of confidence in the client, or even in yourself as a coach. You would never want your own needs or insecurities to suggest that the client should continue in a coaching relationship with you.

Ideally, the ending point is an opportunity for your own development. It is a chance for you to reflect on your growth as a coach, identify gaps in your abilities, and consider future experiences you would like to have. These reflections are likely to be tied to perceptions about your client's relative success and what you might have done to make it a stronger experience. While under some circumstances you may discuss some of these observations with clients, they are topics best discussed with your case supervisor or coaching mentor. Your openness about endings presents a real opportunity for your own development, reflecting a parallel with the process established between you and your client.

Other Considerations

As mentioned previously, be sure to provide adequate time in the coaching process to accommodate your client's possible reactions to the ending. Some clients prefer a definitive break, while others want to know that there will be follow-up contact. You also need to negotiate what form the follow-up will take. Some coaches like to build in follow-up contact(s), by phone or in person, within one to three months to ease the transition and provide the client an opportunity for course adjustment; others invite the client to reach out to them on a more ad hoc basis.

While contact will be significantly reduced after formal coaching has concluded, it is important for you to continually maintain the role and confidentiality boundaries established during the engagement. If you feel a pull to shift your relationship with a client in a different professional or even a personal direction, you should discuss this with your case supervisor. In any helping profession, deviating from the boundaries of a contracted relationship is fraught with complexities and should be avoided, even if it has been a long time since the engagement ended.

These boundaries may be especially difficult to monitor and maintain in the age of social media. Clients may ask coaches to be linked in various networks to keep in touch or be part of the client's social media contact list. While some amount of social networking involvement may be harmless, coaches need to be self-aware and mindful about such contacts with clients. There are no definitive answers about where coaches should be in the client's list of contacts, but there is a growing concern about becoming a *friend* or a *buddy* on various websites or online networks. It is easy to see how these connections, however innocent, could erode boundaries and diminish the value you had in your client's professional life, not to mention potential violations of confidentiality.

Often your client's general self-efficacy is enhanced through coaching, even though it is not an overt goal. As part of the closure process, consider asking your clients what attitudes and beliefs have strengthened during coaching that will allow them to better weather the ups and downs of organizational life. You might encourage clients to reflect on what self-perceived limitations have been confronted and disarmed, or what client characteristics have been empowered to face future challenges better. Such questions tap into implicit learning from coaching and support the client's future resilience.

Another aspect of closure may be considerations involving your client's legacy. Depending on your client's life and career stage, coaching can trigger a pull toward leaving a stronger legacy. Clients further along in their careers may also wonder how they can foster others' growth and give back more to those they care about. These feelings may reflect a shift in the client's priorities as a side effect of coaching and raise questions about who the beneficiaries of that shift should be. Not all clients will want to reflect on these legacy issues, but for those who might, you should be prepared to facilitate their thinking and capitalize on the moment.

Involving Sponsors

You can also help sponsors, and especially the client's manager, anticipate the end of coaching by being transparent about the coaching process. As coaching moves toward closure, your contacts with sponsors can anticipate questions about challenges to future development, the post-coaching relationship between you and the client, and ad hoc follow-up support. As mentioned , you can structure and then facilitate a closing meeting with the client and sponsors to encourage open discussion of these same questions with everyone present. Usually, such a meeting will focus on acknowledging the employee's progress, but it should also identify areas needing more work and engage the sponsors in actively supporting your client's continuing development. Sponsors appreciate your initiative in scheduling such events because, unless these meetings are built into the process, they may not feel empowered to call for them. It is in both your immediate and longer-term interests to build and maintain positive relationships with sponsors, and ending provides an opportunity to do so.

Ending is a phase of coaching that is challenging in several respects, yet is very important to both the integrity of the process and the affirmation of the gains the client has made. As a coach, get in touch with your own feelings about endings, both positive and negative. Use these reactions to create an ending process with clients that instills positive closure, confidence in the future, and a support structure that encourages continuing development.

CASE ILLUSTRATION: PLANNED ENDINGS NEED FLEXIBILITY

Many coaches have a clear structure to their process and set the closing session date well in advance. This provides clarity to all concerned, but it may not provide enough flexibility to accommodate changes in plans. As a result, there can be misunderstandings that occur between you and your client about closure. Here is how one coach sought to close that gap.

Josh had been coaching Meredith, a partner in a management consulting firm, for approximately six months. The engagement had gone well, and Josh was looking forward to their final session. Unfortunately, Meredith had to cancel two sessions in a row because of a major commitment to an out-of-town project. This postponement left Josh in a bit of a quandary. The next session was scheduled to be their final meeting, yet there were several important topics to follow up on, and they had never really discussed Meredith's reaction to ending coaching. Josh sent Meredith an e-mail confirming their next meeting, mentioning the open topics to cover (including closure), and suggesting that they needed at least one additional meeting.

Meredith did confirm the appointment but did not address Josh's suggestion about an additional meeting. She actually began the session by noting that it would be their final meeting. Josh was taken aback because he had conveyed to her that there wasn't adequate time in one session to cover everything they needed to discuss in order to effectively end the coaching. Her action also triggered self-doubt and even a feeling of rejection, although

Josh had been assured by Meredith and the sponsors that the engagement had gone well. After a pause, he was able to note that they had missed the previous two sessions, and he thought they needed to schedule another session to bring the coaching to proper closure. Meredith resisted, saying she thought they could get it all done today. Josh relented and said, "We'll try."

As Meredith described the developmental actions she had been taking, Josh began thinking about closure in Meredith's life. He knew she was struggling to support aging parents and that a big project was nearly concluded while others were waiting in the wings. Thinking about these other closure issues, he grew more uncomfortable with the prospect that this session was unlikely to provide Meredith with a productive closure to their coaching. He recognized that he had his own feelings in response to her officious agenda, but he could put those aside and was still convinced that it was truly not in Meredith's best interests to shortchange the closure of coaching.

As she came to a pause in her update, Josh stopped her and expressed his concern that they would run out of time in the session and not do justice to both open items and the need to discuss the closure of coaching. Going on, he said he wanted to ask Meredith two questions: First, he asked her, "What's a good ending?" He paused to let her think about her answer. She responded with a sense of achievement, goals met, acknowledgment, and similar points. Second, he asked her, "What's a bad ending?" Again, he waited for her response, and she took a few moments to consider it. She mentioned terms like "unexpected," "no resolution," and "final." Josh paused and then asked her which of those words would describe the end of coaching if they concluded without adequate discussion.

Meredith anticipated where this line of inquiry was going and she was willing to concede that Josh was making an important point. While he knew that she had many pressures in her life, truncating an end to coaching would reduce the positive impact of what they had achieved together. Josh articulated what he felt they were both thinking by recommending that they schedule another coaching meeting dedicated to a productive end to their coaching. Meredith paused, then smiled and agreed.

Supervisor's Observations _____

Both coach and client had the best of intentions in planning the coaching process and scheduling the last session well in advance. However, the client's work life interfered with their schedule and there had not been enough contact between them to adjust and plan a new ending date. As a result, they were in different places as the last scheduled coaching meeting began. While the coach assumed that they could extend to another session to deal with closure issues, the client preempted him by pushing to keep to their original schedule. Meredith's behavior also confused, and possibly hurt, Josh, which gave him a lot to deal with. We may wonder why a client might want to end coaching prematurely, but there are many reasons, especially when a client is feeling overwhelmed by work and sees the end of coaching as one less thing to schedule. Even though she had a very positive experience in coaching, Meredith's absence from the process for several weeks and other pressures led her to put the utility of a quick closure ahead of the value of a good closure process.

There are many things Josh could have done to reassert the need for a more productive end to coaching. Before he could decide what to do, however, he had to listen to his own feelings. He knew Meredith had exerted unexpected control over the last session, and his general tendency was to try to accommodate a client's preferences. But he also became more certain that ending without adequate discussion was not in her best interests, not to mention his own. He also reminded himself that he had a positive and trusting relationship with Meredith that he could draw on. He could have made these points directly with Meredith, and this might have been successful. Instead, however, he felt that a more indirect, rhetorical method would help him to persuade her. So, he spontaneously introduced two questions designed to get the client to draw new conclusions. This tactic bought him time and gave Meredith insight into Josh's concerns. Their appropriate recontracting gave Josh the process he was seeking and slowed Meredith down to remind her of what was truly important.

Takeaways

- Closure is a definitive step in the engagement that coaches plan for, and it is best if understood and anticipated from the beginning.

- Closure provides a clear opportunity for celebrating success, considering extensions of the coaching, and for handing off development from the coach to the client's manager.

- The closure process needs to include honest discussion of progress, gaps, and the challenges of post-coaching growth.

- Clients interested in extending the coaching must gain agreement with you and the sponsors about how extended coaching will work.

- Endings may be emotionally evocative and demand heightened self-awareness and self-management from you as well as from the client.

- Be sure you are clear about post-coaching supportive contacts with clients. These contacts may be planned or ad hoc in nature, but they must always maintain the boundaries and the professionalism of the relationship.

- It is important for you to thank and obtain feedback from the client and sponsors and reflect on your own learning from each case.

18

What Happened: Self-Reflection and Evaluation

T THE TIME THAT YOU ARE INTERVIEWED FOR A POSSIBLE COACHING ENGAGE-
MENT, YOU MAY BE ASKED HOW YOU EVALUATE THE EFFECTIVENESS OF YOUR
COACHING. THIS QUESTION IS NOT AN INVITATION TO DISCUSS THE LATEST
research on coaching outcomes, although some sponsors may find that an
interesting topic. Instead, it is an opening for you to demonstrate your credibility as a coach. Those who hire you want to be assured that you are seriously committed to achieving results. Also, the criteria you use for evaluation
are an indication of what you see as important aspects of coaching. Lastly,
your own observations and feedback from others on how well the process
worked are invaluable for your own continued learning and development. It
makes sense that your approach to evaluation be built in from the start of
coaching.

Here are some of the important points to remember about how to evaluate your coaching effectiveness:

- Learning from your coaching experience assumes intentionality about
  your choices and awareness of what has happened during the engagement.

- One way to inform self-reflection is to be direct and ask your clients what they are experiencing during coaching—both what works and what could be done better.

- As coaching progresses, there are usually opportunities to gather feedback from the client, sponsors, and other colleagues.

- Your post-coaching self-reflection can be informed by more formal data gathering using questionnaires aimed at getting feedback from both clients and sponsors.

Being Intentional: Coach and Client

The convergence of your client's behavior change and the development objectives you have helped to set largely determine the effectiveness of the coaching. However, goals are often broad and aspirational and are unlikely to be fully accomplished during the time frame of a coaching engagement. For instance, if a client's development objective is improving her ability to inspire others, her development plans would include intermediary behavioral steps to reach that goal. Both clear goals and specific behavioral indicators are key to evaluating progress.

Your own subjective judgment of your client's progress is the first step in evaluation. This begins with self-reflection as you compare what your client was trying to do with what you believe actually happened: To what extent did the client act on the commitments embodied in the development plan? Many coaches seek to capture their thoughts, reflections, and feelings using their own *notes to file* methods. As was suggested in the Introduction, some coaches keep a journal about coaching sessions, with both client-specific and more general points. This is an excellent means of establishing a self-monitoring discipline to help you evaluate progress as you go and adjust accordingly. Journaling often addresses such questions as: *What did I intend to do in a session? What do I believe happened for my client? What happened for me? How will what happened show up in the client's behavior in the organization? What might I do differently during the next session?* While answering these questions is purely subjective, your responses can be surprisingly accurate as to what is going well and what needs more of your attention. Also, your self-evaluations do become more accurate as your coaching experience increases.

Sources of Information for Evaluating Coaching

Just as feedback was used to create your client's development plan, it can also be used to help determine client progress. As an engagement advances, your client's behavior during sessions with you is an important indicator of progress. Being prepared, keeping appointments, following through on commitments, and other behaviors are telling signs of client progress. In addition, your client's and other stakeholders' observations about the effectiveness of coaching are important sources of evaluative data.

After your self-reflection, evaluation focuses on your client. That is why it is especially important for you, as coach, to ask your clients about their experiences during coaching: *What insights or learning did they have during the session? How might it affect their behavior? What should the two of you spend more time exploring?* While these types of questions are essential to tuning into your client and adjusting your approach, they also model openness to feedback and a learning posture that support the client's development.

In some coaching engagements, you may have the opportunity to observe your client directly during business meetings (a technique described previously as *shadowing*) or less formally by simply being present in their offices. These situations put you in a position to observe the client's behavior in person, *in the moment*, with others, and while dealing with workday challenges. While these are useful coaching interventions, they also allow you to evaluate progress that may inform adjustments to your coaching approach.

As coaching progresses, there may be various opportunities to hear from your client and others about behavior changes. You and your client can contract about the frequency that feedback should be asked for and whether you, the client, or both of you should make those inquiries. For some coaches, empowering clients to obtain and integrate ongoing feedback is an important element in their Personal Models. For other coaches, it can be accomplished as a more joint effort, consistent with your responsibility to keep in contact with sponsors after a development plan is in place. Their opinions and observations about your client's behavior are important guideposts for your work. Whatever way the observations are obtained from sponsors, you and your client can compare what others are saying about progress and together strategize adjustments that may be warranted.

Formal Approaches to Gathering Evaluative Information

During the 1970s, a psychologist named Donald Kirkpatrick identified four types, or levels, of variables to use in evaluating the impact of training interventions.[1] These also are appropriate criteria for evaluating coaching. They are:

1. *Reactions or Relative Satisfaction.* This first level addresses evaluation in a completely subjective way: How satisfied were clients and sponsors with the coaching program that you delivered?

This is a relatively easy level to measure. Clients and sponsors can be surveyed about their satisfaction after coaching is completed with a simple questionnaire or with a few direct questions in a discussion. While these surveys are sometimes discounted as *applause meters*, they can be useful in identifying important positive and negative reactions.

2. *Learning or Retention.* Focusing on cognitive change, this level of evaluation attempts to answer the question, What did clients actually learn during coaching? Although concern about cognitive growth reflects Kirkpatrick's roots in training, it is not formally measured in coaching, where cognitive learning is not the main focus. Coaches do not focus on intellectual growth as one might do in a training program. However, to the extent that a coach uses readings, books, or conceptual models (such as situational leadership, emotional intelligence, or listening skills), learning may be an important outcome—at least for the client. Such learning could also be queried on a post-coaching questionnaire aimed at the client.

3. *Behavioral or Observable Changes.* This level of evaluation address-es the primary focus of coaching by asking to what extent the client has changed in terms of the stated objectives and behavioral actions in the development plan.

Development plans lend themselves to being transformed into a cus-tomized multirater form (i.e., a full 360-degree survey of stakeholders, manager alone, or some other sample) or conceptually tied to a standard-ized multirater (360-degree) questionnaire. Although these are not strictly measurements of behavior (they express others' perceptions of the client's behavior), most people consider them as close as we can get to actual behavior.

At the same time, this type of evaluation is very sensitive to how long others have had the opportunity to observe the client's new behaviors. The client's behavior may have changed based on the coaching, but the aware-ness of others will naturally lag behind those changes. Therefore, while this level of evaluation is clearly aligned with what is typically in a development plan, it should only be applied later, well after the client has implemented behavioral changes and others have opportunities to observe them.

4. *Organizational Results or Return on Investment (ROI).* This level of evaluation estimates whether coaching has yielded tangible benefits to the organization; for example, increased revenue, more customers, or more effi-cient and cost-effective processes. ROI evaluation aims to provide a tangible link between the cognitive and behavioral goals of coaching and organiza-tional value.

This is a difficult connection for coaching to make, not because coach-ing lacks a bottom-line impact, but because coaching is always a one-at-a-time endeavor whereas organizational results always involve others. While you might believe that the big new account or the creative breakthrough of the team is a result of your client's coaching, this hypothesis would be spec-ulative at best. A stronger argument could be made if there were several clients whose coaching-sparked activity coincided with business success. Improvements in your client's performance appraisal, promotion, or talent management review could be used as part of this level of evaluation, although these results may not align closely with the coaching time frame.

The first and third levels of Kirkpatrick's hierarchy (satisfaction and behavioral change) can be routinely evaluated during and after coaching programs. More practically, you can always have your evaluative antennae up, seeking information about how the client is doing from all sources available to you.

Kirkpatrick' s four levels of evaluation can also be used to prepare you for the question that began this chapter: How do you evaluate the effectiveness of your coaching? You may be asked this question both before coaching, as a way of evaluating the sophistication of your approach, as well as after coaching, to tap your ability to tune into coaching outcomes. Consider answering such questions by describing your focus on the satisfaction, learning, and behavior change of your clients, based on input from all perspectives—the client's, the sponsor's, and your own. Whether you want to reach for organizational impact evaluative metrics will depend on the scope of your engagement and your own rhetorical skills.

In large organizations where many coaching assignments may be active, internal research programs may exist to evaluate the effectiveness of coaching. These programs may use satisfaction and behavioral change measures (as described previously), but they do not usually involve feedback from coaches. In addition, if sufficient numbers of coaching cases exist, they may study the longer-term impact of coaching at the ROI level, such as changes in client performance ratings, awards received by clients, retention rates of clients, and so forth. When such research is being done, you can still conduct your less formal follow-up evaluation and later request the results of the organization's efforts. Both approaches can be very useful for you to reflect on. Just as with clients, your learning depends on feedback, reflection, and adjustment.

For those coaches who are interested in conducting research or being published in coaching journals, outcome studies of coaching do exist and can be replicated.[2] They usually use a sizable number of cases so that statistical analyses can be applied. Data is typically collected both before and after coaching using the same 360-degree survey of client performance. More of these types of rigorous outcome studies would be of wide benefit to the field of coaching.

CASE ILLUSTRATION: INTERIM EVALUATION HAS MANY BENEFITS

Asking your client and sponsors about changes in the client's behavior should occur periodically in the normal course of coaching and it is helpful on many levels. It provides feedback so adjustments can be made; it provides indications about whether developmental changes are being noticed; and it encourages all to be committed to the development plan. Coaches, however, have to make decisions about who should ask for feedback, and there are some subtle considerations that the coach in the following situation is incorporating into the inquiries that she and her client are making.

Kathy and Jim were well into their coaching engagement. They had built a productive relationship based on Jim's sincere interest in growing into his new VP role. Kathy had conducted informational interviews and organized the information into strength and development themes. An action plan that Jim was implementing had emerged. Their biweekly sessions had established a rhythm: discussing actions Jim had taken, debriefing results, looking for insights about his behavior or the situation, and then targeting opportunities likely to arise in the coming two weeks. These were tied to the goals in the development plan, but Jim was also learning that implementation was fluid and could be tailored to what he faced day-to-day.

Kathy felt it was time to get some feedback on his progress. She was cognizant of the time lag between a client's own sense of improvement and when others begin to perceive it, but she felt that input at this point could be very useful in knowing whether to stay the course or make adjustments in Jim's efforts.

They discussed how to collect this input, and Kathy determined that Jim hadn't yet asked anyone, even his manager, for feedback. They decided that at this point, Jim could ask for his manager's observations as part of their weekly one-on-one meeting. They also identified a peer who had a lot of con-

tact with Jim and who had been included in the original data-gathering process. In addition, Jim's HR generalist was well aware of the process and may have observed Jim during staff meetings or picked up something through others' comments.

Jim was comfortable about approaching all of them directly. Kathy and Jim rehearsed a contextual statement as a lead-in to one or two questions. He would explain that he was actively implementing his development plan, and while it was early, he was open to their feedback and would welcome hearing what they noticed in his performance. If they hadn't noticed anything at all, Jim would be interested in knowing in what aspects of his behavior they would expect to see changes. Kathy and Jim also discussed remaining non-defensive and appreciative, whatever the feedback was.

They agreed that he could show the peer the actual development plan, if he needed a prompt as to what the peer might look for. The manager and HR person had received the revised plan after the development planning meeting. Kathy and Jim agreed that Jim would reach out to them in the next two weeks and that Kathy would follow up with the manager and HR person a few weeks after that. Kathy chose this sequence of feedback requests to empower Jim more about owning his plan fully and flexing it as situations occurred. The fact that Jim hadn't asked for feedback from his manager during the six weeks since the development planning meeting was an indication to Kathy that he was holding the plan too tightly. Even though she would be asking for feedback too, she decided to make the responsibility of having a regular dialogue about his developmental efforts with his manager a priority for Jim.

It also sounded to her as though the manager needed a little prompting since he hadn't inquired about Jim's progress either. She knew that managers are often inhibited to ask questions about how coaching is going and what the client is getting from the process out of a misplaced fear of interfering. Actually, their questions facilitate that shift in responsibility from coach to client that should occur as coaching progresses.

At their next session, Kathy and Jim reviewed what he had discovered in asking others for feedback. The peer hadn't noticed anything, but he and Jim had a useful conversation about what Jim was trying to do and what opportunities there were to make changes. Jim's manager and the HR person were encouraging, and they had noticed Jim handling interactions differently and being more active during meetings. Kathy also took the opportunity to ask

Jim about his self-perceived progress in making changes. That question, combined with Jim's data gathering from others, seemed to raise his ownership of the plan. They discussed several adjustments Jim would make in his developmental efforts. Kathy praised his new attitude about the plan and encouraged him to make it a topic for discussion with others.

Supervisor's Observations _____

Thinking about evaluating coaching, whether during or after an engagement, is usually framed in terms of answering the question, *How effective was coaching in achieving the results envisioned?* Behavioral data is very relevant in determining what the client is actually doing differently as a result of coaching. Gathering behavioral feedback from sponsors, as well as from the client himself, keeps the sponsors engaged and provides just-in-time data to support your efforts with clients.

Kathy decided to use the timing of interim feedback collection as a way to encourage the client to take a stronger role in his own development. Some clients need that push and hopefully it extends beyond coaching in empowering clients and sponsors to take a more proactive role in the client's development. Coaches are also interested in asking sponsors for feedback about progress, but Kathy decided to delay her outreach in favor of making the client's efforts more prominent with the manager.

An unstated but important goal of coaching is to increase the client's feedback-seeking behavior and the manager's feedback-giving behavior as part of instilling a developmental mindset. In addition to encouraging Jim's outreach to others, Kathy built on his feedback-seeking behavior by asking him to reflect on his own view of what he was getting out of coaching. Doing so may help Kathy in her coaching because her client's self-perceptions about what is making the difference for him can provide fascinating insights for the coach.

In this case, since the client is actively implementing a development plan, it would be interesting to get his feedback about how he sees himself differently, what he has learned about himself, and what is still emerging for him. Clients report greater self-awareness, an appreciation that even good intentions are often not visible to others, and increased confidence that they can change their behavior for the better. The impact of these self-perceptions cannot be measured, but coaches do recognize their value, especially as cognitive-behavioral approaches to change have been successfully applied to coaching. While coaches are fostering observable behavioral change in clients' performance, intangible cognitive changes are happening too. Coaches have a unique opportunity to highlight both of those kinds of changes for clients. Not all clients are going to be interested in this consciousness-raising, but for many the additional insights will help sustain motivation to change and they will inform your learning as well.

Takeaways

- While the evaluation of coaching is a frequently discussed topic, within individual cases, evaluation is based on perceptions—yours, your client's, and those of stakeholders.

- Those perceptions are useful on many levels, including adjusting developmental efforts, confirming your coaching focus, empowering others' involvement in development, and instilling in clients a curiosity about the impact of their efforts.

- Your self-reflections about client progress and encouraging clients to assess their own efforts are always useful; insights on many levels can emerge from those discussions.

- After coaching has ended, clients and sponsors can be surveyed more formally about their satisfaction with the coaching and the results of the process on the client's behavior.

- Evaluation, unless done for research purposes across a number of cases, can inform your learning. How your coaching efforts are facilitating change and growth in a client is very useful in shaping your development as a coach.

19

Professionalism and Responsibility

FOR ALL THE GOOD THAT COACHING CAN DO, THERE ARE NO GUARANTEES. YOUR OPTIMISM NEEDS TO BE BALANCED WITH A REALISTIC AND PRAGMATIC PERSPECTIVE ABOUT CLIENTS AND ORGANIZATIONS. ALONG THE WAY, THERE MAY be situations that challenge your values as a coach—unfulfilled commitments, goals that shift unpredictably, or pressure to reveal protected information. While these situations are unusual, you need to be prepared to deal with them as well as other challenges. Consider the following reminders.

- First of all, do no harm. When your sense of fairness is aroused, be careful about being too activist and becoming a client-crusader. Consider all the possible risks of your actions. Doing less is often the best response.

- Put what is best for the client and sponsors ahead of your own needs for professional activity. Align the coaching process with their expectations.

- Become familiar with professional guidelines about ethical behavior, commitments to clients, confidentiality, and role boundaries for executive coaches or from related fields of practice.

Challenges the Client and the Organization Pose

Occasionally, every experienced coach has to deal with challenges to his or her operating values. In the spirit of prevention and to keep such challenges to a minimum, it is best to explore potentially negative factors when you are contracting a coaching engagement. Organizationally specific negative indicators to the success of coaching include ambiguous or qualified support for the client's development (e.g., threat of termination looming over the client); an absent, oppositional, or skeptical manager (e.g., manager expresses little optimism that coaching will help the client); organizational upheaval and uncertainty (e.g., downsizing and mergers); and a highly political, low-trust organizational culture (e.g., aggressive internal competition where your loss is my gain). There may be other organizational factors that threaten to distract your client from a developmental focus. If you encounter any of these challenges, remember that it is easier to delay or step away at the outset than after coaching begins. At the very least, you can contract to build in needed organizational support—such as more contact with sponsors, adequate time for coaching, checkpoints with all participants, or even an early process review meeting—in response to the challenges that your contracting conversations reveal.

In addition, not all clients will be able to use coaching to the same degree or, in some cases, at all. Clients may have characteristics that make them unlikely to benefit from coaching. While there may be some indication of client-specific challenges to coaching in your pre-coaching interactions, they are more likely to surface in the early stages of the process. They can include a personal or family crisis, extreme defensiveness, emotional fragility, or low motivation to understand and change behavior. If these characteristics are apparent during the contracting phase, you may decide to step away, delay, or adjust your contract. If you do move ahead, contracting a coaching process that provides more latitude can help to mitigate these client-based risk factors. There are times when you must adjust expectations for progress downward so that a client with significant limitations can make productive use of coaching. You may find it in your client's best interest to slow the pace, draw in more involvement of others, or redefine progress indicators to be more in line with what that particular client can manage. The aim is to make your coaching process robust enough to accommodate needed adjustments.

For a summary of both organizational and client-specific variables that can compromise coaching, see Figure 19-1.

Figure 19-1. Coaching caveats[1]

Organizational Context

1. Equivocal organizational commitment to the client's development
2. Organization upheaval, such as merger, downsizing, or reorganization
3. Quality of the sponsor/manager's relationship with the client
4. Internally competitive, ends-over-means organizational climate
5. Coaching tied to a larger organizational program, such as leadership training, 360-degree feedback, or talent management process

Client Characteristics

1. Significant personal or familial problems, upheaval or upset in the client's life
2. Risk tolerance: the willingness to try new approaches and tolerate some discomfort and vulnerability
3. Emotional resilience: the ability to accept feedback, depersonalize setbacks, and stay motivated
4. Psychological curiosity and insight
5. Motivation to change

Coaching Challenges

There are also several temptations and vulnerabilities inherent in the coaching role that require both self-awareness and self-management on your part. For executive coaches, confidentiality is one issue requiring special vigilance. This begins with being very clear in distinguishing between confidential information (generally whatever the client, or anyone else, tells you, as well as your own observations) and that which can be shared (coaching objectives, general statements about progress, and the development plan).

While in principle these are easy to separate, in practice the boundaries may be challenged, even inadvertently. A sponsor may ask you how the client handled 360-degree feedback; an HR person may ask when the client will be ready to move into an open position; a colleague may express extreme distrust and animosity toward your client. In these awkward moments and others that may arise as you come in contact with the organizational context, you need to remain confident in your role, even if that means sidestepping the implied demand or pressure for information. It is always safe to listen, restate what you are hearing, ask clarifying questions, and if need be, reassert the requirements and boundaries of your role. You need to be willing to disappoint, or even frustrate, whoever is making the request, confident that in doing so, you are honoring your commitment to the client and the process. Even when you are clear about the ethical response, however, these moments can be lonely or even unsettling, and you would benefit from discussing them with a trusted colleague or your case supervisor.

Therapists and other helping professionals use the concept of *containment* (introduced in Chapter 13) in creating safety for clients and coaches can borrow it to expand their grasp of confidentiality. As a coach, you are the container of your client's hopes, fears, resentments, and other difficult feelings. You provide a safe place where the client can explore these reactions.

Contracting about confidentiality is the first element of providing that safe container, but there are three others. The second element is your competence as a coach. This arms you with knowledge about coaching practices so that you can anticipate challenges and adjust the process accordingly. The third element is self-management, which asks you to know your own vulnerable moments, anticipate them, and respond intentionally rather than impulsively. Lastly, if you are to provide your clients with a structurally sound *safe container*, you must have your own safe haven in which to discuss quandaries and challenges. This means that you have established a relationship with a coaching mentor or case supervisor in advance of when you need it. These four mutually supportive elements provide the professional support that you need to create a safe and productive relationship with clients even when faced with unexpected difficulties (see Figure 13-1).

In every engagement, preserve the integrity of your relationship with the client. To do this, you need to protect the boundaries between providing consultative expertise, facilitating client self-insight, and empowering change. Difficulties arise if your clients are particularly needy, bereft of ideas, and pressure or tempt you to provide recommendations or answers. There may be rare times when it is appropriate to be more directive; for example, if your client is engaged in blatant self-sabotage (e.g., emotional outbursts, verbal attacks on others, or being overtly oppositional). In the majority of situations, however, the power inherent in your role as coach is best used to cultivate the client's self-efficacy instead of responding to momentary pressure to *save* the client or solve the client's problems.

There are also challenges to your boundaries that arise after the engagement is concluded. The guiding principle is the importance of being sensitive to your client's potential exposure and vulnerability even after coaching has ended. It is also vital to demonstrate responsible handling of a former client's feelings. For example, you will be expected to maintain confidentiality *indefinitely*. Continue to treat your clients as clients even after coaching has ended. This means avoiding social contact or any change in your relationship with them (related matters are discussed in Chapter 17 on closure). In this regard, consulting projects that happen to have a client in an important role can be especially challenging, and it may be best to delay your participation until after coaching has concluded. If you have former clients in an organization where you are currently coaching or consulting, consider informing them in advance that you may be observed on their premises and reaffirm your confidentiality commitments to them.

Your own personal needs may also exacerbate boundary challenges. In becoming an exceptional coach you assume responsibility for a higher level of self-monitoring and self-management. You should not seek to satisfy your own needs for companionship, acceptance, credit, admiration, or even more business through a coaching relationship. However, all coaches have human frailties and want to be helpful, so there may be times when you feel weaker in terms of your commitment to the values inherent in the role. Some of those times are predictable, as when you remind yourself that being too helpful with needy clients is less valuable than supporting and empowering them. Other especially sensitive challenges to your role that may tap into your own needs can emerge from your contacts within the organizational context: with the HR manager who controls your future work in the organization and who asks to know what the client thinks of him; with the manager who asks you to convey her evaluation of the client because she doesn't have the time; with a client who asks you to discuss the development plan with his manager because they have a strained relationship. These individuals and others will challenge you to stay within the boundaries of effective coaching.

In maintaining boundaries and confidentiality in coaching, internal coaches have a more complex task than external coaches. Most internal coaches have responsibilities besides coaching: leadership development, training, talent management, organization development, and HR generalist activities, for instance. As a result, internal coaches often have multiple contact points with coaching clients or their client's colleagues and direct reports. (This subject is presented in detail in Chapter 20 on the role of the internal coach).

Some internal coaches seek to reduce such contact points by providing coaching services only to divisions of their organizations where they have no other responsibilities. However, it is the responsibility of the organization to create an overall structure that protects the role of its internal coaches. Clear, organizationally supported guidelines for internal coaching can be very helpful, and these policies need to be clarified and confirmed each time an engagement is contracted.

An anchor in navigating difficult situations is to become familiar with practice and ethical guidelines in larger and more established helping professions, such as psychology, social work, medicine, and so on. Whether or not you are a member of one of these professions, their ethical standards are usually broadly applicable to coaching and may help guide your choices in difficult situations.

CASE ILLUSTRATION: WHEN COACHES FACE TOUGH CHOICES

There are times when clients make requests that are heartfelt but that would take you outside of your coaching contract. While empathy is an important capacity for coaches, so is sound reasoning, and at times these two characteristics are in conflict. Ultimately, your professional judgment must focus on what is in the long-term best interests of the client, and compromising your role is unlikely to meet that criterion.

Fred is the VP of corporate communications for a high-profile cosmetics company. He has grown up in the company and now, after twenty-five years, he needs to make some changes because he is being pressured to do more with less. He is also challenged by a younger, female direct report team. HR determined coaching would have the best chance of helping him improve his respect toward the managers on his team and empower them more. Steve, an external coach, had a lot of experience with the client organization and was engaged to work with Fred.

As was customary, Steve spent the first few coaching sessions getting to know Fred, identifying self-perceived strengths and development areas, and building trust. It was clear that, given the organization's felt needs, input from Fred's team was essential. So he and Steve planned the data-gathering process. Steve followed his usual protocol in interviewing members of Fred's team, along with a few of his peers, and then carefully pulled themes together. He knew from looking at the results that Fred would have a tough time accepting the feedback, much less using it productively, but that was why Steve had been called in to coach him.

During the feedback discussion, Steve had a difficult time drawing Fred out; his client seemed genuinely deflated by the developmental recommendations. While Fred's strengths were expressed too, he tended to dwell on themes having to do with his need to be more accepting of new ideas. He was upset that people sometimes experienced him as an obstacle to innovation. Both direct reports and peers were in agreement about Fred's "rain on their parade" responses. Steve and Fred briefly covered what he could do differ-

ently in response to other's ideas, but his motivation seemed low. Steve encouraged Fred to review the summary on his own, indicating they would dig into action ideas during their next session.

At the next session, however, Fred surprised Steve by handing him his résumé. He requested that Steve help him revise it because he had reached the conclusion that he just didn't fit in at the firm anymore and that he probably needed to find a job elsewhere.

While taken aback, Steve had faced these types of client requests before. He knew that actually helping with résumés was not within his coaching boundaries, and more important, such requests were often expressions of vulnerability and a veiled request for a different type of help.

Steve did not respond directly to Fred's request and instead asked about his response to the feedback. What actually upset him the most was that he wasn't getting the respect he felt he deserved. Steve made the connection that ironically, the staff's reactions mirrored Fred's own feelings; in their view, Fred wasn't adequately respecting their ideas. Since both sides were focused on the same issue, Steve pointed out that the way to get his staff's respect was to learn what he needed to do to model more respect by showing respect for them.

The feedback contained a lot of ideas and suggestions about how to do that, and Steve was ready to work with Fred on trying them out. Before they embarked on this exploration, Steve pointed out that coaching was like a living laboratory where Fred could experiment on his team leadership, which would be useful now and in the future, no matter where he might go. Fred paused and then smiled, "I guess you won't be helping me with my résumé, but then again, maybe I won't need it."

Supervisor's Observations

There are many facets to coaching as well as many potential pitfalls. Here, Steve bumped into a very common one—when a client asks a coach to go outside the established contract to do something more personal or instrumental for him. It's not uncommon for clients to ask for recommendations or consulting help, rather than coaching. Help with résumés sometimes comes up in response to frustration on the job, conflicted relationships with more senior leaders, or a values clash with the manager. As a coach, however, your agreement with the sponsoring organization is to help clients develop in their context, not to help people leave the company or change the organizational culture.

On the other hand, clients do sometimes have legitimate reasons to aspire to an internal move, promotion, or even job reconfiguration. As long as you determine that these desires are aligned with the client's career direction and are not a flight reflex caused by a difficult situation, coaching can continue very productively. The goal may shift toward strategizing and empowering the client to build the necessary relationships and have the needed conversations with decision makers. Ideally, this shift is led by your client, transparent to the sponsors and supported by them.

Again, it is part of your role as coach to help bring alignment between your client's actions and the situational expectations, even while you are primarily supporting the client in stretching toward his or her aspirations.

Takeaways

- ⊙ There are organizational and client-specific challenges to effective coaching; to the extent possible, try to size them up during contracting and design a robust process that can accommodate adjustments.

- ⊙ It may be prudent to withdraw yourself from consideration for a coaching assignment when you sense mixed organizational support and a client with significant limitations.

- ⊙ Containment is a broad concept supporting confidentiality. It includes clear confidentiality guidelines, knowledge of effective coaching practices, knowledge of our own vulnerabilities, and the availability of a case supervisor for those times when you need professional support.

- ⊙ If you are an internal coach, you need to pay particularly close attention to confidentiality, boundaries, and contracting. In addition, organizational policy support for the internal coaching process is vital, given the multiple roles that internal coaches perform and the many relationships they have in their organizations.

◉ Review ethical guidelines from other professions, especially those you are part of, to help anchor your coaching practice; tailor those guidelines to your Personal Model of coaching and then adhere to them.

◉ Utilize a coaching mentor, case supervisor, or coaching colleague as a discussion partner when cases are at risk of crossing boundaries or you are experiencing pressure to do something that does not feel right to you.

CHAPTER

20

The Role of the Internal Coach

HE TERM *EXECUTIVE COACH* CONJURES AN IMAGE OF A PROFESSIONAL ENGAGING WITH CLIENTS IN A VARIETY OF ORGANIZATIONS, BUT THIS IMAGE DOES NOT FULLY REFLECT THE REALITY OF HOW COACHING IS DELIVERED. As mentioned in the previous chapter, coaching services are increasingly provided by professionals internal to the organizations in which they work. Our definition of *executive coaching* in Chapter 3 encompasses both internal and external coaching engagements, and several of the case examples in Part II of this book focus on the work of internal coaches. In addition, if you are, or aspire to be, an internal coach, the following points should be considered:

- Effective internal coaches need to have the same sensibilities and competencies as external coaches.

- Well-conceived coaching methods and processes apply equally to external and internal engagements, with several important adjustments to contracting and boundaries.

- In keeping with the premise of this book, your particular approach to internal or external coaching can be accommodated within an articulation of your Personal Model.

⊙ Internal coaches benefit from organization knowledge but must carefully manage multifaceted relationships with clients, sponsors, and other colleagues.

The growth of internal coaching reflects both increased organizational need for coaching and its perceived value to the organization. As summarized in Chapter 3, individual development planning components have been added to many training, feedback, and leadership development processes. Traditionally, these one-to-one components were delivered by external coaches brought in especially for that purpose. Triggered by logistical and budgetary challenges, these arrangements were examined more closely to reveal that organizations often have internal staff whose interests and skills are similar to external coaches.[1]

With that realization, organizations have invested in professional development for those internal resources to more directly build their coaching skills. For example, a typical short engagement for internal coaches is to help managers analyze the results of 360-degree feedback to facilitate creating detailed development action plans. The internal coaches delivering those engagements need interpretive skills for the particular assessment instrument used, and more important, they need coaching skills to engage clients in creating a much more actionable and motivating development plan than would have happened on their own.

As internal coaches have proved they are useful and cost-effective, their activities have expanded to cover engagements more traditionally covered by external coaches. These engagements include on-boarding or transition coaching, individual development as follow-up to leadership courses, facilitating manager-client development planning meetings, and development through action learning projects. In organizations where internal coaching has several long-established practitioners, they also may take on three- to six-month coaching assignments usually handled by external coaches. This growing use of internal coaches does not appear to have adversely affected the amount of external coaching being provided; in a sense, both internal and external coaching have benefited from the expansion of coaching. The result is that coaching is available to more managers, deeper in organizations, and as enrichments to larger initiatives. Some organizations have embraced this trend and made it a cornerstone of their organizational identity, labeling it a *coaching culture* and bringing other developmental initiatives under that umbrella.

While internal coaches feel gratified by their popularity, there are obstacles and challenges to overcome. A frequent one is finding the proper balance between time devoted to coaching and other responsibilities that are part of their jobs. In our experience, internal coaches must carve out coaching time from other roles, such as learning and development (L&D) or organization development (OD) responsibilities. Other internal disciplines also produce internal coaches, such as Human Resource generalists, talent management specialists, and performance management experts. Even line managers or executives get involved by setting aside time to devote to coaching outside their usual chains of command. Providing coach training to managers from many different backgrounds is certainly a challenge, but an even bigger one is securing the time and structure to support their coaching activities. Nothing undermines an internal coaching initiative faster than launching it only to find that none of the coaches have time to actually coach.

Another challenge for internal coaches is that definitions of their roles vary greatly from organization to organization. While in some organizations, internal and external coach roles are almost interchangeable, more often internal coaches are expected to deliver very specialized services reflecting specific organizational needs. For example, an organization may have internal coaches deployed to help salespeople make better presentations, support managers to improve their own coaching skills, or explain and coach about a customized 360-degree feedback tool that is being rolled out. The specificity and diversity of internal coach accountabilities means that training them requires customization. This is especially true if the internal coaches are being drawn from disciplines that do not have a history of one-to-one helping experience, such as leadership development, OD, or talent management.

Other special challenges attached to internal coaching are due to the coworker relationship between coach and client. An internal coach is likely to have continuing contact with a client even after an engagement is over, even if that contact is casual or informal. Internal coaches need to anticipate how to handle unplanned contact with clients and client managers. For example, an internal coach may, as part of her other duties, deliver a training program that a client is attending or facilitate a team-building exercise that includes a past client. In both cases, the coach needs to keep the coaching separate from other activities and to reassure clients about the boundary between the activities.

Informal interactions between internal coaches and a client's colleagues may also be common, and innocent questions can lead to awkward situations for internal coaches (e.g., "How's the coaching going?" or "Are you guys still meeting?"). More complex challenges to confidentiality can occur when a coaching client is being considered for a promotion or other change in employment status. Internal coaches need to have both the organizational support and their own backbone to diplomatically sidestep involvement in those discussions that would erode the boundaries of their coaching roles.

Creating and following clear confidentiality guidelines is critical for internal coaches. Just as with external coaching, not everything is confidential, but defining protected information needs to be clear and supported by the organization. If an internal coach is treated as just another HR person, clients may participate in coaching, but they are likely to hold back on making significant revelations out of uncertainty about where that information might end up.

The effectiveness of internal coaches, therefore, cannot be separated from the organizational context in which they work. The accountabilities, goals, and structure of the internal coach role need to be described in detail, in policy guidelines supported by senior executive sponsors. These guidelines need to be included in coach training and communicated to managers and clients before a coaching engagement begins. Unless such guidelines are in place, clients are less likely to trust an internal coach's assurances about confidentiality.

Organizational guidelines for internal coaching can include a definition of the internal coach role, a description of the types of engagements internal coaches will be delivering, and confidentiality definitions in terms of what is protected information and what can be shared (such as development plans). Other details might include how to determine when internal coaching is appropriate, directions and processes for how to access those services, and a coach-client matching process that reduces overlap between their job contexts. In organizations where internal coaching is more ad hoc and initiated by informal request, contracting between coach and client becomes especially important, while still relying on formal support of organizational policy. Figure 20-1 outlines the advantages of internal coaching, and some of the cautions and accommodations that must also be taken in these arrangements.

Internal coaching can be customized to organizational needs but there are several trends in how it is used. First, internal coaches tend to coach at varied levels in the organization, from supervisor to middle manager, and much less likely in executive ranks. As a result, their clients are often earlier in their careers and therefore these coaches may provide more basic managerial skills building. This is not a problem, and it can be very gratifying to help clients at more formative stages, but it does mean that internal coaches need to be well versed in a wide range of managerial topics. Often they will draw from concepts and models used in the organization's management training programs. In fact, this type of engagement may be formalized when internal coaches do follow-up facilitation after clients attend a management or leadership training program. Similarly, internal coaching engagements are often shorter and more targeted than those of external coaches. They may stipulate a specific number of sessions or a tangible deliverable, such as interpreting results of a 360-degree survey or drafting a development plan.

Second, internal coaches are often involved in engagements that capitalize on their intimate knowledge of the organization, its culture, and its key leaders. This foundation is especially useful in on-boarding new managers who are coming in from outside the organization, but it can also be applied to significant promotions and transitions that internal managers make. One could make a case that the organizational knowledge of an internal coach provides an advantage over an external coach for this transition support work.

Figure 20-1. Internal coach considerations

Advantages of Internal Coaching	Cautions for Internal Coaching	Internal Coaching Accommodations
Cost-effective for the organization.	➤ There are complex matching considerations for client and coach: the client's level and function, organizational unit, and relationships present confidentiality challenges. ➤ Some clients view external coaches as more credible, having more experience; external coaches are more likely to work at senior levels.	➤ Establish guidelines for client-coach matching and addressing each request for a coach on its own merits. This builds credibility of both internal and external coaching within the organization. ➤ There will always be engagements better served by external coaches.
Internal coaches know the business or segments of the business, culture, and managers, and may have familiarity with the challenges the client faces. *Internal coach insights may support faster initial progress toward a developmental agenda.*	➤ Regardless of what an internal coach knows about the organization and brings to the coaching, it is important to understand the client's experience and viewpoints. ➤ Relying too heavily on an internal perspective may interfere with the client's need to explore, discover, and take a new direction.	➤ Deciding when to use internal perspectives and when to reach for other insights is a particular challenge for internal coaches. ➤ Having a neutral perspective, as an external coach, might be an advantage in some politically fraught situations.
Internal coaches have ready access to information and the client's stakeholders.	➤ Gathering available information may be too easy and the usual contracting may get over-looked and the information may be unbalanced. ➤ Clients may be uncomfortable with the amount of access that the internal coach has to colleagues.	➤ Contracting for information gathering is always important even if the internal coach has ready access to the information (e.g., performance reviews or talent assessments).

(continued on page 214)

Figure 20-1. Internal coach considerations (continued)

Advantages of Internal Coaching	Cautions for Internal Coaching	Internal Coaching Accommodations
	➤ Internal coaches may be tempted to act on their clients' behalf instead of fostering client action. ➤ Internal coach notes and records may be considered property of the organization.	➤ Internal legal opinions and internal coach guidelines may be useful in terms of how records and coach notes should be handled.
Internal coaches may have independent relationships with a client's manager, peers, or direct reports due to current and past work contact.	➤ Well-established relationships of the internal coach around the client can provide information but the internal coach needs to keep an open mind and tap the client's perspective. ➤ Stakeholders may approach the internal coach directly to give or request information about the client, challenging confidentiality agreements.	➤ Coaching requires deepening relationships with clients rather than benefiting coach relationships with stakeholders. ➤ Confidentiality and other boundaries need to be explained and written into internal coach policy. ➤ Internal coaching should not unsettle existing relationships between client and colleagues; they should be encouraged to deal with each other directly.
Internal coaches are more likely to have informal opportunities to observe clients in action.	➤ While not all contacts with clients can be anticipated by internal coaches, shadowing or observing clients, especially on behaviors targeted for development, should be contracted with clients. ➤ Internal coaches need to anticipate unplanned contacts with clients, such as being in the same meetings, casual contact in the elevator or cafeteria, and know how to deal with those situations.	➤ Early in coaching relationships, internal coaches need to be transparent about roles that they are in so that they are known to clients and the best way to handle them can be determined.

Figure 20-1. Internal coach considerations (continued)

Advantages of Internal Coaching	Cautions for Internal Coaching	Internal Coaching Accommodations
	➤ Internal coaches can use their observations about clients, even in casual or social situations, in support of development progress.	
The multiple roles of the internal coach bring with them advantages in understanding clients' situations and also responsibility for keeping the roles clear and separate.	➤ Clients may be unsure about how to deal with their internal coach in other contexts. ➤ Internal coaches' other roles may create questions for clients about confidentiality. ➤ Internal coaches may need to step away from other roles when there is overlap with the client's department or abstain from participating in decisions affecting the client. ➤ Internal coaches may possess information from their other roles that could be useful to clients; confidentiality needs to be respected in all directions.	➤ Role boundary issues are always present and challenging for internal coaches to manage; organizational support for the role is important. ➤ In general, having the internal coach and the client in different chains of command or even business units can reduce boundary confusion. ➤ Experienced internal coaches try to be sensitive to even the appearance of conflict of interest or boundary concerns with clients. ➤ Anticipation of situational conflicts and transparency are useful strategies; avoiding and abstaining from some situations may be warranted. ➤ Internal coaches should probe client feelings and reactions to any boundary challenge that occurs, even when there is no actual threat to the role.

A third trend is that, once assigned to the role, internal coaches are likely to be asked for counsel, advice, and other guidance outside the boundaries of an actual engagement. These ad hoc consultations may draw on the coach's skills in listening and offering a different perspective, but strictly speaking, they are not coaching relationships because no process has been agreed upon. Internal coaches use their judgment about whether an ad hoc counseling session is sufficient or if a coaching engagement should be contracted. When there appears to be need and interest in a coaching process, the internal coach would discuss with the potential client a design for a coaching engagement, which may include the usual steps, such as data gathering, sponsor involvement, and development planning. The challenge for internal coaches is to move these interactions either into an actual coaching engagement or refer the colleague to other helping resources. Continuing to meet and talk without contracting next steps in an actual engagement is an inefficient use of both coach and client time. Unfortunately, internal coaches can be in high demand for these counseling conversations, eroding their avaliability for actual contracted coaching. While it is always flattering to be sought out, counseling conversations that do not result in productive next steps are a significant risk to the productivity of internal coaches.

For those readers interested in internal coaching, the considerations presented in this chapter are intended to provide a glimpse into the breadth of the role and its challenges. If you are already operating as an internal coach, apply the contents of the preceding chapters to your internal coach activities and shape a personal model for your coaching that supports your work and is aligned with your organization's needs. You may discover important ways in which your internal coaching can be more effective and satisfying. You may also discover ways in which your organization needs to better support your internal coaching work. Both your skills and your organization's policies must be well developed for an internal coaching program to succeed. If you are an external coach, being familiar with the details of the internal coach role will make you a better partner with them.

Part I of this book built the foundation for becoming an exceptional executive coach by introducing the idea of creating a Personal Model based on three inputs and three outputs. Input 1 is your own self-assessment about characteristics you bring to executive coaching. Input 2 prompts you to think about strengths and experiences you bring to working in organizational contexts. Input 3 asks you to consider key topics, practices, and options in executive coaching using the content chapters in Part II of this book. The next chapter begins Part III, which describes how to articulate the three outputs that constitute the more public aspects of your Personal Model: (1) your approach to delivering executive coaching engagements, (2) how you might build your coaching practice, and (3) what your plans are for further developing your coaching skills.

At this point in your learning, you may feel that drafting the outputs of your Personal Model of coaching is a stretch. We acknowledge the challenge of that task, and our students experience similar concerns. At the same time, the sooner you begin to articulate your Personal Model, the better you will be able to both promote your practice and deliver effective coaching services. This is not to pressure or rush you, but instead to help you make tangible progress at whatever level you can manage. Your model will continue to evolve as you accumulate and reflect on new coaching experiences. It would not be desirable or expected for your coaching abilities and approach to remain static. As you celebrate the emergence and continued evolution of your model, you can anchor it in the self-awareness of where you are now, while consciously adjusting as circumstances and your preferences interact.

Chapter 21, highlighting Output 1 of your Personal Model, offers guidance on how to articulate key aspects of your approach to delivering executive coaching services. Chapter 22 focuses on Output 2: how you will secure the coaching work that you seek. Chapter 23 offers suggestions about your continued growth and development as an executive coach; your professional development plan is Output 3. While these three outputs overlap conceptually, each has unique elements for you to consider. Finally, Chapter 24 presents a composite but realistic description of a newer coach on a journey toward learning coaching skills and creating her Personal Model.

PART

III

ARTICULATING THE OUTPUTS OF

YOUR PERSONAL MODEL

Output 1: Your Approach to Executive Coaching

A S YOU READ THE PREVIOUS CHAPTERS, YOU STARTED BUILDING A FRAME-
WORK FOR YOUR PERSONAL MODEL BY REFLECTING ON WHO YOU ARE AS A
PERSON, WHAT YOU BRING TO WORKING IN ORGANIZATIONAL CONTEXTS,
and your preferences for coaching concepts, practices, and techniques.
Putting these three inputs together informs this first and most comprehensive output of your Personal Model—a description of your approach to
coaching.

Integrating all of the elements mentioned surfaces a surprising number
of issues. Many of these tap directly into the coaching process options that
were described in the chapters of Part II. Your understanding of that content,
filtered by your own preferences and experience, gives you a basis for choosing how you operate as a coach.

Statements about coaching approaches are as varied as the coaches
making them. We encourage you to find ideas and concepts that appeal to
you and articulate the elements that go into your approach to coaching.
Some coaches emphasize the ways they help clients; others focus on the
theoretical lenses they use to understand clients, or they put a primary
emphasis on their relationships with clients. Every coach brings his or her

own history and character into the relationship, and some reflect on these as a starting point for explaining a preferred approach.

The following statements are excerpts from the first output of Personal Models we have read, sorted into several categories. They may be helpful as you think about this first output for yourself.

Helping Clients

Coaching is helping someone maximize his impact and effectiveness.

The development plan will be a dynamic statement of my client's aspirations and ideas for getting there.

My approach to coaching is a results-oriented process that helps clients discover and implement solutions to meet their leadership challenges.

Theory Preferences

I think about change in cognitive terms while always aiming for behavioral outcomes. Thoughts and feelings come through in our words and language, which in turn determine behavior and job performance. Along the way we will surface client assumptions, causative beliefs, and other mental models.

I use emotional intelligence as a core framework to help clients target their learning opportunities.

My primary approach to coaching involves leveraging mindfulness to fully investigate, understand, and empathize with the client's intentions. Each session with a client should encourage unstructured conversation about thoughts, feelings, events, and challenges.

Relationships with Clients

The coaching process allows me to run alongside the moving train that the client is already on, so for a while we can move at the same speed. I will be a journey partner for my clients, drawing out stories and looking at situations from a variety of perspectives to unlock new possibilities.

For me, the cornerstone of effective coaching is the coach-client relationship. My first challenge is to build trust, which I do by being fully pres-

ent and an active listener. I need to move along the continuum of empathizing with the client versus challenging her, based on what a client needs at any particular moment.

Acknowledging How Personal Style Affects the Coach-Client Relationship

I have tools that I use with clients, such as goal evolution, informational interviewing, and use of self. Importantly for me, I also have tools that stay inside my head to guide what I do: organization development/process consultation values and existential psychology or the importance of client choice.

My approach to coaching is anchored in my naturally friendly and disarming style. My demeanor makes people feel comfortable and reduces obstacles to openness.

Learning and Change

My coaching presence tunes into what a client needs at each moment to learn and grow. I work with clients to build awareness about needed change, gather others' perceptions, explore interpretations, commit to change, and implement new behaviors.

Clients are always in a state of personal and professional transition. Their current story needs to be reframed into the next story, and my job is to help them make conscious choices about what to do and what to leave behind.

As a coach, I see myself as a catalyst for the client's lifelong learning and change effort. I believe people are capable of doing this at any age. With my support, the client can keep experimenting until the desired change becomes internalized.

As an internal coach, I focus on coaching leaders during change initiatives. This requires that I juggle the organization's objectives and the individual leader's strengths and gaps.

The Coaching Process

I collaborate with my client and the sponsors to determine a coaching process that fits their needs. If they charge me to design the process, it would have the following steps: determine readiness for change, gather and interpret information about the client, implement the change process, check for progress, and sustain the change.

My approach is collaborative and customized. I want to ensure that the client's experience is productive and that the organization sees the effort as value-added.

I think that it will help clients, sponsors, and me if I write up a guide to the coaching process and share that with everyone. It will include the following steps: discussion of process and boundaries, discussion of felt needs with client and manager, start of coaching with self-discovery and data collection, feedback to client and goal setting, three-way meeting with manager to gain consensus on goals, writing action plan, implementing the plan and having the client get feedback from the manager during regular one-on-one meetings, targeting end point to the coaching and reaching closure.

With those examples as a springboard, below is a series of questions that will help you be comprehensive in articulating Output 1 of your Personal Model. Your answers to these questions represent the core of your approach to executive coaching. Writing answers to these questions may take several pages or more, depending on the detail you wish to include. A visual image, diagram, or flowchart might be useful and illustrative of your approach. Bulleted points, descriptive paragraphs, and your own examples may be helpful in capturing the essence of what process steps and coaching methods you want to include. Working on Output 1 of your Personal Model will prepare you to answer the question that clients and sponsors are likely to ask, "What's your approach to coaching?"

Your Presence as a Coach. Envision yourself working as a coach and reflect on any coaching or helping experiences you have had: What stands out as unique about you? How do you use your own feelings and reactions to understand others (*use of self*) during coaching interactions? What is likely to be your interpersonal style with clients?

Your responses:

Your Boundaries as a Coach. Where do you prefer to help clients focus on the continuum from personal insight to organizational results? In your view, what topics, roles, and activities are key parts of your executive coaching, and which ones are not? How prepared are you to create clear coaching contracts with sponsors and clients? What are your preferences in handling confidentiality and other aspects of containment?

Your responses:

Your Approach to Relationship Building with Clients. What facilitation skills will you apply to building a relationship of trust and discovery? How might you use client stories as an intervention? What are your self-management issues and how will you address them? How will you address reluctance and difference issues that may arise with clients?

Your responses:

Your Approach to Sponsors. In what ways will you include the stakeholders in immediate proximity to your client and those somewhat more distant? How will you balance individual development goals with organization expectations for coaching outcomes? In what ways will you support the client in enlisting resources for development after your engagement is concluded?

Your responses:

Your Current Coaching Process. What types of coaching are you attracted to delivering and what sequence of steps do you envision using? What elements of a coaching process would you contract for and how would you structure coaching sessions? What may be milestone events in your coaching process?

Your responses:

Your Use of Assessment Methods. What assessment tools and methods do you expect to use and which ones may be optional for you? How much emphasis will you place on assessment within coaching and how interested are you in expanding your repertoire of assessment tools? What is your approach to providing feedback to clients so that assessment results inform development goals?

Your responses:

Your Dialogue/Conversation Methods and Eliciting Stories. What questions and facilitation techniques will you use to engage clients and facilitate openness? What will you do to take their answers to a deeper and more reflective place? How will you foster and interpret their stories? What questions will you use with sponsors?

Your responses:

Your Grasp of Leadership Concepts and Issues. What leadership ideas and models appeal to you and how might you use them with clients? What level of leadership do you feel ready to coach? How firm is your grasp of management and leadership competencies to help define client development goals? What will you do to help leaders leverage the stories they tell followers?

Your responses:

Your Approach to Development Planning. What is your approach to helping your clients evolve and structure compelling development goals? Describe how you will help translate those goals into on-the-job action ideas that can result in observable change. What process will you and your clients use to share development plans with sponsors?

Your responses:

Your Approach to Evaluation. How will you know if your coaching is effective, both during the process and after? What methods will you use for progress checks and post-coaching evaluation? What will you do to capitalize on evaluation for your own learning?

Your responses:

Organizing Principle

Some coaches find that in reflecting on their approach to coaching, a unifying theme emerges that links the elements together in a cohesive way. We call such a theme an *organizing principle.*

An organizing principle for a Personal Model tends to be a simple statement that connects coaching with your personal view of what matters most in finding fulfillment and effectiveness. This statement is often anchored in your values. As such, it can offer a useful way to tie the elements of your approach together and foster clarity in your work. It also offers a powerful way to explain your coaching approach to others.

Some examples of organizing principles are:

I believe everyone is responsible for making their own choices, and my role in the relationship is to help clients clarify their options and support new choices.

In my view, learning is a continuous process and an underpinning of all change.

To my way of thinking, the synergies and possibilities of combining action and reflection are enormous.

My core belief in coaching is that managing oneself is invariably linked to managing others.

My coaching emphasizes the struggle to bring an honest understanding of complex feelings into day-to-day roles.

Because I approach clients as whole people, it is important for me to help clients find a work/life ratio that feels right to them.

If an organizing principle emerges for you, it may be useful to incorporate it into your explanation of your approach. In practice, there is no set script to use in communicating your approach. All executive coaches are similar in some ways, but a Personal Model helps to identify the ways in which you are unique and different from other coaches.

Having articulated your best thinking about Output 1 of your Personal Model, you are in a much better position to explain your approach to coaching to clients and sponsors. In addition, your approach to coaching provides a foundation upon which your model can grow and evolve as you gain more experience and become a more confident coach.

22

Output 2: Your Executive Coaching Practice

THIS CHAPTER SUMMARIZES THE BUSINESS OR PRACTICE ASPECTS OF EXECUTIVE COACHING AND PROMPTS YOU TO CREATE A PLAN TO INCREASE YOUR COACHING WORK. THIS IS THE SECOND OUTPUT OF YOUR PERSONAL MODEL. IT extrapolates from Output 1—your approach to coaching—into your future as a coach. It asks you to reflect on how to integrate coaching with your other professional activities. You may be an internal or external coach with varying interests and opportunities to do coaching. Whichever aspects of the profession you choose, it is essential that you secure real-world application to continue to build your coaching skills, whether your coaching services are fee-free or income-producing.

Since most coaches are also consultants, they usually provide a range of services. This means that your coaching work must be given conscious planning and prominence within the services you offer. Otherwise, coaching risks being overshadowed by the other services (such as consulting or training) that you have traditionally provided. It is never too early to begin considering and planning how you will make the time available to structure, promote, and deliver your coaching services.

Getting Started with an External Practice

There are dozens of books on how to start consulting practices and how to add new services to your list of offerings. There are no universal answers. Because very few coaches make all of their income from coaching, it is usual for coaching to be included with other consulting services (e.g., training, facilitation, HR consulting, recruiting, or career counseling).

Here's how some external coaches have described building the coaching part of their practices:

I will finish my website so that it is engaging and describes what I do, make sure clients know that I have expanded my practice to include executive coaching, leverage my experience with branded 360-degree tools, and focus on getting development plan coaching assignments. I also plan to create a small group of peer coaches for mutual support and joint business development.

I will reach back to my well-established network of contacts. By making repeated contacts I will make sure they are aware of my ability and interest in taking on coaching cases.

During the next year or two, I would like to have had about ten coaching clients. I will put gaining the experience ahead of getting my full fee. That will give me the flexibility to offer coaching to mid-level managers who have been promoted to larger leadership roles.

I will start as an external coach as soon as I officially retire from my current job. In anticipating that, I need to pay much more attention to building an external network, becoming involved in professional associations, and gaining more exposure through speaking and writing.

Targeting Your Marketing

No coach can market services to every segment. How focused should your practice be? That's a simple question with a complicated answer. Many coaches try to focus on a niche because it taps into the input side of their

Personal Models in terms of interests and experiences. They may also have more contacts in a particular market segment or industry.

Here are a few examples of targeted marketing statements:

> *I especially hope to coach people in transition, such as newly hired leaders, those newly promoted, leaders going through career transitions, and leaders in organizations where significant change is occurring.*

> *I will target executives focused on improving their leadership skills, and on executives new to an organization, such as assisting foreign nationals on assignment here in the United States and assisting executives who are preparing for retirement.*

> *I have a particular interest in coaching entrepreneurs. These engagements may have a different process than the usual coaching assignment because the client may be the sponsor. Entrepreneurs often are hungry for feedback.*

Getting Started with Internal Coaching

Coaches working inside of organizations have to think about how they are going to find coaching opportunities since their job titles may not mention coaching. The issues here include making time, getting support, managing boundaries, and finding ways to promote one's services internally.

Sample statements from practicing internal coaches may be useful in formulating your own plan:

> *I will remain an internal coach for the next four years, taking on about one client per quarter to keep in practice. Then I expect to become an external consultant and offer coaching as part of my mix of services.*

> *I am very excited to be putting on my 'coaching hat' and using these skills internally. I have a clear understanding of when I can offer my coaching services and how to contract the process, so there should be ample opportunities for me to be a coach. I have strong support from my boss for this work.*

As an internal resource, I will work with management on the talent iden-tification process and bring coaching to the high-potential pool. Development plans can be individualized while also having elements that are shared with other high potentials.

Your Practice Plan

If you are committed to growing your coaching practice, there are several important specifics that you'll want to consider. By thinking through answers to the following questions and discussing them with colleagues and case supervisors, you will be closer to having a plan to build your practice:

- How much time do you have or can you make available to both deliver and pursue your coaching interests?

- What industry, function, or client type will you specialize in?

- What do you need to do to become comfortable in describing your approach to coaching (i.e., Output 1 of your Personal Model)?

- What types of coaching services do you want to offer and what coaching examples can you provide to support those offerings?

- Where (e.g., your office? client's office? other locations?) and when in your usual schedule will you deliver coaching?

- What forums, groups, or professional associations would be most useful for you to participate in to promote your coaching?

- What exposure opportunities do you have to present yourself as a coach? What speaking, writing, or teaching opportunities may there be for you?

- If fee-based coaching is not available to you at this time, how might you secure fee-free coaching assignments in order to build your experience?

- How might you approach existing or new sponsors/clients to offer them a service that is different from other services you have delivered?

Marketing coaching services often involves networking. There are coaches of many types, so it is not always easy for buyers to differentiate them. This makes it more difficult for prospective sponsors to source, meet, and hire a coach, whether new or experienced. Often, the pivotal difference that allows you to stand out from other coaches is who you know and who they know. This is classic networking, used in many service fields, as well as in finding full-time employment. Networks reflecting your education, career, professional identity, interests, life stage, and others all may be sources of coaching work directly or indirectly. These can now be accessed more easily through various online sites.

Effective networking starts by making lists of contacts and relationships, independent of any immediate prospects for work. To make them pay off, the lists need to be as long as possible.

Here are some questions that may remind you of contacts to build your list:

- Who should be informed about your work as a coach?
- Who might have contacts that you'd like to reach out to and include in your network?
- What can you do to increase the number of names on your list?
- How can social media be useful to you (e.g. webinars and podcasts)?
- Consider creating your own website or expanding the one you already have.
- What can you learn by looking at the websites of other coaches and professionals who are effective at marketing their services?

Regardless of what you do with online marketing, you still need to prepare and keep on hand descriptions of your services in hardcopy form. Sometimes it is simply easier and more immediate to hand a biosketch or brochure to someone you have just met at a professional gathering or conference, or to send a digital copy by e-mail. It should be clear and descriptive of the services you offer. Review the materials of successful executive coaches to get ideas about how to structure these and what to include.

What is most important is that you commit to promoting your coaching services actively in whatever market segments you identify. Some coaches retain advisers or consultants who specialize in marketing professional practices. Whatever methods you choose, gaining coaching experience, even if fee-free, and persisting in the marketplace are essential requirements. Prepare your support documents, online resources, and articulations of your coaching approach and let people know that you are offering coaching services. That direct contact will help you refine your presentation, and hopefully land coaching business.

23

Output 3: Your Professional Development Plan

HE THIRD OUTPUT OF YOUR PERSONAL MODEL IS A DEVELOPMENT PLAN FOR YOURSELF AS COACH. THIS PLAN TAPS INTO THE STRENGTHS AND GAPS OF BOTH YOUR APPROACH TO COACHING AND YOUR PRACTICE PLAN FOR GETTING more coaching work. Addressing your areas for growth strengthens your approach and potentially increases your effectiveness in the marketplace.

Every coach should have a personal agenda for becoming a better coach. Below are developmental ideas from other coaches' Personal Models that reflect their awareness of competencies that need to be developed. They tend to be more interpersonal and emotional competencies than cognitive ones.

> *I need to upgrade my listening and communication skills in order to be an effective coach. I need to be able to listen without jumping in with advice. Similarly, I need to really consider what a client is saying, without judgment or forming an immediate opinion.*
>
> *As a coach, I need a much more reflective, calmer style than in my usual roles.*
>
> *I need to have a stronger presence with those leaders who have big egos.*

> *Whether clients or managers, they tend to dominate conversation and put me into a passive mode. I need to have strategies for holding my own with them and leveraging my point of view.*

> *To be a more effective and versatile coach, I need to remain sharp and present when I am tired or distracted. I tend to move into my comfort zone of consulting and advising.*

> *A challenge I have is to become more comfortable with silence and giving the client time to really think about what we are discussing.*

There are skills, knowledge, and abilities that may benefit your coaching practice as well, as expressed in these sample statements:

> *My plan for ongoing development as a coach includes learning more about positive psychology, exploring the topic of psychological loss, and becoming certified in an emotional intelligence instrument and a 360-degree feedback tool.*

> *I need to understand more concepts about leadership and management so that I can listen actively and respond with substantive ideas, yet stay away from providing answers.*

> *My development plan includes learning more about theoretical models such as appreciative inquiry. Also, I want to get experience with cross-cultural coaching by securing an international client.*

> *I will become certified in several of the psychological and interpersonal-style assessment techniques that are often used in coaching engagements.*

All coaches have their own preferred way of learning. These methods might include study, courses, peer learning groups, or an arrangement with a case supervisor. Here are some practicing coaches' reflections on their learning methods:

> *Every engagement holds the potential for learning. I have used journaling to make my reflections more productive. I will continue to journal, but in future cases, I will target my journaling on several key questions aimed at each coaching assignment: What am I learning about*

myself? What feels risky with this client and what should I do about it? What needs to happen so that the balance of responsibility is tipped toward the client? What about this client is unclear and what can I do about it? To what extent am I modeling what we are talking about?

My meditative discipline outside of sessions is an important contributor to being less reactive and more present during sessions. I would also like to identify a set of mindfulness exercises to use before I meet with clients.

Since I learn best by doing, I will use my coaching work to be my teacher. It will take a disciplined approach to reflection, which I plan to do in three contexts: on my own, after each session, and at milestones; with a peer-coach support group of three to four colleagues; and with a more senior case supervisor, on more complex cases or when I feel stuck.

The following questions are designed to help you consider your own future learning:

- Reflecting back on your current experience, what areas of coaching would you like to improve?

- What personal or professional characteristics would you like to address because they hold you back as a coach?

- What can you do to expand your interpersonal range with clients?

- What types of clients do you find most difficult or challenging?

- How can you learn to work more confidently with a wider range of clients?

- Building on your practice plan, what personal strengths can you build on?

- As you consider approaching the groups, business sectors, and types of organizations that you would like to work with, what hurdles might you want to overcome?

- What might you do to expand your repertoire of coaching methods?

- How would you assess your listening skills, and what about them do you want to further leverage?

- What questions do you have about theories, principles, or concepts that are linked with coaching?

- What models, approaches, or coaching techniques (Part II of this book) do you want to learn more about, and how might you experiment with them?

- What personal development areas may hold you back from being the coach you envision?

- How might you work on your own personal growth as you do coaching?

- What learning resources might you access to further your professional development (e.g., case supervision, support or professional learning groups, tutorials), and how will you contract them?

- What challenges do you face as an internal coach in terms of time, boundaries, senior leader support, program definition, case supervision, and continued investment in your growth as a coach?

- How might you address and get support in addressing internal coach challenges?

As you develop as an executive coach, you will find that your approach expands and becomes more robust. At the same time, working on your development plan will enhance your presence in the marketplace and add to the overt skills needed for coaching assignments. As with the rest of your Personal Model, it is meant to be fluid and changeable as you grow and gain more experience. Even senior coaches maintain development plans, although with less of a focus on skill areas and more attention given to theories or new approaches. Most important, your development plan links you with your clients' struggles to learn and grow so that you can better identify with their experiences during coaching.

24

Becoming an Exceptional Executive Coach: Amber's Story

Pᴇᴏᴘʟᴇ ᴄᴏᴍᴇ ᴛᴏ ᴇxᴇᴄᴜᴛɪᴠᴇ ᴄᴏᴀᴄʜɪɴɢ ꜰʀᴏᴍ ᴍᴀɴʏ ᴅɪꜰꜰᴇʀᴇɴᴛ ᴇᴅᴜᴄᴀᴛɪᴏɴᴀʟ ᴀɴᴅ ᴘʀᴏꜰᴇꜱꜱɪᴏɴᴀʟ ʙᴀᴄᴋɢʀᴏᴜɴᴅꜱ. Tʜᴇ ᴜꜱᴜᴀʟ ᴘʀᴏꜰɪʟᴇ ɪɴᴄʟᴜᴅᴇꜱ ᴇᴅᴜᴄᴀᴛɪᴏɴ ɪɴ ʜᴇʟᴘɪɴɢ ᴘʀᴏꜰᴇꜱꜱɪᴏɴꜱ ᴏʀ ɪɴ ᴏʀɢᴀɴɪᴢᴀᴛɪᴏɴᴀʟ ᴅɪꜱᴄɪᴘʟɪɴᴇꜱ ᴀɴᴅ ᴇxᴘᴇʀɪᴇɴᴄᴇ in leadership development, talent management, or human resources. Less frequent is the line manager or executive who aspires to become an executive coach.

In order to illustrate the range of backgrounds that coaches come from, this chapter profiles the experience of one of those line managers who felt a calling to become a coach and found a way to make it happen in her career.[1] We hope Amber's story helps you understand and anticipate what you may experience in becoming an exceptional executive coach.

Amber had many years of experience as a manager in a large corporation and enjoyed her career, although not always the work itself. She had known from an early point that she got more satisfaction from helping a staff member learn and grow than she did from her own technical assignments. People at work seemed to gravitate to her when they had a problem or a quandary, and she had developed a reputation as an excellent listener and idea generator. "I knew my style and interests were different from other managers," she said, "and I had a reputation as a talent developer, but I didn't think much about it in terms of my career."

Over the years, these qualities and skills became integrated into her managerial style, and she had more recently embraced the mission of nurturing and supporting others in the advancement of their careers. This mission was even more pronounced outside of work in organized activities she enjoyed in her community. In those organizations she was often called upon to resolve sensitive interpersonal and leadership challenges.

Amber had heard about executive coaching at work and at times she wondered, "Am I doing coaching or is it just my need to help others?" That question sparked her to learn more about the profession of executive coaching. She became convinced that what coaches did was what she now wanted to do. Synchronicity was in her favor since she expected to be offered a package as her employer cut staff.

Amber targeted coaching as a second career and investigated various executive coach training courses. Since she didn't have the usual background of coaches, Amber decided that she wanted an in-person class experience where she would be provided with a coaching approach to channel her natural helping style and a managerial client to gain practical experience doing actual casework. As she noted, "At that point, I was actually hoping for some type of magic formula for how to coach and keeping my fingers crossed about whether I would be good enough to use it."

She took a deep breath and signed up for such a course. She dove into the pre-reading, including books on executive coaching, and she completed several self-assessment instruments and reflective questions. The appeal of that content was counterbalanced by doubts that became stronger as the program approached: "Can I actually do the type of coaching work described in the books? What can I bring to a client I have never met before? Who would hire me to help a client change? Am I just fooling myself?"

These doubts and anxieties are not unique to Amber. To varying degrees, they are part of every new coach's experience. In fact, the anticipation of meeting a client can spur a new coach on to becoming serious about learning. Amber channeled her anxieties into a search for the definitive guideline for effective coaching, but she hadn't found one when the course began.

Amber's anxiety increased when she met her classmates on the first day of the program. They were an impressive group with many years of corporate HR or professional helping experience. There were even therapists and counselors who had graduate training and deep understanding of personality and change. They were gracious and interested in her technical background and business career, but she definitely felt less prepared than they were. She was convinced that if this group represented the norm in new coaches, she would never measure up.

However, the course included one-on-one time with a faculty member who served as Amber's case supervisor. Meetings with her supervisor allowed Amber to share her initial fears. This was helpful in easing her concerns and reminding her that she had many practical organizational and managerial assets to bring to coaching.

In the early class sessions, Amber was surprised to discover that everyone had doubts about their ability to become an executive coach. Even the experienced HR people were worried that, stripped of the credibility of their usual roles, they would have no leverage with clients. Each student seemed to have areas of self-perceived deficiency, but all could be summed up under the heading, *What makes me think I can help anyone else, let alone a manager or leader I have never met?* Everyone in the class felt very insecure about providing value to a client and dealing with the complexity of sponsor agendas and organizational dynamics.

Amber was able to explore her concerns with her case supervisor. She knew from her other helping experiences that she tended to be reactive to other people's problems. Sometimes this tendency led her to be overly helpful and to take action on another's behalf. Given how committed she was to helping, she saw herself becoming frustrated when others didn't act on her well-meant advice. She didn't know how to fix these tendencies, which added to her worry. "I knew I had some natural abilities I could apply to coaching," she observed, "but there were so many unknowns: the client, the organization, and how to conduct myself as a coach. It was intimidating!" Still, she pressed ahead and took on faith both the guidance she was receiving and the prospect of working with an actual client.

The initial client meetings were surprisingly gratifying to Amber. She was struck by how unique her client's challenges were—a complex mix of skills, gaps, aspirations, and situational constraints, all in an organizational culture that was completely unknown to her. She lost interest in a coaching "formula" and began to see the wisdom of more genuine responses within the context of the coaching engagement. Instead of working to adhere to a predetermined path, she was able to focus her full attention on her client. Her confidence was bolstered by her keen listening skills, which led to moments when her questions made her client pause to think, or when her observations were a useful reframing of what the client was experiencing. With her supervisor's encouragement, she found that she could draw on her business experience to ask incisive questions. Her grasp of organizational dynamics and corporate politics informed her understanding of the client's challenges. As she noted, "I was discovering my own way of helping my client; it was me, but tailored to fit within the boundaries of the coaching relationship. I was surprised at how freeing that was."

When new coaches begin to apply their listening and interpersonal skills in the context of a coaching process that has structure and goals, they begin to feel they are making progress in learning to coach. It confirms both that they can be an agent of change with their clients and that there is no one right way to do it. This can be a liberating moment even though there is still much more to learn. Doubts begin to ease and are replaced by the challenge of becoming more intentional about choices with clients.

Amber and her supervisor examined those choices and expanded her range of options: "I was feeling more confident in the role, but I knew I still had a lot to learn—about my own blind spots, such as my tendency to help too much, about how to handle sponsors and get to a development plan that everyone could support. I had to accept that my learning would have some dips."

Amber also realized that the ups and downs of her confidence level contained clues to her Personal Model. Reflecting on these fluctuations would enable her to articulate her approach to coaching. When she saw the client getting excited about insights or behavioral progress, she got confirmation that what she was doing was effective. On the other hand, when she felt herself trying too hard, feeling unsure, or saying things she regretted, she would analyze why those moments had happened to target what she needed to do differently. While the task of articulating her Personal Model still felt quite daunting, she was beginning to accumulate insights that would inform it.

To Amber's credit, she was open with her supervisor about ineffective tendencies. As she had anticipated, she did talk too much when nervous or unsure of what to do next with the client. More challenging was not going into *savior mode* in response to requests for help: Her habit was to solve the problem. "I was always the go-to person at work, but I was learning that it wouldn't fly in a coaching relationship," she observed. Since her client would have been happy to have her solve his problems, Amber faced significant pressure in avoiding that entrenched behavior in herself.

She and her supervisor had rich conversations about that struggle. Amber's first challenge was to change her attitude about jumping in to help by accepting that it conveyed a lack of confidence in the client's own abilities and reduced his commitment to what he would do differently. As Amber incorporated these ideas, she grew less focused on solving the client's problems. Instead, she tried using inquiry to facilitate the client's ideas and keep the lines of responsibility clear. She also found that when she ignored the implied demand to provide solutions, she had more time to think creatively about the client, making associations between the specific problem they were discussing and others, helping him voice his doubts and fears, exploring payoffs and risks in making a change, and reframing specific challenges as opportunities to make progress on his development goals. She was surprised to find that this way of thinking turned out to be more exciting than trying to satisfy his need for help.

It also allowed her to discover that her intuition about the client's mental state, and why, was usually on target. Encouraged by this feedback, Amber took more risks in making observations about how he might be feeling, how she experienced the client, and what the client did in their sessions that reminded her of his development needs. She hadn't known that she could use her *self* so actively, and it gave her a stronger presence with her client. She realized that other characteristics—her warmth and optimism particularly—worked in concert with her intuition, providing a nurturing environment in which the client was safe to consider Amber's sometimes pointed observations.

She and her supervisor labeled this *her tough but caring style*, and it became the organizing principle for her approach to coaching. Having an awareness of it was the beginning of articulating her own Personal Model of coaching, and it buoyed her confidence more than any formula ever could have. According to Amber, "I remember starting to feel that, if I could be my best self, then effective coaching would follow. Suddenly it started to feel possible."

Looking back on this process, reflection, discussion, and experience combined to create insights. In the early stages, as Amber became more accepting of herself as a coach, she became aware of experiences, values, and abilities that she could bring into the role. Some of these qualities have been mentioned, but one that emerged later was a strong emphasis on understanding the client's motivation. She had taken a psychology course in college that emphasized the motivational roots of all behavior, and she had applied this model in her own life. She found that she was naturally inclined to use a motivational viewpoint to better understand her client: What did he really want? What were the hidden forces shaping his motivation, or lack of it? How might she explore those variables with him? By putting a motivational lens in her model, she felt more empowered to use it in her questions.

In addition, a message from her childhood kept coming back to her: *Never forget how hard it is to try something new.* Her father had been particularly patient with her when she was learning a new sport or skill. When she later asked him about it, he explained that he had wanted her to experience both the challenge and the excitement of learning, and that meant he had to back off and let her succeed and fail at her own pace. Recalling those past interactions helped her shift her usual push for results to a *pull* toward learning. Both curiosity about motivation and an appreciation of how to empower learning became aspects of her Personal Model.

Shaping a Personal Model also includes insights about fears, gaps, and ineffective tendencies. Amber believed that there was more to be gained in fostering discovery than providing answers, but at first this didn't ease the pressure she felt when she sidestepped the client's clear request for more direct help. In the past, when she heard "What should I do?" from a colleague, it would have brought out all of her problem-solving resources. Now as a coach, that question, whether overt or implied, made her hesitate and look for a different direction. Sometimes the client's distress or dissatisfaction made her doubt she could provide help in a new way. As a result, she wasn't always able to do what she intended. However, these situations were opportunities for reflection and her courage and versatility increased over time.

Amber also found that she needed to build more skills in how to involve sponsors appropriately in her client's coaching. She needed to find ways of listening to sponsors neutrally so that she could more fully understand the client's context and put aside her inclination to protect or advocate for her client. "It surprised me how defensive I felt when my client's boss told me she hadn't seen much change. But I took a deep breath and asked more questions."

Her client also challenged her in unexpected ways. As is usual in executive coaching, she and the client had been meeting in a conference room near the client's office. Unexpectedly before the next session, he sent Amber an e-mail requesting that they meet in a local coffee shop. While Amber's tendency was to accommodate this request, her intuition told her that she should be careful. She had learned that clients sometimes test boundaries, drawing coaches into topics or relationships that may not be appropriate for executive development.

When they did meet in the coffee shop, Amber wasn't surprised that the client requested her help with his interviewing skills because another firm was recruiting him. Her preparation allowed her to reflect on how she felt about this request and how not to simply comply. She had decidedly mixed feelings about what he was requesting and she was able to voice her concerns clearly but empathetically. She told him that she appreciated his confidence but was not comfortable taking a position on his interest in another job. At the same time, she brought their focus back to making the most of his learning opportunities in his current job. "That was a very tough moment for me," Amber recalled. "I thought, 'What's the harm in helping him with interview skills?' But I couldn't do it. My worst fears flashed before my eyes: Would he storm out of the coffee shop if I refused? Would he reject me as a coach? I guess I chose the lesser of the two evils in keeping our focus where it was." Amber felt proud about how she had handled the situation, and her supervisor summed it up: She hadn't let her drive to help overwhelm the importance of keeping coaching boundaries clear.

Shaping a Personal Model of coaching serves many functions. In Amber's situation, it served as a quality-control mechanism on the boundary challenge that her client made. She had accumulated insights about *use of self*, acquired the learning that she needed about coaching practices and choices, and considered the type of coaching she aspired to deliver. Although her model had not yet been written, the process of creating it had given her important guidelines for what she needed to do in handling a difficult situation. "I was so glad I didn't get off track," Amber said. "In the end, I think I had a stronger relationship with my client because I stayed the course. He respected my decision and maybe it gave him an anchor to have a more reasoned response to being recruited."

A Personal Model has many other practical implications. It can serve as a source for statements about what distinguishes Amber as a coach. "I bring a wealth of real-world organizational experience to inform the discovery process I use with clients. I also bring a willingness to provide direct feedback in a safe relationship that supports tangible progress on development."

Sponsors and clients expect coaches to be articulate about their approaches, but it is also important to present approaches in distinctive and engaging ways. There are also times when awareness of her model may help Amber avoid engagements that do not suit her—for example, if the time frame is too short for her or the opportunities for coach-client relationship building are limited.

After coaching for a period of time, Amber understood that these public dimensions of her model would not exist without a lot of private work. Her Personal Model is much deeper and more faceted than clients or sponsors need to hear, but the sample of it that she shares with them is tied directly to those variegated roots. As she has observed, "Personal Models reflect a lot of influences and contain many elements, and I guess I will always be honing mine. But even as a work-in-progress it has increased both my personal self-awareness and my outward confidence as a coach."

Amber also appreciated the broader philosophical benefit of creating her Personal Model. Every client can be thought of as having his or her own implicit model for leadership or change. Having shaped her own coaching model, Amber is more attuned to exploring the components of her clients' mental models of how they see the world.

Amber did eventually draft her model: her approach to executive coaching, her practice plan for getting more coaching work, and her development plan. She had mixed feelings about formally writing it down because to do so felt too final, whereas she, and the model itself, remained works in progress. The discipline of actually having to describe her model to others, however, was beneficial in pushing her to take the articulation of her model, and therefore her coaching, to the next level.

Amber found that there were similarities between her model and those of other students in the class. For example, many people drew upon their experiences of leadership in the real world of organizations, their core facilitation skills, and the newfound facility in using their own reactions to the client as part of the helping relationship.

However, there were important differences among models, too. Some were grounded in particular theories of adult change, such as cognitive, behavioral, or emotional intelligence. Some emphasized a structured process; others were more emergent. Some took an activist role in facilitating the client/sponsor relationship. Of course, the internal and external coaches had very different plans to get more coaching work.

In the end, having a tangible Personal Model was both an appropriate benchmark for Amber's learning experience and a foundation for launching her new career as an executive coach: "I guess we all expect clients to beat a path to our door, but that isn't realistic. Coaching is a competitive field, and I won't stand out if I don't know what I stand for. My Personal Model helps me meet prospective clients, size up engagements, work with sponsors, and most importantly, be a change agent in my own way in my role as coach."

All executive coaches have unique ways of approaching the challenge of helping clients change. For the reasons reviewed in this chapter, it is valuable to make these conscious and intentional choices. However, that is not an easy task and Amber is a case in point.

Hopefully this book has fostered your thinking about your own unique blend of knowledge, experience, and intuition as they might apply to becoming an exceptional executive coach. The book has been designed to reflect the process that Amber and others have gone through as they create Personal Models of coaching. Its content should allow you to begin creating your own Personal Model and start or expand your coaching practice.

Ultimately, your model will always be a work-in-progress. It is iterative, based on formal learning, coaching experiences, case supervision, and your own career interests. Nonetheless, in the spirit of every journey beginning with a few steps, we hope that the principles we have provided here start you toward your Personal Model, so that you can become the exceptional coach you are capable of being.

Exhibits

Exhibit 1. (Chapter 3) Distinctions Among Executive Coaching, Personal Coaching, Therapy, and Consulting

	EXECUTIVE/ LEADERSHIP COACHING	PERSONAL COACHING	PSYCHOTHERAPY	CONSULTING
Types	Coaching managers and executives within organizational context. Manager, HR, and organization support and sponsor the coaching Typically provided by independent coaches, coaching organization, or internal coaches and conducted on organization premises	Personal, Life, and Career Coaching Other specific forms of coaching on personal or career topics Typically provided via independent practices, career services firms, and outplacement organizations	Personal counseling and therapy on a wide range of personal, familial, emotional, and behavioral issues Various approaches: cognitive, behavioral, hypnosis, Gestalt, psychoanalytic, etc. Typically provided via licensed independent clinicians, clinics, social service organizations, and hospitals	Wide range of topics and technical or professional specialties providing expertise and advice to individual clients and client groups within organizations and at many levels Typically contracted and provided by independent consultants or consultants associated with a consulting organization Also provided internally by designated internal consultants
Participants	One-on-one coach and client Also, periodic meetings with sponsors	One-on-one coach and client	One-on-one with "patient"; spouse, family, and group combinations as the issue warrants	One-on-one or a group of consultants with individuals or a group of organization representatives
Focus	The client within the context of his/her organization Focused on behavior change, skill enhancement, work transition, leadership, and on-the-job action learning Here and now perspective with coach and client very active	The client's personal life or career Centers on changes in one or more areas of client's personal life Career coaching centers on career direction, job search, and job satisfaction	The patient's emotional health and overall functioning Insight and uncovering/ solving problems in patient's character traits or long-standing ways of thinking and behaving Most therapies explore early life experiences; patient histories are used to understand and interpret stressors and patterns of thinking or acting	An individual client or groups within an organization often centered on strategic change and implementation Consultants conduct individual and organizational assessments and provide expertise on process and/or content

Continues on page 250

Exhibit 1. (Chapter 3) Distinctions Among Executive Coaching, Personal Coaching, Therapy, and Consulting (continued)

	EXECUTIVE/ LEADERSHIP COACHING	PERSONAL COACHING	PSYCHOTHERAPY	CONSULTING
Time Frame	Contracted periods usually from 3-6 months to one year Renewable	Contracted periods or open-ended	Long-term psychotherapy or a variety of brief therapy approaches	From brief projects to long term—multiple years effecting organizational change
Sponsor/ Payer	The employer	Individual client; career services may be paid by employer	Patient, health insurance, family	The organization
Roles	Partnership between the coach and the client Most coaches have the understanding that much of the expertise for the client's development lies within the client himself/herself Coach guides the process Pragmatic and behavioral; coach/client relationship is a means to move action forward and not studied in its own right	The coach is a guide, expert, advisor	Largely follows a medical model that the person has a problem around which help is sought The psychotherapist, depending upon the type of therapy, is seen as an authority, transference object, healer, and expert Much of the work of psychotherapy involves dealing with painful experiences A certain amount of suffering is viewed as part of the process to move forward in therapy	The consultant may assume a variety of roles in the course of a contract including strategic, tactical, and personal Consultants may at times be treated as part of the organization and at other times outside the organization Consultants may serve as advice givers, thought partners, "coach," and more
Target Population	Managers and executives in the context of their work	Individuals seeking to make concrete behavioral changes in personal or professional lives and who are willing to fund coaching Individuals in job/career transitions	People with a wide range of problem areas including addictions, emotional difficulties, and relationship challenges, both mild and major	Individuals, groups, often leaders of major functions in organizations

Exhibit 1. (Chapter 3) Distinctions Among Executive Coaching, Personal Coaching, Therapy, and Consulting (continued)

	EXECUTIVE/ LEADERSHIP COACHING	PERSONAL COACHING	PSYCHOTHERAPY	CONSULTING
Boundaries	Shares tradition of helping with psychotherapy and of putting the client's interests ahead of one's own as the coach Coaching should be avoided if active addiction including alcoholism, drugs, eating disorders, gambling, moderate to severe emotional illness, disabling phobias, anxiety disorders, physically abusive to self or others, medical crisis in self or family Organization circumstances may render the coaching inappropriate (e.g., during a chaotic merger or downsizing)	Shares tradition of helping with psychotherapy and of putting the client's interests ahead of one's own as the coach Coaching should be avoided if active addiction including alcoholism, drugs, eating disorders, gambling, moderate to severe emotional illness, disabling phobias, anxiety disorders, physically abusive to self or others, medical crisis in self or family	Clear standards of boundaries and confidentiality including proper use of information, avoidance of personal relationships, and reporting of abuse or threats to self or others	Varies with the nature of the contract, which includes confidentiality guidelines, noncompetes, and others as determined by the hiring organization
Provider Background and Licensure/ Certification	Coaching usually requires some psychological curiosity, work of organizations, organizational development concepts, and Human Resources functions Not licensed but various certifying bodies; many coaches follow the principles, ethics, and best practices of their original profession and/or the emerging coaching professional organizations	Coaching usually requires some psychological training and/or experience as a counselor Not licensed but various certifying bodies; many coaches follow the principles, ethics, and best practices of their original profession and/or the emerging coaching professional organizations	Typically professionals licensed by the profession and the state in which they reside: psychologists, psychiatrists, clinical social workers, psychiatric nurses Practice and legal protections apply	Wide range including clinical, management, HR, organization development, technical business and professional expertise Role often emerges after many years of specific expertise Licenses/ certifications, if any, related to respective professions
Case Supervision	Recommended, especially in training	Recommended, especially in training	Strongly recommended and/or required	Recommended, especially in training

Exhibit 2. *(Chapter 5) Sample contract*

NOTE: This sample contract is one that takes place after the coach has met once with the HR Director and client's manager and once with the client. It is written directly to the client; a separate document would be prepared for the sponsors containing fee and payment information.

Sandra Storey, CSW
Executive Coach
Two Connecticut Drive
Jersey City, NJ 00000

Judith Coasten
STL Company
77 Sixth Street
New York, NY 10000

LEADERSHIP DEVELOPMENT PROPOSAL FOR JUDITH COASTEN

PURPOSE

To provide a tailored six-month Leadership Development program for you, Judith Coasten, to help you capitalize on your leadership competence and develop your leadership strengths and influence.

Your program will be informed by Key Development Points, emerging from prior conversations with Robert Heally, SVP of Human Resources, Terrence Thompson, your manager, you, and myself. These Key Development Points are the starting places from which we will narrow down more precise development areas.

KEY DEVELOPMENT POINTS

- Increase self-awareness of your communication style and preferences, your tendency to "react," and for you to learn ways to pace and adapt to styles different from yours
- Increase your confidence, poise, and competence while making presentations
- Increase your ability to manage difficult relationships with greater finesse
- Learn how to translate your vision into "digestible" and logical steps so that your manager and others can more effectively manage your high-bar expectations

ONE-TO-ONE CONFIDENTIAL MEETINGS

Your program will involve confidential meetings between you and me. For the first four months, we will meet on a weekly basis and twice a month thereafter. Our meetings will take place at your offices/conference room, which you will arrange, and/or in my office. These meetings will last from 90–120 minutes, depending upon schedules, calendars, and needs. In addition, during the course of this program, you will have ready access to me by phone, fax, or e-mail for any questions or support you may need.

Periodically, I will share with your manager where we are in the process. It will not contain the content of our sessions, which is private.

Exhibit 2. (Chapter 5) Sample contract (continued)

ASSESSMENT INSTRUMENTS

We may select one or more of the following tools to assist you in increasing your self-awareness and your leadership preferences so you can develop the ability to leverage your strengths and focus on areas for development.

1. Listening Skills Profile
2. Leadership Assessment Report
3. Videotaping for feedback on your style and delivery
4. At least one shadowing meeting
5. Stakeholder interviews for input and anonymous feedback

While it is important to have feedback, it is also important to realize that your progress is a process that will become visible to others incrementally.

ASSIGNMENTS

Judith, you will have weekly assignments designed to help you practice the new behaviors, skills, and techniques. Applying them in selected situations and with selected people will help to make each developing skill more natural for you and visible to others.

During your program, we will schedule a three-way in-person conference with your manager and me to share perceptions and assess, support, and sustain your progress. These meetings are key to your progress, since feedback can be invaluable as you move forward.

One of the key deliverables/outcomes of this program is for you to create a strategic Professional Development Plan (PDP) that will emerge from our discussions of the Key Development Points as well as integrating the results from the assessment steps including stakeholder interviews. Your PDP will also act as reinforcement of your developing strengths and as a personalized roadmap for the future.

At the end of the program, we will have a completion meeting where you will present your ongoing PDP to your manager.

It will be critical for us to keep a steady, predictable, and reliable schedule, to the best of our capabilities, since it will be important to keep the momentum of your progress.

"COACHING JOURNAL"

I will also ask you to start and maintain a "Coaching Journal" for the length of your program. Here, you will log and capture your reactions, observations, and any questions that arise during the course of the program. It will act as a log for your successes in your leadership growth; competence and confidence in interactions with your clients, internal staff, and management; and ultimately be your "resource guide" for the future.

Continues on page 254

Exhibit 2. (Chapter 5) Sample contract (continued)

FINAL REPORT

I will ask you to write a Final Report on the effectiveness of this program, from your perspective. This report will cover all the Key Development and Learning Points and your evaluation of the total program. The final report may come from the notes from your "Coaching Journal" as well as from any other experiences and reflections.

After the program has been completed, I will provide two follow-through phone meetings, to help ensure your continued success.

FEES

Inclusive fees and billing arrangements have been discussed and approved with your management and will be activated upon signing of and full agreement to this proposal. Payment will be made in two installments, half of which will be paid upon acceptance of this proposal.

TERMINATION

The above outlined Leadership Development Program for Judith Coasten can be terminated with a four weeks' notification period during this program. Should STL terminate this program, Sandra Storey will return any fees for unused coaching services, minus the four weeks required to terminate the program.

Signed:_____Date:_____

Signed:_____Date:_____

Exhibit 3. (Chapter 5) Sample contracting letter to HR sponsor

Roberta Lopez, LLC
Executive Excellence
Five Plate Street
New York, NY 10001

Date

Alan Linux
Global Human Resources
GIB Co.
1700 Beechum Place
New Town, NY 23456

Hello Alan,

Thank you for your call today, and your offer for me to work with GIB Co. and you in regard to coaching Peter Kim. This e-mail will serve as a Letter of Agreement between us for this purpose.

I will provide individual executive coaching to Peter in connection with his current work setting. The general goal, as I now understand it, will be to partner with him as he considers how to manage the conflicts in his work setting.

This Agreement will be effective as soon as you approve it, and will continue for six months. We can consider renewing the contract for another six months as the initial contract comes to a conclusion.

The specifics of how often, for how long, and where Peter and I will meet will be discussed by us at our first session. The typical pattern, however, is for me to meet with clients each week for two hours or so in the early weeks, and somewhat less frequently as time goes on—perhaps two or three times a month. Sometimes there are longer sessions in the beginning of a coaching relationship. Most of these meetings will be in my office but some will be in his office location. Inevitably there also are telephone sessions and e-mail exchanges.

It will be essential to meet with Peter's manager, Athena. It may also be appropriate for me to meet with or talk by phone with others in GIB, as agreed by Peter and myself.

Periodic "progress" reports will be communicated to you and/or Athena, with the understanding that the content of the coaching conversations will remain confidential to Peter and myself.

The fee for the coaching is $xxx. I prefer to submit one invoice, approximately a month into the engagement.

These are the major items for our Agreement. If you wish me to sign a Nondisclosure Agreement, I'll be pleased to do so.

Please let me know if you have questions about this Agreement. I look forward to working with you!

Sincerely,

Roberta

Exhibit 4. (Chapter 5) Sample proposal

Mitch Evans, Ph.D.
Executive Coach
18 West Avenue
New York, NY 10001

Date

Ron Smith, Controller &
Laurie Franks, Director HR
XYZ Capital
1 West 50th Street
New York, NY 10020

Dear Ron and Laurie:

I really enjoyed meeting with both of you this morning to discuss the possibility of providing leadership coaching to Ron. I have been providing coaching services to managers and executives for over 20 years and have a 30-year career as an organizational psychologist (you have my biosketch). I am currently engaged in a variety of coaching assignments in financial services companies.

As Ron and I discussed, he has a long-standing commitment to his professional growth and development but has not had formal courses on leadership or management. In addition, he would like help in expanding his managerial repertoire so that he can be more direct when the situation requires it. His openness to learning coupled with his awareness of areas he would like to work on are very positive predictors of growth through coaching. In addition, it may be useful for Ron to attend a leadership development or managerial skill course, possibly later this year, which would build on his progress in coaching.

I will use this letter to outline steps and fees for the type of coaching program that Ron and I discussed. For clarity, I have separated coaching into two connected phases, with a third phase of follow-up support to be structured later. The initial two phases are: *1. Relationship Building and Needs Assessment 2. Active Coaching. Each is described below.*

1. Relationship Building and Needs Assessment

This phase includes the following steps (some steps could overlap):

- Assuming Ron and I are in agreement to proceed, we would meet again to confirm steps in the coaching process and discuss in more detail his career, challenges, strengths, gaps, and aspirations to begin shaping possible development themes and action ideas
- I would interview Ron's manager, Bill, to gather his perspective about Ron's strengths and development areas
- Coaching often taps peers and direct reports to get the most complete picture of how the client is viewed so I would also interview Ron's direct reports and a sample of peers and internal clients
- If there is interest, I can also provide standardized assessments to Ron using

Exhibit 4. (Chapter 5) Sample proposal (continued)

tools such as the MBTI (Myers-Briggs Type Indicator) to add to the self-insight process

- I would analyze the results of the interviews and other information and distill themes into a feedback summary, which would be presented to Ron for a thorough discussion
- Based on that information, Ron and I would draft a development action plan aimed at strengthening and broadening his leadership style. It would identify 2–3 key development goals as well as on-the-job action ideas to make progress on those goals
- We would share that draft development plan with HR and Bill to reach consensus and get everyone's active support for implementing Ron's development efforts

> This phase would involve 12–18 professional hours (the range reflects unknowns about numbers of interviews and other elements). Fees: XXX

2. Active Coaching

Building upon the development plan, this phase increases developmental activity:

- Ron and I would meet biweekly (every other week) for coaching meetings of 1–2 hours each, in a conference room at XYZ
- The focus of these meetings would be to make progress on the developmental objectives by implementing the action ideas outlined in the development plan; support for and adjustments in action ideas would also be made to take advantage of emerging situations
- Discussions would focus on the application of new self-insight and management tactics, approaches to current work challenges, adjustments in leadership style, overcoming challenges, and other topics
- I would be available to Ron via phone and e-mail for just-in-time consultation on management, leadership, or other questions that arise
- I am prepared to teach management, leadership, and other skills that support the changes envisioned in the plan
- I would recommend management and leadership books and other materials as helpful adjuncts to the development plan; management and leadership courses would also be identified
- Regular contacts by me with HR and Bill to get feedback on progress and understand any emerging organizational issues relevant to Ron

> Assuming an overall six-month timeframe for both phases, this phase would involve 15–20 professional hours. Fees: XXX

3. Follow-up Support

A supportive follow-up phase is often part of coaching. It usually involves a less intensive schedule between coach and client while still providing guidance and

Continues on page 258

Exhibit 4. (Chapter 5) Sample proposal (continued)

support. It can be structured in many different ways (e.g., monthly meetings, phone contact, quarterly meetings, e-mail). We can determine how to structure this phase to meet Ron's and the organization's needs and interests when we are closer to it.

This would be especially important after Ron attends a leadership development course, possibly later this year, that would build on his progress in coaching. Follow-up coaching would help him assimilate the learning from the course and apply it to his leadership responsibilities. Such a course would also be useful in evaluating his progress on development since it usually includes a 360-degree survey as pre-work.

I prefer to invoice monthly for direct professional time rendered in my coaching work and my invoices describe the work that was performed during the past month. I invoice using my company name and would be happy to provide whatever information is required for your vendor system, including signing a W-9 and Non-Disclosure Agreement (NDA). The upper limit of the estimated range for each phase is calculated based on my hourly rate and represents a ceiling; unless we were to discuss special circumstances, you could assume that hours and fees would not exceed that amount and may in fact be lower, depending on progress.

The only items not included in the fees above are: 1. out-of-pocket expenses associated with travel or other direct expenditures (assessments, books, etc.), 2. actual time I am required to travel to deliver coaching services, and 3. appointments canceled on short notice. Here is how I handle each of these: 1. Out-of-pocket expenses, such as test fees, travel, and meals are simply included on my invoices with the required documentation. For work in Manhattan there would be no travel expenses. 2. For my travel time, my practice is to invoice for half of the actual time I am in transit, after the first 30 minutes each way. In other words, there are no fees for normal commutation to the client's site in Manhattan. 3. Finally, I reserve the right to charge, based on my hourly rate, for appointments canceled on short notice (less than a week). Should any of these 3 items apply, they would be in addition to the fees outlined above for delivering the coaching services.

The contents of all coaching conversations, feedback reports, and assessment results are confidential between Ron and me. The development plan, however, is not confidential and is meant as a guide for all parties invested in Ron's development. Obviously, I would seek regular contact with Bill and HR to gain views on Ron's progress and discuss ways in which to support that progress.

I hope this proposal letter adequately outlines the executive coaching that Ron and I discussed. Let me know if any questions arise. I am prepared to begin working with Ron in the next week, pending the appropriate approvals.

I look forward to working with XYZ on Ron's development.

Sincerely,

Mitch Evans, Ph.D.

Exhibit 5. (Chapter 10) Verbatim feedback report

CONFIDENTIAL

Informational Interviews on Behalf of Rachel Munez

NOTE: In choosing to use verbatim comments made by participants across perspectives in the informational interviews, the coach believed it was important for Rachel to hear the frequency and consistency of positive comments and suggestions. The coach noticed that Rachel, while competent in her work, had a consistent thread of self-doubt and displayed a lack of confidence. The coach believed that hearing the exact words rather than summarizing or consolidating responses would be the best way to show Rachel that others not only believed in her, but wanted more of her observed effective behaviors. The perspectives of Group #1 Colleagues/Internal Clients, Group #2 Senior Managers/Leaders, and Group #3 Her Direct Manager were virtually the same and also reported to her verbatim.

What are the activities or areas where Rachel functions most effectively? What would you like to see continue?

In what areas are there opportunities for Rachel become more effective? What are areas for improvement?

Suggestions/Professional Development In what new areas would you like Rachel to get involved or further leverage her skills?

GROUPS #1, 2, and 3

Strengths/Effective

- Go-to person for problem resolution, having created comfortable and direct relationships
- Takes care of problems: gathers facts; walks through the process; provides emotional support
- Relates well to employees and managers; makes others feel comfortable around her
- Makes it seem like you can go to her for anything; not intimidating
- Clearly maintains confidentiality; listens well; good sounding board
- Reacts quickly to concerns and needs; very responsive in person and e-mails
- Her responses show concern and interest
- Has a strong focus on the organization and what's important
- Easy to reach out to, to talk to, and trust even if have differences
- Checks out the buzz; asks about what might be less visible to her and what managers are hearing
- Follows up; explores, plans, conducts thorough due diligence; gets back to you
- Probes others' thinking
- High professionalism; demonstrates honesty and integrity beyond reproach
- Gives feedback that is useful and without judgment; strong at having difficult conversations; can deliver tough information sensitively and in the least hurtful way
- Shows patience with frequent conversations; encourages opinions and stretch
- Friendly and open to casual conversation, which can lead to additional guidance/suggestions

Exhibit 5. (Chapter 10) Verbatim feedback report (continued)

- Acknowledges strengths in others; helps them feel important and encourages contributions
- Inspiring and a model for tough yet compassionate work
- Aggressive in dealing with knotty issues
- Nonjudgmental, open, accessible, and interested
- Assesses tough situations; explores alternatives; and involves the manager and employee in seeking solutions
- Diplomatic and takes the middle ground, balancing the company's interest and mine
- Helps clarification of goals; guides and advises in reaching a solution
- Counsels managers to be more effective in handling individuals (who are new to the organization and those around a long time)
- Conducts herself objectively; doesn't seem to allow friendships to get in her way
- Creates trust and confidence and respects confidentiality
- Provides concise, well-defined advice
- Creates an atmosphere of warmth, comfort, and uses humor; interacts on professional level that is also casual, fun, and welcoming
- Gives clear presentations reflecting preparation; fields questions
- Demonstrates positive forward thinking and collaboration
- Brings a level-headed perspective; sensitively helps manager work through challenging situations
- Checks in with managers to see what may be cropping up

Areas to Become More Effective
- Could be more proactive/frequent in checking out if there are unaddressed wants and needs
- Meet even more frequently with managers to provide more unsolicited but helpful feedback to managers
- Can help me in defining more junior people's skill sets
- Because of her talent making sense of issues, it would be nice if she could spend more time learning and checking on subtle staff needs and issues and raising them with managers
- Informally get to know the staff more to create more access and further enhance services

Suggestions/Professional Development
- Continue being out there and knowing what's going on within the organization
- Use more of her capacity for providing support
- Create more opportunities to work with managers to uncover areas in which she can be additionally helpful
- Might be more deliberate and frequent checking in with managers
- Manage expectations on big projects—clarify status; give more frequent updates
- Raise self-confidence level while working on new initiatives

Exhibit 6. (Chapter 10) Feedback summary

Personal and Confidential

Feedback Summary
Thomas Jones
Large Company Inc.
September 2010

This summary is based on 14 confidential interviews conducted by your executive coach: 5 were with outside Board members, plus the Chairman of the Board, and 8 were with members of the Executive Committee. On average, interviews lasted 45 minutes. A consistent interview format was utilized that focused on strengths to continue leveraging, gaps or areas to improve, as well as targeted questions about fostering greater teamwork and key short-term priorities. Interpretations are derived as closely as possible from interview content, consistent with capturing insights and protecting individual interviewee identities.

Unless noted, themes were highly consistent across all interviewees.

Strengths to Continue Leveraging

- Embraces COMPANY history and committed to maintaining the COMPANY culture
- Deep operational experience and project management expertise
- Tough minded re project plans and budgets
- Analytical; considers issues logically and thoroughly
- Willing to face tough organizational decisions fairly and in a timely manner
- Honest, credible, trustworthy; puts the well-being of COMPANY as a whole first
- Steady, stable, and dependable; stays the course and reduces risk
- Open to learning and addressing areas for professional growth
- Command attention; executive bearing

There were many unsolicited comments about trust and respect for you. While this has been a difficult period of time, there was unequivocal support for your leadership.

Gaps or Areas to Improve for Enhanced Effectiveness

Nonetheless, interviewees were very forthcoming with suggestions about how to fulfill your role. Not surprisingly, under this topic outside Board members had a somewhat different focus than the Executive Committee members, which can be summarized as external/big picture vs. internal leadership style issues. The Board emphasized the first four bullets while the Executive Committee emphasized the second four bullets, but feedback overall was highly consistent.

- Shape the vision of the future COMPANY and the resulting medium to long-range plans.

Exhibit 6. (Chapter 10) Feedback summary (continued)

- Shift focus from US operations to Global COMPANY ventures; must fully delegate leadership of the areas you know best.
- Represent COMPANY in industry, customer, and professional associations and meetings.
- Increase market and marketing focus in extending COMPANY's reach to customers.
- Decision process could be more collaborative by having more give-and-take during discussions and more iteration as your views are being formed.
- More often choose relationship building rather than progress on your own tasks; take advantage of opportunities to interact with others even if unscheduled or informal.
- Channel your frustration and disappointment into words about the gaps between what you expected and what you got; angry e-mails, voicemails, or public "dressing downs" drive others away.
- Reach out and seek help on areas that would benefit from input and/or are not strengths (e.g., overseas ventures, and other thorny issues); such input can come from many sources including internal staff, outside Board members, outside advisers.

Exhibit 7. (Chapter 11) Sample development plan

Confidential

Kile Smith
Director, Systems Development
Big Bank USA, Inc.

This document is based on data-gathering interviews, standardized self-development questionnaires, and information supplied directly by Kile to provide a foundation for growth and development.

Strengths

- Intellectually quick; grasps details rapidly and thoroughly
- Analytical skills in evaluating alternatives; logical
- Grasps the big-picture view of projects; strategic
- Savvy understanding of business applications; financial rationale (ROI)
- Accountable; committed to delivering results; gets things done
- Project management skills: tasks, dates, paths, and stakeholders
- Able to partner with others; collaborative problem-solving skills (with some inconsistency)
- High standards for self and others
- Concise communication; gets to the point efficiently

Development Goals and Representative Actions

I. Upgrade skills in managing the performance of others.

Start/Increase:

- When work is delegated, contract with direct report about due dates, check points, and deliverables; conduct this contracting as a discussion and hear out concerns even if there is little flex in expectations
- Adjust your delegation style to fit the readiness of the direct report for the task, shifting from hands-off empowerment to closely monitored/directive as indicated by Situational Leadership
- To the extent possible, explicitly link assignments to a direct report's gaps, interests, or career aspirations; where possible, make clear the developmental value of an assignment
- When your expectations are disappointed, provide timely and frank feedback to direct reports; listen to their reactions and together shape an improvement plan
- When priorities change or unanticipated tasks infringe on already contracted work, discuss overt adjustments in the commitments made; agree on new time frames
- Provide a big-picture perspective for task or project goals
- Acknowledge accomplishments one-on-one and as a group

Exhibit 7. (Chapter 11) Sample development plan (continued)

Stop/Reduce:
- Criticizing or making comments that could be interpreted to undermine direct reports when others are present
- Ignoring changes in priorities that have delayed attention to contracted tasks
- Dictating how something should be done when there are multiple acceptable paths; overcontrol

II. Consistently build collaborative relationships.

Start/Increase:
- Get to know others beyond the essentials for task delivery.
- Signal your approachability with both verbal and nonverbal cues, especially with new team members and those you haven't worked with before.
- Consider the extent to which your e- and voice-mail messages invite involvement or distance others from you.
- Where possible, expand your contacts by talking with people you don't know well.
- Apply active listening skills to explore others' points of view, and keep an open mind to new ideas, even when in your own thinking you favor a particular approach.
- When others have not lived up to your standards, use listening skills to understand rather than judge them; at the same time, express your reactions honestly using "I" language.
- Monitor your stress/fatigue; try to ameliorate feelings of high pressure/stress, especially anticipating situations not under your control.
- Push back/renegotiate priorities when unexpected but important work disrupts previously made plans; avoid repeatedly sacrificing work/life balance.

Stop/Decrease:
- Nonverbal cues that signal frustration or anger
- Verbal tone or comments that imply blame and negative judgment
- Clipped, demanding, "all business" interactions with others

Exhibit 8. (Chapter 11) Sample development plan

DEVELOPMENT OPPORTUNITY PLAN: BY VICTORIA DEAN
OCTOBER 20XX

DEVELOPMENT OPPORTUNITY	FEEDBACK I WANT TO ADDRESS	BEHAVIORS TO FURTHER DEVELOP AND PRACTICE
Communication Pay attention to how things are said, contemplating how unintended interpretations or reactions can be avoided	"Can take a less demanding, less harsh tone in both oral and written communications" "Can be more supportive in giving direct feedback" "Under pressure, watch for tendency to be caustic and directive/demanding and too succinct"	• Focus on understanding others, before confirming that they understand me • Work to ensure I understand others' points of view, indicate what I agree with before expressing my doubts, if any, and reasons why • When feeling that I do not agree with someone, look to replace "I don't agree" or "That's not correct" with "I have some concerns/questions." • Prior to sending, take time to review e-mails to ensure that they are not harsh or demanding in tone
Collaboration Develop more collaborative and informal relationships with direct reports, peers, and other executives	"Work more on building close working relationships "Let more of the personal aspect come out; initiate informal contact" "Notice impact on others" "Continue building relationships at more levels"	• Increase use of open-ended questions including words such as "elaborate," "compare," "illustrate," to encourage in-depth exchanges of information and to make conversations livelier • Identify key individuals for relationship building • Utilize more face-to-face discussions of issues as opposed to e-mail • Focus on initiating more informal conversations, in public areas and by stopping into offices of others • Seek guidance (a mentor) to help with expanding executive presence and to negotiate with a positive posture • Continue to develop personal/trusting relationships through informal conversations, speaking highly of individuals when appropriate

Exhibit 8. (Chapter 11) Sample development plan (continued)

DEVELOPMENT OPPORTUNITY PLAN: BY VICTORIA DEAN
OCTOBER 20XX

DEVELOPMENT OPPORTUNITY	FEEDBACK I WANT TO ADDRESS	BEHAVIORS TO FURTHER DEVELOP AND PRACTICE
Acknowledgment of Others Find a range of ways to recognize/involve staff	"Regularly keep team more closely apprised of company-wide initiatives/status" "Delegate responsibility with even more accountability" "Allow people to feel even more empowered"	• Include informal, but important mention of employee's significant personal accomplishments at the monthly staff meetings • Give more frequent specific and direct feedback to junior staff regarding their work accomplishments • Include staff in more strategic and policy meetings • Work on assigning stretch projects that provide visibility for staff members

Exhibit 9. (Chapter 11) Sample development plan

		My Developmental Plan				Dec 20XX
Continue to make a significant contribution to SSS Corp						
What areas do I want to develop?	Actions I will take	Resources and Support	Obstacles	How will I know I am making progress?	Where do I need to be most aware?	What is my target date for completion?
To become more present with others	• Keep goals in forefront • Stay present with people • Keep longer horizon in focus • Take more time to observe • Pay attention to details • Continual creativity • Take things less personally	Jeff Greene Harry Gable My staff	• Schedule too hectic • Not enough downtime • Too many priorities Rx: Pause more. Step back. Remember goals	• Better quality of life • Better decisions • Higher morale of associates • Better trusting relationships with peers • Sought after as a resource	• XXX staff meetings • Client staff meetings	04/02/2011
Become a facilitator rather than controller	• Increase receptivity to future ideas • Take time to listen to others • Set up regular team member meetings • Trust that others can make wise calls	My team leaders	• Tight deadlines • Lack of trust in direct reports Rx: Step back and have candid dialog	• Better team morale, better results and more trusting relationships • More receptive to ideas • Better coaching opportunities	• My staff meetings • Technical meetings • When I lead a project • Engineering meetings	Continual
Improve mentoring	• Spend more time with LX • More frequent check-ins (proper timing) • Investments in staff training • Less telling, more asking • Provide stretch assignments • Provide empathic listening	Direct Reports Regional Managers Staff	• Hectic schedule • Lack of knowledge • Jumping to conclusions Rx: Gain knowledge, ask more questions	• More opportunity for their advancement • Better results • Improved trust	Throughout	12/12/11
Improve listening	• Stay focused on one task at a time • Do not always have to provide a solution • Give others time to think • Stay open to new ideas	Direct Reports Staff Members Peers	• Multiple priorities • Not being open-minded • Short-term focus Rx: Prioritize: Urgent or important	• Better decisions • Better results • Better team involvement	Throughout	Continual
Strategic thinking / planning	• Slow down to speed up • Delegate day-to-day issues more • 5–10 year time frame • Dedicate one day a month to just think about the future	Vicki Schneider Lorraine Schultz	• Day-to-day business • Economic stresses • Structural changes Rx: Prioritize and slow down	• Team buy-in and increased alignment	• Monthly assessment	Monthly

Notes

Chapter 3: Foundations and Definitions

1. Mary Beth O'Neill, *Executive Coaching with Backbone and Heart: A Systems Approach to Engaging Leaders with Their Challenges*, 2nd ed. (San Francisco: Jossey-Bass, 2007), 5.

2. David L. Dotlich and Peter C. Cairo, *Action Coaching: How to Leverage Individual Performance for Company Success* (San Francisco: Jossey-Bass, 1999), 18.

3. James Flaherty, *Coaching: Evoking Excellence in Others*, 2nd ed. (Burlington, MA: Butterworth-Heinemann, 2005), xviii and 9.

4. Robert Hargrove, *Masterful Coaching*, 3rd ed (San Francisco: Jossey-Bass, 2008), 17.

5. Eric de Haan and Yvonne Burger, *Coaching with Colleagues: An Action Guide to One-to-One Learning* (Hampshire, UK: Palgrave Macmillan, 2005), 5.

6. Richard R. Kilburg. "When Shadows Fall: Using Psychodynamic Approaches in Executive Coaching," *Consulting Psychology Journal: Practice and Research* 56, no. 4 (2004), 246–68; Manfred Kets De Vries, Konstantin Korotov, and Elizabeth Florent-Treacy, *Coach and Couch: The Psychology of Making Better Leaders* (New York: Palgrave Macmillan, 2007); and Harry Levinson,' "Executive Coaching," *Consulting Psychology Journal: Practice and Research* 48, no. 2 (1996), 115–23.

7. Daniel J. Levinson, Charlotte N. Darrow, Edward Klein, Maria H. Levinson, and Braxton McKee, *The Seasons of a Man's Life* (New York: Ballantine Books; 1978), and Steven D. Axelrod, "Executive Growth Along the Adult Development Curve," *Consulting Psychology Journal: Practice and Research* 57, no. 2 (2005), 118–25.

8. Marshall Goldsmith and Laurence Lyons. *Coaching for Leadership*, 2nd ed. (San Francisco: Pfeiffer, 2006).

9. Daniel Goleman, Richard Boyatzis, and Annie McKee, *Primal Leadership: Realizing the Importance of Emotional Intelligence* (Boston: Harvard University Press, 2002), and Martin E. P. Seligman. *Authentic Happiness: Using the New Positive Psychology to Realize Your Potential for Lasting Fulfillment* (New York: Free Press, 2002).

10. Flaherty, *Coaching: Evoking Excellence in Others.*

11. Daniel White, *Coaching Leaders: Guiding People Who Guide Others* (San Francisco: Jossey-Bass, 2005); and David B. Peterson and J. Miller, "The Alchemy of Coaching: 'You're Good, Jennifer, but You Could Be Really Good,'" *Consulting Psychology Journal: Practice and Research* 57, no. 1 (2005), 14–40.

12. For learning models, Eric de Haan, *Relational Coaching: Journeys Towards Mastering One-to-One Learning* (West Sussex, UK: John Wiley & Sons, 2008); for system approaches, O'Neill, *Executive Coaching with Backbone and Heart.*

Chapter 7: Building Early Relationships with Clients

1. D. D. McKenna and S. L. Davis, "Hidden in Plain Sight: The Active Ingredients of Executive Coaching," *Industrial and Organizational Psychology; Perspectives on Science and Practice* 2, no. 3 (2009), p. 244–60.

2. C. C. DiClemente and J. O. Prochaska, "Toward a Comprehensive, Transtheoretical Model of Change," in *Treating Addictive Behaviors*, 2nd edition, ed. W. R. Miller and N. Heather (New York: Plenum Press, 1998), pp. 3–24.

3. William R. Miller and Stephen Rollnick, *Motivational Interviewing: Preparing People for Change*, 2nd ed. (New York: Guildford Press, 2002).

Chapter 12: Encouraging Dialogue and Stories

1. Dan P. McAdams, *The Stories We Live By* (New York: Guilford, 1993).

Chapter 13: Strengthening the Partnership

1. McKenna and Davis, "Hidden in Plain Sight," 244–60.

Chapter 15: Coaching for Leadership

1. Sarah N. King, David G. Altman, and Robert J. Lee, *Discovering the Leader in You*, 2nd ed. (San Francisco: Wiley, 2011).

2. Lori Silverman, *Wake Me When the Data Is Over: How Organizations Use Storytelling to Drive Results* (San Francisco: Jossey- Bass, 2006).

3. Robert E. Kaplan and Robert B. Kaiser, *The Versatile Leader* (San Francisco: Pfeiffer, 2006).

Chapter 17: Closure

1. Martin E. P. Seligman, *Authentic Happiness* (New York: Free Press, 2002).

Chapter 18: What Happened: Self-Reflection and Evaluation

1. Donald L. Kirkpatrick, "Evaluating Training Programs: Evidence vs. Proof," *Training and Development Journal* 31 (1977), 9–12.

2. Kenneth P. De Meuse, Guangrong Dai, and Robert J. Lee, "Evaluating the Effectiveness of Executive Coaching: Beyond ROI?" *Coaching: An International Journal of Theory, Research, and Practice* 2, no. 2 (2009), 118–35.

Chapter 19: Professionalism and Responsibility

1. Michael H. Frisch. "Coaching Caveats Part 1: Characteristics of the Organization," *Human Resource Planning* 28, no. 2 (2005), 13–15; and Michael H. Frisch, "Coaching Caveats Part 2: Characteristics of the Coachee," *Human Resource Planning* 28, no. 3 (2005), 14–16.

Chapter 20: The Role of the Internal Coach

1. Michael H. Frisch, "The Emerging Role of the Internal Coach," *Consulting Psychology Journal: Practice and Research* 53, no. 4 (Autumn 2001), 240–50.

Chapter 24: Becoming an Exceptional Executive Coach: Amber's Story

1. Amber's story is a fictional composite of student experiences in becoming executive coaches; quotes are invented. Like all stories, some of Amber's story reflects her individuality, since coaching encompasses a diverse population. Largely, however, her experience of becoming an executive coach is typical and intended to illustrate key milestones along that journey.

Glossary

ACTION PLANS Specific, on-the-job actions to be taken by a client to make progress toward development objectives; they focus on new behaviors and other actions that can be applied in the context of day-to-day work but may also include suggestions for courses, readings, and other development activities.

ASSESSMENT CERTIFICATION Formal training in how to administer and interpret a particular assessment tool, with certification of satisfactory completion usually under the auspices of the publisher of the tool and covers the uses and limitations of particular assessment; for some tools, certification is required in order to purchase and use it with clients.

ASSESSMENT INTERPRETATION Using the results of an assessment tool to make inferences about a client's work style, interpersonal approach, or other characteristics with on-the-job implications.

ASSESSMENT TOOL OR INSTRUMENT Researched questionnaire eliciting perceptions of oneself (self-report) and/or others' feedback about a client (multirater assessments); when results are analyzed, the tool or instrument yields a structured report about a client using concepts and terminology unique to that instrument; available from assessment publishing and consulting firms with appropriate certification.

CLIENT In a coaching context, usually refers to the person in the relationship with the coach seeking professional growth and the focus of the coach's efforts.

CONFIDENTIALITY The safeguarding of privileged client information: oral, written, and electronic; in coaching, there must be a clear understanding of what information can be shared with sponsors since all else would be considered confidential.

CONTAINMENT A broad construct that includes confidentiality, coach self-management, case supervision, and coach knowledge of coaching practices, all aimed at creating a safe and supportive process for client learning and development.

CONTRACTING Process undertaken early in coaching in which coach, sponsors, and client reach consensus about the coaching process, the roles of key participants such as the manager and the client, mutual expectations, assessment tools, milestones and confidentiality.

DEVELOPMENT PLANNING After assessment steps have been completed and results are interpreted coach and client identify key themes or development objectives and then brainstorm action plans for each objective and record the results as a written draft.

DEVELOPMENT PLANNING SKILLS A skill set that includes interpretation of assessment results, insight into the client and the client's situation, articulation of key themes that represent compelling growth objectives for the client, and suggestion of practical on-the-job actions that will further the client's development goals.

DEVELOPMENT THEMES OR GOALS Fairly broad, positive, behavioral statements (e.g., "Build stronger relationships with peers," or "Dedicate more time to coach and develop direct report team") that articulate where the coach and client agree there is the most payback from invested developmental effort; sometimes referred to as *designed objectives*.

EMPATHY The ability to imagine oneself in another person's situation and feel what the other person might be feeling; an important element of emotional intelligence.

EXECUTIVE COACHING A one-to-one development process formally contracted between a professional coach, an organization, and an individual client who has people management and/or team responsibility, to increase the client's managerial and/or leadership performance, often using feedback processes and on-the-job action learning.

FACILITATION SKILLS A broader term for active listening skills, as in drawing out and helping to expand the ideas of others, using both verbal and nonverbal skills; the goal of facilitation is to help people fully express themselves.

FEEDBACK SKILLS Skills and sensibilities in selecting and phrasing interpretations of assessment results or other observations so that they can be understood by a client and motivate the client to reach conclusions about strengths and development areas.

INFLUENCING SKILLS The ability to present observations and interpretations in ways that persuade others as to their relevance; motivating efforts to change behavior; although a very broad topic, in the coaching context, influencing often involves overcoming defensive or deflective responses to difficult feedback.

INTERNAL COACHING A one-to-one development intervention provided by an employee of the same organization of those who are coached and formally supported by organizational policy and guidelines; internal coaches are empowered to design and deliver programs aimed at individual professional growth, although usually at different levels or containing different features than typical executive coaching engagements.

LIFE or PERSONAL COACHING Similar process to executive coaching except it is contracted and funded directly by the client without sponsor or stakeholder involvement and the goals may or may not be work-related.

PRESENTING ISSUE In coaching, the initial concern(s) described by sponsors or clients that motivated them to seek coaching; often rephrased and made more specific and actionable during the early stages of coaching; sometimes referred to as a *felt need*.

PSYCHOLOGICAL CURIOSITY A basic interest in understanding why people do what they do; an important capacity for coaches and useful in clients.

SHADOWING Contracted process whereby the coach observes the client in day-to-day meetings and other leadership activities for the purpose of providing immediate feedback as well as evaluating progress on development goals.

SPONSOR(S) Usually refers to those within an organization who contract with the coach to provide services to the client; usually the client's manager and human resources representative. In larger organizations, sponsors may include those involved in managing the use of coaches or talent development processes.

SPONSOR MANAGEMENT SKILLS Experience and skills in keeping in touch with sponsors during a coaching engagement; getting information and observations from sponsors and sharing contracted information such as progress reports and development plans.

STAKEHOLDERS General term for colleagues of the client who have an interest in the client's development and may be included in the data gathering about the client and in the follow-up to evaluate progress on the development plan; stakeholders might include the client's direct reports, peers, internal customers, among others.

SUPERVISION In coaching, a more experienced coach guiding less experienced coaches, usually through case review discussions, primarily to aid the growth of the coach but also to benefit the cases under discussion; supervisors are bound by the same confidentiality commitments made by coaches to their clients.

For Further Reading

Books

Bacon, Terry R., and Karen I. Spear. *Adaptive Coaching*. Mountain View, CA: Davies-Black Publishing, 2003.

> *The authors present models of communication between coach and client written in an accessible style. Their coaching process reflects effective coaching practices and includes many examples, both for executive coaches and for managerial coaching.*

de Haan, Eric. *Relational Coaching: Journeys Towards Mastering One-to-One Learning*. West Sussex, UK: John Wiley & Sons, 2008.

> *Eric de Haan tackles the core questions in coaching: Why it works, what the critical moments are, and how coaching looks from the client's perspective. He has an engaging chapter on the continuing development of coaches.*

de Haan, Eric, and Yvonne Burger. *Coaching with Colleagues: An Action Guide to One-to-One Learning*. Hampshire, UK: Palgrave Macmillan, 2005.

> *This book provides impressive insights into how coaching conversations can be helpful. The authors review several major approaches to coaching and conclude with chapters on a coach's capabilities, learning challenges, and the limits of coaching one's colleagues. Their scope is wider than executive coaching.*

Flaherty, James. *Coaching: Evoking Excellence in Others*. 2nd ed. Burlington, MA: Butterworth-Heinemann, 2005.

> *Flaherty's approach to coaching is based on insights about human existence, as applied to executives. Some coaches absolutely love this approach, and others find it confusing because it throws a very wide philosophical net around coaching.*

Hargrove, Robert. *Masterful Coaching*. 3rd ed. San Francisco: Jossey-Bass, 2008.

> *This is a popular text, well written and comprehensive. Hargrove emphasizes a "transformational" approach that encompasses elements of an executive's total life.*

Kilburg, Richard R. *Executive Coaching: Developing Managerial Wisdom in a World of Chaos*. Washington, DC: American Psychological Association, 2000.

> *Kilburg's text is a very thoughtful integration of psychodynamic and systems theories as applied to executive coaching. Insightful but challenging to absorb.*

O'Neill, Mary Beth. *Executive Coaching with Backbone and Heart: A Systems Approach to Engaging Leaders with Their Challenges*. 2nd ed. San Francisco: Jossey-Bass, 2007.

> *This well-received popular text on coaching offers good, practical advice for the new coach. O'Neill places coaching within the context of other organization development activities.*

Underhill, Brian O., Kimcee McAnally, and John J Koriath. *Executive Coaching for Results: The Definitive Guide to Developing Organizational Leaders*. San Francisco: Berrett-Koehler Publishers, 2007.

> *Based on their consulting experiences, the authors offer a useful overview of the coaching field, with handy summaries and tables—all in an efficient format.*

Valerio, Anna Marie, and Robert J. Lee. *Executive Coaching: A Guide for the HR Professional.* San Francisco: Pfeiffer, 2005.

This is a practical guide for people involved in coaching—the coach, the client, and the organizational sponsor. Highly practical, it contains useful samples and lists, as well as five first-person stories from clients.

White, Daniel. *Coaching Leaders: Guiding People Who Guide Others.* San Francisco: Jossey-Bass, 2005.

This book is a comprehensive text for learning to be a coach. It includes many examples and short cases. There is good explanation in here of the cognitive-behavioral approach to coaching.

Whitmore, John. *Coaching for Performance: GROWing Human Potential and Purpose: The Principles and Practice of Coaching and Leadership.* 4th ed. London: Nicholas Brealey Publishing, 2009.

Whitmore's first edition was one of the pioneering books in the coaching field in 1992. His GROW model is simple and applies to many types of coaching conversations.

Articles and Excerpts

Kilburg, Richard. "Individual Interventions in Consulting Psychology." In *The California School of Organization Studies Handbook of Organizational Consulting Psychology: A Comprehensive Guide to Theory, Skills, and Techniques,* edited by Rodney Lowman. San Francisco: Jossey-Bass, 2002.

Kilburg's chapter is a very thoughtful analysis of how coaching reflects the issues of consulting at the individual level. He examines human development, emotions, diagnostics, supervision, and related topics.

Peterson, David B. "Executive Coaching: A Critical Review and Recommendations for Advancing the Practice." In *APA Handbook of Industrial and Organizational Psychology,* edited by Sheldon Zedeck, PhD. Washington, DC: American Psychological Association, 2010.

Peterson's chapter is a review of what has been happening in the coaching field and within a coaching relationship. The literature review is extensive, and the critiques are incisive.

Ting, Sharon, and E. Wayne Hart. "Formal Coaching." In *Center for Creative Leadership Handbook of Leadership Development,* edited by Cynthia McCauley and Ellen van Velsor. San Francisco: Jossey-Bass, 2004.

This chapter provides a succinct framework for formal coaching by expanding the Center for Creative Leadership's well-known development model into a coaching model. The authors outline a practical approach to assessment and feedback.

Edited Collections

Broom, Gina Hernez, and Lisa A. Boyce, eds. *Advancing Executive Coaching: Setting the Course for Successful Leadership Coaching* (JosseyBass SIOP Professional Practice Series). San Francisco: Pfeiffer, 2011.

A collection of chapters, each written by coaching experts addressing major topics in executive coaching. Comprehensive treatment of the field.

Fitzgerald, Catherine, and Jennifer Garvey Berger, eds. *Executive Coaching: Practices and Perspectives.* Palo Alto, CA: Davies-Black, 2002.

Over a dozen experienced coaches address important issues in coaching, such as being a reflective practitioner, coaching senior executives, setting up coaching within organizations, and working with entrepreneurs.

Goldsmith, Marshall, and Laurence S. Lyons, eds. *Coaching for Leadership: The Practice of Leadership Coaching from the World's Greatest Coaches.* 2nd ed. San Francisco: Pfeiffer, 2006:

The twenty-six chapters in this book are by a range of professionals with business, leadership development, and consulting backgrounds, as well as a number of professional executive coaches. Several of the chapters reflect Goldsmith's own approach to coaching.

Kilburg, Richard, PhD, and Richard Diedrich, PhD, eds. *The Wisdom of Coaching: Essential Papers in Consulting Psychology for a World of Change.* Washington, DC: American Psychological Association, 2007.

This coffee-table-size collection reprints many of the coaching articles from Consulting Psychology Journal *from 1996 through 2007. The thirty-nine articles explore definitions, approaches, and challenges, and offer case studies from seven practitioners.*

Coaching Psychology Resources

Palmer, Stephen, and Alison Whybrow. *Handbook of Coaching Psychology: A Guide for Practitioners.* Oxford, UK: Routledge, 2008.

Peltier, Bruce. *The Psychology of Executive Coaching: Theory and Application.* 2nd ed. Oxford, UK: Routledge, 2001.

These two books published by Routledge each review the field of psychology and show how various theories and approaches apply to executive coaching.

Journals

Coaching at Work. A UK-based online and print magazine that provides articles, an up-to-date reference archive, practical tips, and a place to exchange news and views on coaching.

Consulting Psychology Journal. The quarterly publication of the Society of Consulting Psychology, which is Division 13 of the American Psychological Association, has been publishing important articles about coaching since about 1996.

International Coaching Psychology Review. This international journal focuses on theory, practice, and research in the field of coaching psychology. It includes research reports and systematic reviews of the literature.

International Journal of Coaching in Organizations. IJCO is a forum for professional coaches focused on the disciplined practice of coaching within organizations. Published quarterly.

Other Resources

The Coaching Commons (www.coachingcommons.org)

As the name implies, this online news site covers all types of coaching and can be informative and stimulating.

Index

About the Authors

Formed in 2004, iCoachNewYork is the organization through which the five authors collaborate to train executive coaches. This includes a three-month certificate-level course, the *Professional Coaching Program,* offered in conjunction with CUNY's Baruch College, and a graduate level course, *Coaching Theory and Practice* at New School University. iCoachNewYork also offers consultation and customized in-house programs for internal coaches and case supervision to support the ongoing development of executive coaches. Up-to-date information about offerings can be obtained from iCoachNewYork.com or by contacting any of the authors directly.

The five authors share long experience as executive coaches, commitment to coach training and development, and professional support for the field of executive coaching. Embodying the Personal Model concept, they differ in background, coaching styles, and coaching interests, as detailed in their bios below.

Michael H. Frisch, Ph.D. Prior to starting his current independent practice, Michael was Senior Consultant and Director of Coaching Services for Personnel Decisions International's (PDI) New York office. Earlier positions include Manager of Management Development for PepsiCo and consulting on leadership development, management training, feedback processes, and individual development planning. During the course of his career, Michael has presented to groups such as The Conference Board and the Human Resource Planning Society and published articles and book chapters on interviewing, performance management, assessment, internal coaching, and executive coaching. Michael received his Ph.D. in Industrial/Organizational Psychology from Rice University and his MS from Georgia Institute of Technology. He is a member of the Society for Industrial and Organizational Psychology, and the American Psychological Association, Divisions 13 and 14. Michael is a licensed psychologist in New York State. MFrischPhD@gmail.com

Robert J. Lee, Ph.D. Bob has been teaching, writing, and speaking on the topic of executive coaching since starting his coaching practice in New York City in 1997. In 2004, he was the prime mover in bringing the current authors together to form iCoachNewYork and create professional training programs for executive coaches that have led to the writing of this book. His prior role was President of the Center for Creative Leadership, the world's largest leadership development and research organization. Before that, Bob helped create and define the career services industry through his founding and then leadership roles with Lee Hecht Harrison. He has co-authored two prior books, *Discovering the Leader in You* [2nd Edition, Jossey-Bass, 2011] and *Executive Coaching: A Guide for the HR Professional* [Wiley/Pfeiffer, 2004]. He holds a Ph.D. in Industrial/Organizational Psychology from Case Western Reserve University and is a Fellow of the Society for Industrial and Organizational Psychology. Bob@BobLeeCoach.com

Karen L. Metzger, LCSW, has been an executive coach, management consultant, management trainer, and supervisor of coaches for many years. Her coaching clients range from high-potentials in leadership succession programs to senior-level executives at risk of derailing and cover a wide spectrum of industry sectors, not-for-profit organizations, and professional specialties. Formerly she was a Vice-President in the Human Resources department at Scudder Kemper Investments, providing internal coaching, consulting, and management development training design. She has also been on the professional staff at Lee Hecht Harrison and other career service firms. She has been a faculty member at the Hunter College School of Social Work and in 1998 she co-founded and has co-facilitated the Coaching Learning Group in New York City. Karen has an MSW degree from Columbia University and completed doctoral coursework at the City University of New York. Karen@KarenMetzger.com.

Jeremy Robinson, MSW, MCC, is a well-known coach and trainer/supervisor of executive coaches in New York City. He was co-creator and co-academic Director of the Wharton Executive Coaching Workshop at the Aresty Institute Executive Education Program at the University of Pennsylvania. Since 1999, he has been the Dean of the Executive Coach Academy. As a coach and coach trainer, Jeremy has specialized in using an Emotional Intelligence Behavioral model in working with his executive clients, many of whom are at the highest levels of their organizations. He also focuses on coaching African-American, Latino, and LGBT executives toward increasing their organizational influence and visibility. He has presented on executive coaching to the American Psychological Association, the Executive Coaching Summit, the Minority Corporate Counsel Annual Conference, and the International Coach Federation. He is a co-author of the Coaching Development Assessment (CDA), a coach self-development tool. He has a certificate in Psychoanalysis and Psychotherapy from the Postgraduate Center for Mental Health, as well as graduate degrees in Social Work and English Literature/Creative Writing. CEOCoachRobinson@gmail.com

Judy Rosemarin, MS, LMSW, is a highly experienced executive coach in the New York City area and has coached senior executives on topics such as leadership development, influential listening, and leadership story telling since 1983. She was the original *New York Post's* "Careers Plus" weekly columnist and continued in that role for six years, writing about career resilience and effective career management. Judy has had wide media exposure, has been quoted in the *Wall Street Journal,* and has been a featured guest on radio and television programs. Judy is an adjunct faculty member of New York University's School of Professional Studies. Building on her Influential Listening and Presentation Skills workshop, Judy has created the highly successful Humaway™ StoryTelling technique to increase leadership impact. Judy holds a Bachelor's Degree in Photography and Journalism, a Masters degree in Counseling from Long Island University, and a Masters degree in Social Work from Adelphi University. Judy@sense-ablestrategies.com

Made in the USA
Columbia, SC
27 November 2020